THE SHAKESPEARE WORKBOOK AND VIDEO

'In a seamless progression from their first and second books David and Rebecca have produced a seminal work for student and professional alike. The depth of their teaching and coaching experience is revealed in a beautifully articulated and artistically supportive methodology of speaking, questioning and acting the text of Shakespeare. Bravo.' *Janine Pearson, Head of Coaching, Stratford Festival, Canada.*

'Rebecca and David teach invaluable ways to sift through the different clues in Shakespeare's poetry and ask the most productive questions. Their coaching has helped me turn prep time into the practice of getting out of the text's way, so that performance becomes the joy of riding language.' *Raffi Barsoumian, Actor*

'This is a book that works, a workbook and a working book. It's meticulous in its attention to detail and methodical in the practicability of its approaches. It's written with an articulacy borne out of two lifetimes of experience in the field of voice and text coaching. The exercises are clear, muscular and transferable. This is a book for actors, students and anyone interested in the mechanics of getting Shakespeare's language off the page and to where it belongs.' *Tim Crouch, Theatre Maker*

'When I think of my time at RADA, the Careys spring to mind immediately. What I learnt from David and Rebecca was invaluable; it was their techniques that most effectively conveyed to me the relationship between text, mind, breath and voice. These techniques are particularly useful when dealing with Shakespeare; their shared ability to demystify it is uncanny.' *Taron Egerton, Actor*

The authors of this work have laid out a rich banquet of experience at which the student of Shakespeare in performance is a truly welcomed guest. At this table, the performer's needs are systematically and comprehensively addressed in such a way as to satisfy not only the appetite for knowledge but also the desire for success. *Jane Boston, Head of The International Centre for Voice, Central School of Speech and Drama*

THE SHAKESPEARE WORKBOOK AND VIDEO

A Practical Course for Actors

DAVID CAREY AND REBECCA CLARK CAREY

Bloomsbury Methuen Drama
An imprint of Bloomsbury Publishing Plc

B L O O M S B U R Y
LONDON • NEW DELHI • NEW YORK • SYDNEY

Bloomsbury Methuen Drama

An imprint of Bloomsbury Publishing Plc

Imprint previously known as Methuen Drama

50 Bedford Square
London
WC1B 3DP
UK

1385 Broadway
New York
NY 10018
USA

www.bloomsbury.com

BLOOMSBURY, METHUEN DRAMA and the Diana logo are trademarks of Bloomsbury Publishing Plc

First published 2015

British Library Cataloguing-in-Publication Data
A catalogue record for this book is available from the British Library.

ISBN: PB: 978-1-4725-2323-5
ePDF: 978-1-4725-3065-3
epub: 978-1-4725-2509-3

Library of Congress Cataloging-in-Publication Data
A catalog record for this books is available from the Library of Congress

Typeset by Fakenham Prepress Solutions, Fakenham, Norfolk NR21 8NN
Printed and bound in India

To our mentors:

Cicely Berry for her passion for language and humanity

Dudley Knight for his inspirational wit and wisdom

CONTENTS

4 Rhetoric and Style 179

5 Preparation for Performance 219

Appendix 1 Vocal Warm-up 241

Appendix 2 Curriculum Choices 247

Appendix 3 Professional Histories 255

Appendix 4 Bibliography and Resources 261

Links to Workbook Video 265

ACKNOWLEDGEMENTS

We would like to warmly thank the following: Nancy Benjamin, Rena Cook, Lyn Darnley, Scott Kaiser, Ursula Meyer, for their advice, encouragement and support. We also want to thank Miles Fletcher for his expertise and patience in creating the video which accompanies this book. And our thanks also go to Anasazi, Royer, Kurt, Erin, Corey and Rusty for their enthusiastic participation and excellent contributions in the workshop that forms the content of the video.

We would like to acknowledge wholeheartedly the contribution that our teachers and our students through the years have made to our understanding of Shakespeare's texts.

Our thanks go also to all at Bloomsbury; in particular, Jenny Ridout and John O'Donovan for their continued support and enthusiasm. Our gratitude also goes to Nick Fawcett for his excellent work on copy-editing our text.

FOREWORD

During my time at the Royal Shakespeare Company (RSC) one of my greatest pleasures has been to conduct text workshops with professional actors, students, amateur actors and scholars. It is not surprising that many new to Shakespeare are initially intimidated by the heightened language, by the verse form and by words that have evolved to have a different meaning. Even trained actors will have spent a limited time working on classical texts as today's actors have to train for film and television as well as for the stage. Their experience may not have included many classical roles. Women especially may have had few challenging roles because of the gender imbalance in the plays. Anxieties include how to handle the verse and the rules actors believe must be adhered to. Many feel there is a 'secret code' that they do not have access to, or that there is a required style of speaking that they are not party to. Such anxiety is fuelled by a misconception of a Golden Age of verse speaking. Performance styles change and this keeps theatre relevant. There was a time in the history of theatre training when verse was at the heart of the syllabus. Through a connection with poetry, actors were able to develop a sense of rhythm, become *au fait* with metaphor and confident with working in verse. The repertory system allowed more on the job experience and a wider variety of texts. Anxiety is restricting, and defusing it with a combination of practical physical work and helpful information is essential. If actors can be helped to defuse their anxiety, they are able to take ownership of the language and to 'free the text' to the point that they are able to bring their individual imagination, invention and motivation to their performance while using the text as the starting point. When this happens the joy and empowerment that speaking the text brings is rewarding to witness.

David and Rebecca Carey have a wealth of teaching and professional theatre coaching experience between them, and have poured
that experience into this book. Their work at the Royal Shakespeare
Company, Oregon Shakespeare Festival, Royal Academy of Dramatic
Art, and Royal Central School of Speech and Drama (among other
prestigious organizations), means they know what it takes to perform
Shakespeare and what actors want and need to know and experience.

I have known David for over thirty years both in the drama training
sector and as an RSC colleague where directors and actors have
always had enormous respect for his knowledge and integrity. As
experienced and gifted teachers, David and Rebecca bring a nurturing
feel to this new book, which follows on from their previous publications,
Vocal Arts Workbook and *Verbal Arts Workbook*.

This practical Shakespeare workbook is a useful addition to texts
currently available. It answers many of the most common questions in
a simple but detailed and practical way. Each chapter clearly presents
a new technical challenge, providing a developmental journey for
the actor. It breaks work down into distinct sections, making this an
accessible text that should help to remove fear and any sense of being
overwhelmed.

The book will be a helpful teaching aid and offers tips for teachers
in schools, the training sector and drama practitioners, and it also
provides a personal guided journey of discovery for actors in the
professional and amateur sectors.

Lyn Darnley
Head of Text, Voice and Artistic Development, Royal Shakespeare
Company (2003–14)

Introduction
HOW TO USE THIS BOOK

The Shakespeare Workbook and you

When young actors and drama students approach Shakespeare, they are often given some variation on the following two pieces of advice: don't diminish the power of the language by bringing it down to your level (i.e. mumbling, pausing and ignoring the poetry); and speak the language with freshness and immediacy (i.e. make it sound like a real person talking, not an actor expounding). These are both sound principles, but you can quickly go crazy trying to do both at once. Honouring the complexity of Shakespeare's text while giving the audience all the emotional depth and behavioural verisimilitude we expect from contemporary acting can feel like a double bind, particularly for the developing actor. *How* to integrate the technical demands of Shakespeare's heightened language with the aesthetics of those modern acting styles that celebrate a natural, personal or 'truthful' delivery is a huge challenge and one that this book is designed to help you meet.

The first step in learning to play Shakespeare with confidence and skill is to accept that his language is *heightened*. It is artificial in the sense that no one actually speaks like a Shakespearean character. But it is also important to realize that no one ever did speak like Shakespeare's characters. Even Shakespeare himself, it is fairly safe to say, would not have gone around ordering ale at the pub in iambic pentameter or using elaborate metaphors and other rhetorical tropes when discussing the Globe theatre's finances with his fellow shareholders. While certain words and conventions of language that are unfamiliar to us would have been common in Elizabethan England, like the use of 'thee' and 'thou', there was never any pretence that Shakespeare was recreating 'ordinary language' in his plays. In fact, he made up hundreds of words – words that have now passed into common usage and so are actually *easier* for a modern audience to understand than they would have been for the Elizabethans, who had never heard them before – words such as *fashionable* or *sanctimonious*. So the language would have seemed elaborate and sometimes strange to them as well. Yet, just as we flock to concerts of singer-songwriters and rap artists who can turn phrases and invent rhymes that are wonderfully clever, unexpected, and illuminating of our emotional lives, so Elizabethan audiences went to the theatre to hear language that was *extra*ordinary. It's fun and inspiring and invigorating to watch people do things better than you can. What are the Olympics, dance performances, concerts and improvisational comedy other than opportunities to watch your fellow human beings transcend the limits of the ordinary, the easy and the prosaic? Shakespeare is an Olympic champion of the English tongue. He could create dense, dizzying, dramatic and delightful language better than anyone, and if we are not constantly striving to live up to the complex genius of his text, we are cheating our audience of the best part of the ride.

The Shakespeare Workbook: An overview

So how *do* we live up to Shakespeare's astonishing language – embody it and own it and capture its explosive energy? It's a tricky thing to do; and it's a tricky thing to teach. The danger in picking out any one principle or rule about 'how to do Shakespeare' is that you end up playing that principle or rule rather than playing the text in the moment. If there isn't a specific acting impulse behind the principle, the performance is pulled out of balance. You may try to drive the energy of the thought forward, which is important, but then rush through the language and iron out the detail and nuance. Or, you try to coin images and phrases freshly, but end up breaking up the text. Committing to the high stakes in a scene can lead to playing a general emotion rather than specific thoughts. Trying to make the most of the poetic sounds and rhythmic patterns in the text can put you in danger of losing the meaning. Well-intentioned efforts to make the language clear to the audience can result in over-explaining it, actually making it harder to grasp. The pitfalls are many and deep. In this book, we will help you develop a methodology that should enable you to keep in balance the multiple demands that performing Shakespeare on modern stages places on you.

The basic sequence of this methodology is:

Speak the text.
Question the text.
Act the text.

In each chapter, we will focus on a particular aspect of Shakespeare's language, such as imagery or rhythm. We will start by simply speaking the text before moving on to questioning that aspect of the text to see what it reveals about given circumstances, intentions, obstacles – all the nuts and bolts of acting – and you will then use what you've learned to act the text.

Speak the text

This sequencing is very deliberate. Traditionally, work on Shakespeare's texts often begins with looking at the rhythm and meter of the verse and/or trying to reach an intellectual understanding of what a character is saying. However, we prefer to engage with the text physically and vocally from the outset, in order to encourage a more holistic approach to the language. We've found that it's important to simply speak the text out loud at least a couple of times before wrestling with what it means and starting to work on it in detail. If you don't, there is a danger that your relationship to Shakespeare's language becomes primarily analytical. Ultimately, to act it well you need to get it into the muscles of your mouth and body as well as into your imagination. Our neighbours while we were writing this book probably thought we were mad, as we spent a lot of time walking around our house reading passages at full voice. We found, though, that our understanding of the texts we were writing about was simply incomplete if we didn't speak and hear them out loud.

With each new piece of text that you will work on, we will begin by inviting you to speak it out loud. Sometimes we'll give some specific instructions about how to do so or how many times; sometimes we won't go into as much detail. Our hope is that you will develop the habit on your own. As you do speak the text, remember that you're still a long way from acting it. It is a particular discipline to speak without imposing a choice or a mood or an interpretation on the text. Don't worry too much about making sense of what you are saying at this stage, and free yourself of the pressure of having to perform the text as if you were in the given circumstances. As you do so, you will find yourself making discoveries that you might not have anticipated. Certain words may gather stress or energy to themselves (i.e. may be 'hot'). Some lines will have a quickness to them, while others will have more weight. Some things that seemed confusing on the page may suddenly make sense when you say them, and other things that you thought were perfectly clear will reveal themselves to be more complicated than you might have suspected. Speaking the text will help you know what kinds of questions you want to ask of it.

There is another pressure which you may feel as you start to speak Shakespeare's text, and that is the pressure to adopt a particular way of speaking – a way of speaking that doesn't belong to *you*. Because the language is heightened, poetic and strange to our modern ears, many students and professional actors feel that they should adopt a more poetic way of speaking it; that somehow their own voices don't sound right with this text; or that there is a correct accent to use with Shakespeare. These feelings often arise because there is a long tradition, particularly in the British theatre, of speaking Shakespeare with a more lyrical vocal quality and in a Received Pronunciation accent. In the United States, this traditional approach to speaking Shakespeare took the form of an anglicized accent known as American Theater Standard or Stage Standard. Actors such as John Barrymore, John Gielgud, Laurence Olivier, Judith Anderson, Peggy Ashcroft and Irene Worth were held up as exemplars of great Shakespearean performers – and indeed they were – but a younger generation of actors and directors has challenged the accepted view of what it means to speak Shakespeare. In our experience, Shakespeare can be spoken just as effectively in, for example, Jamaican, Australian, Japanese and Indian accents as well as all varieties of British and American ones.

You may encounter individuals who maintain, or you yourself may feel, that a certain accent is not 'suitable' for Shakespeare, but we don't subscribe to the view that any accent is deficient. Rather, we believe that Shakespeare's language can be vibrant and active on any tongue. As you move on to developing roles, you may choose to use an accent that is different from your own because you feel it suits the character, but at this stage we encourage you to speak the text in a way that belongs to you, which doesn't feel artificial and which you can own. Ultimately, what matters is muscularity, commitment and fullness of sound, whatever accent you are using.

Question the text

After you have had the experience of speaking it several times, the first question you will probably want to ask of the text is what the words mean. We will give you definitions of words that may be unfamiliar in the passages that we will work on, but it's very important that you get into the habit of doing your own homework in this regard. If you want to continue working with Shakespeare, we recommend that you invest in a good lexicon, a collected works that has good glosses (explanations of difficult words and phrases) and/or well-glossed individual editions of any play you may do. As we discussed in the *Verbal Arts Workbook*, it's virtually impossible to commit truthfully to and play a text if you don't know what it means. Don't stop with looking up words that are entirely foreign; if there's a word or a phrase that you 'kind of' know or are even quite sure that you know but can't quite make sense of in context, look it up. The word 'merely', for example, has come to mean 'just' or 'only', but in the Elizabethan era was most commonly used to indicate 'absolutely' or 'totally'. So in the line 'Give up yourself merely to chance and hazard' (from *Antony and Cleopatra*), the definition of 'merely' that you are most familiar with doesn't quite sit right, which would be your cue to find out what it meant to Shakespeare. Once you have a good grasp of how each word fits in, you'll be able to play the line with a clarity of intention that your audience will be able to grasp, even if they don't have lexicons in front of them. It's also important to look up allusions to historic or mytho-logical figures – knowing the significance of Phaeton or who Pompey was may make a considerable difference to how you play a scene.

Once you know what you are saying, you can start to ask the really interesting questions. Everything that you need to know to play a scene or a speech or build an entire performance is right there in the words that make up the play. Do you want to know how broad a scene is? How delicate? How public or private? Do you want to know how smart your character is? What he wants? (Note: we will use both 'he' and 'she' interchangeably throughout the book to refer to individuals of unknown gender.) What her relationships to the other characters are? What obstacles he faces? How clear-thinking she is? Playful? Cautious? In control? Out of control? From moment to moment, the answers are all there in the text.

When we say that Shakespeare's text provides concrete answers to the questions of what each character is doing and experiencing from moment to moment, however, we in no way mean that it prescribes any one 'correct' way of playing that moment. Rather, we mean that Shakespeare is fantastically good at giving you parameters in which you can create successful performances. We have seen over and over again in classrooms and rehearsal rooms across the world that creativity thrives on structure and limits. Anyone who has ever done the simplest of improvisation exercises knows that if a scene can go literally anywhere, it will most likely go nowhere. The rules of the improv game and the given circumstances introduced into it create a tightly defined arena in which the performers are free to be inventive. The boundaries stimulate and focus their imaginations. We believe that the same applies to all kinds of theatre and particularly to Shakespeare. Because the Shakespearean actor is working with a very specific and brilliantly constructed set of given circumstances, he is able to make choices that are specific, clear and alive, rather than general or forced.

The process of questioning that we will do in this book could also be described as a process of focused, practical exploration of the text to discover what intentions, actions, obstacles, tactics, hesitations, intensifications, etc. are embedded in it and what it feels like to begin to embody them. We use the word embody very deliberately here; the exercises are designed to help you develop an experiential understanding of the text by engaging your body and your imagination together. Many of them will be physical, so please wear clothes that you can move in and come to class or to your individual session warmed up and physically ready to work.

The kinds of questions that we will explore will vary, but we are always concerned to relate them to your work as an actor. For this reason, we begin in the first chapter with a focus on **language and action**: how to make Shakespeare's language active by finding and pursuing the intentions that are embedded in the text. This is the most fundamental principle of acting Shakespeare; it's what brings energy, specificity and truthfulness to your performances. In the second chapter we'll look at the role **imagery, sound and story** can play in helping you deepen your understanding of the character and play your intentions more fully and with more variety. Next we'll examine Shakespeare's use of **rhythm and meter**, which are important for embodying the subtle shifts of thought and feeling in the language. As we noted above, work on Shakespeare often begins with a consideration of rhythm and meter, as if that's the most important aspect of his language for an actor. However, we believe that this goes against the grain of how an actor prepares and can lead to fear of making a mistake. We prefer to explore the verse rhythm at a later stage, once the actor has an idea of what they are saying and why they are saying it. In this way, the actor can be open to the more delicate nuances that the verse is suggesting. The fourth chapter on **rhetoric and style** will help you play a wide range of Shakespeare's texts with confidence and clarity. And finally we'll consider what's involved in **preparation for performance**, which will give you the opportunity to draw on the work of all the preceding chapters.

As you work to discover how and why different aspects of the text illuminate your character and his journey, we will encourage you not to settle for easy answers. The most powerful discoveries are often ones that can't be easily explained: they have great resonance and a kind of emotional logic, but they aren't always the result of an intellectual process. They also come most reliably when one puts aside the question: 'What would *I* do or feel in this situation?' If this is what you are looking for, you will limit yourself to a rather shallow pool of possible answers. Ask instead: 'What kind of response to these circumstances is Shakespeare revealing here that I might never have imagined?' As you do so, you will find that you gain ownership of the language. It will make sense to you – even feel necessary – to say the exact words you have been given. Trust that Mr Shakespeare knows what he is doing and that if you pay close attention he will help you be a smarter, more agile, more interesting and more powerful actor than you ever knew you could be.

Act the text

That brings us to acting the text, which is very deliberately saved for last. Speaking the text and questioning the text are building blocks to give you a solid foundation on which to construct your performance. Delivering the performance itself is its own skill, and so we strongly advise you to memorize the speeches for the Act work, as you will then be able to get most out of the exercises. Once you have memorized the text, the work on acting a speech will give you an opportunity to integrate the discoveries you've made about the language as you imaginatively enter the given circumstances. The exercises will help you get a feel for the acting choices that are available to you in the speech or scene. Do not, however, think of this section as an opportunity to set 'how you are going to do' the text in stone. It is another stage of exploration where you can learn, through repetition and trial and error, how to play freshly in the moment by making the most of the technical work you've done in your preparation. If you are working in a class, endeavour to support each other's process rather than focusing on product as you work together. If you are working alone, use the opportunity to exercise your imagination and focus on the given circumstances rather than on yourself. Every time you speak the words, be it in a classroom, in your bedroom, in rehearsal, or in a thousand-seat theatre, is another opportunity to find and connect more deeply to the living pulse of Shakespeare's drama.

We would also note that working on the text is not the only preparation necessary to act effectively. One's body and voice also need to be well trained and warmed up. We've included a brief vocal warm-up, which includes some physical work, in Appendix 1. If you don't have much experience with voice and movement training, we would encourage you to enrol in a class or find a good private tutor, and to work your way through any of the books on those subjects in Appendix 4.

Working with *The Shakespeare Workbook*

As with our first two books, *The Vocal Arts Workbook and DVD* and *The Verbal Arts Workbook*, the chapters are divided into several sections. Each begins with a Framework section which will give you useful background information, define terms that we'll be using and discuss how the topic of that chapter fits into the bigger task of acting Shakespeare. An Exploration section will invite you to start exploring the relevant topic by focusing on the opening lines from Mark Antony's famous speech from *Julius Caesar*: 'Friends, Romans, countrymen, lend me your ears'. The Exercises section forms the bulk of each chapter (more on that to come). Next is a Follow-up section which will invite you to investigate how the work of that chapter can be applied to other material. Finally, we provide a list of Further reading. There is a huge body of excellent literature about acting Shakespeare, and we encourage you to read widely in the field. With a subject so vast, exposure to many techniques and multiple points of view will help you refine your own sensibilities.

This book also comes with links to video footage where you can see us working with a group of students and young professionals. We've selected several speeches and with each one we include a range of speaking, questioning and acting exercises from the first four chapters. This video footage is in no way meant to demonstrate the 'correct' way to teach or perform the exercises. Rather, it is intended to give you a sense of how the work might proceed and how this process can help you grow in confidence and clarity as you systematically explore various aspects of the language. We hope the video will also encourage you to be creative in your exploration; you will see that when we are working with actors, we are constantly adapting to what is happening in the room. The underlying principles and structures remain constant, but the fact that no exercise ever develops the same way twice is the thing that makes this work so consistently valuable and engaging. Please see pp. 265–6 for the full list of links.

A few words about the exercises in this book. In *The Verbal Arts Workbook* – our book on the expressive potential of language – many of the exercises did not use a set text, or if they did, that text was

used to help get at a wider principle. This is a more specialized book, and it takes a more specialized approach. Our central thesis is that the actor needs to grapple with the specifics of every word and line of Shakespeare that she speaks in order to perform it as effectively as possible. Accordingly, the practical work in this book will use set texts to demonstrate how you can do this. However, the work on any specific text can be applied to many other speeches. We give examples of how you can achieve this in the Follow-up exercises, and would also encourage you to relate the work of this book to any monologue you are working on. Within the Exercise section of each chapter, there is a series of subheadings – particular aspects of the broader topic. Under each subheading, we will work on two to three speeches or short scenes. There will be a variety of speaking, questioning and acting exercises for each piece of text, each one marked with a Roman numeral. As written, we estimate that it would take between an hour and an hour and a half to do all the exercises that we have included for each speech or short scene, but it is not necessary to do the complete sequence in order to grasp the fundamental principles. We provide two suggested outlines for programmes of work in Appendix 2. However, as you work with this book, please feel free to use the source material to design your sessions as appropriate to your circumstances. Whatever those circumstances may be, we would encourage you to always do at least some of the speaking, some of the questioning and some of the acting exercises with each piece of text.

You will find that we often do exercises that require you to speak the text more slowly than you might otherwise so that you can discover the mental and emotional processes that lead the character from one word or phrase to the next. This is necessary work – it will help you make the language and your acting specific and fresh from moment to moment. Without this kind of work, when it comes time to act, there can be a tendency to rush the text; the character's active process of making specific choices can get lost in a general playing of the character's emotional state. Once you have done the work of investigating the path that leads you from choice to choice, however, it's important to remember that in real life we move from one impulse, one tactic, one thought to the next very quickly. It's often said that Shakespeare's characters 'think on the language', and it's true. They don't have to stop and contemplate the next thing they say. One phrase drives them to the next which stimulates the next which leads them to the next, and so forth. They are not, however, particularly unique in this regard. When you get talking about something that really engages you, chances are that you don't often hesitate or take pauses at all. You move from thought to thought, point to point, until you have created an effect that satisfies you, or someone cuts you off, or you give up. When it comes time to move from questioning the text to acting the text, therefore, challenge yourself to keep the momentum of the speech or scene moving forward. You may find that you go too fast and run over important transitions. If you do, go back and try again. Mental and emotional processes proceed very quickly; we often use the word 'microsecond' when talking about the space necessary for them to happen. The more thoroughly you have explored the movement from one thought/action to the next in your questioning work, the more quickly and truthfully you will be able to embody those transitions when it comes time to act.

This book differs from our first two in another respect. Initially, we wrote *The Vocal Arts Workbook and DVD* because we felt there was a need for a book expressly designed to be used for teaching and learning voice in a classroom situation. This was the genesis of the **Teaching Tip** sidebars which you will also find in this book. While we hoped that it and *The Verbal Arts Workbook* could fruitfully be used by individuals as well, many of the exercises they contained would be difficult to do alone. This book addresses teachers and students and is structured so that it can be used in a classroom, but it would also lend itself particularly well to individual study. Acting Shakespeare is truly a life-long discipline, and while graduates of many drama schools and departments will have had some instruction in it, often there's no more than one class over a term, which is not enough time to build a deep skill set. For that reason, we have endeavoured to make it as easy as possible for the developing professional actor to use this book on his or her own. Many of our exercises ask you to work with a partner so that you have someone to whom you can address the text, but you can just as easily work with an imaginary partner. Similarly, when we invite you to discuss discoveries you have made, take that time to reflect or write rather than discuss if you are on your own. When we have exercises that are addressed to groups or require a more active partner we have included **Working Alone** sidebars in which we will give suggestions for how you can adapt the work to suit your circumstances.

The exercises in this book are not physically rigorous, but if for any reason you find yourself unable to do one or unable to do it safely, please do modify or skip it. If you are working in a class and are physically limited because of injury, illness or disability, talk with your instructor about what you are able to do and what you will need to work around. We have taught a number of differently abled students and have found that, with a little ingenuity and mindfulness on our part, they have been able to participate fully in every aspect of the class. We have also worked with a great number of students and professional actors who are dyslexic, and have found that they are in no way compromised in their ability to comprehend and perform Shakespeare's heightened language. If you are dyslexic, or suspect you may be, though, it's worth consulting with a dyslexia specialist who can recommend strategies to make getting the words off the page and memorizing them easier. We've had the good fortune to know some excellent specialists and have learned from them the following tips, which we recommend teachers adopt as standard practice, as you may or may not know when you have a student with dyslexia in your group:

- Distribute texts before the session in which you will be using them so that students can look them over first.

- Print texts on coloured paper (pastels are good). If you are dyslexic, you may want to try getting a coloured transparent overlay to read through.

- Print texts in a 'sans serif' font such as Calibri, Ariel, Verdana or Comic Sans.

- Print texts in a larger font size, such as 12 or 14.

- Use 1.5 instead of single spacing.

- You may also choose to read the text out loud to the class rather than having students read it silently to themselves.

Shakespeare in *The Shakespeare Workbook*

We talk at great length in this book about Shakespeare's text as if it were in some way definitive, and the fact is, it isn't. Not a single one of Shakespeare's plays has come to us directly from a draft in his own hand. It is true that some of his plays were published in his lifetime in single editions (known as 'quartos', from the size of the book), and it is possible that Shakespeare's handwritten manuscripts of the plays were used as the basis of the text in some instances. However, many of his most famous plays – for example, *Julius Caesar*, *Macbeth*, *Twelfth Night*, and *The Comedy of Errors* – were only published for the first time by his colleagues several years after his death in a collected edition of his plays known today as the First Folio (also from the size of the book). Moreover, even though the quarto and folio publishers may have been working from drafts, fair copies or playhouse scripts of the texts, it was the job of the compositors (or typesetters) to set the text for printing, and they brought their own spelling and punctuation skills and preferences to the task. And so it is impossible to say with any certainty that a quarto or folio version of the text is definitive, in the sense that it represents precisely what Shakespeare wrote and intended.

Over the centuries since the quartos and the First Folio were published, academic editors (including the poet, Alexander Pope, and the famous critic, Dr Samuel Johnson) have attempted to unravel the various knotty textual difficulties created by the typesetters, but in so doing they have also changed words, spellings, punctuation and line endings to fit their interpretation. For this reason, it's worth using an edition that sticks closely to the original sources (though most modernize spelling) and notes when there are variations between them. We have found that the Arden editions are very thorough in this regard and have used them as our source for the passages we've included in this book.

Conclusion

Between us, we have worked on Shakespeare's text with students and professional actors on three continents. We have worked in tiny black box theatres and thousand-seat outdoor amphitheatres. We have coached productions that were set in contemporary Britain, Renaissance Italy and 1970s inner-city America, among other places, with directors whose expectations of how the text should be spoken varied widely. We have witnessed first-hand that no nation, generation, training programme or school of acting has any particular claim on Shakespeare. We have found that everywhere contemporary actors want very much to find a way to 'own' Shakespeare's language – to have a connection to it and feel they have a reason to use the characters' words in the characters' given circumstances. There is, of course, no universal formula to make this happen. Each line, each play, each production presents its own challenges to each actor. And, of course, the text is so rich and open to so many interpretative choices that the possibilities for discovery are nearly infinite, which is precisely what makes it rewarding to work on even after four hundred years. We have found, however, that a systematic, practical exploration of the text – the actions and characterizations it suggests as well as its images, sounds and rhythms – can open the door for discoveries that are exciting and useful. Work on Shakespeare is never finished, but we have found these steps to be a good place to begin.

1
LANGUAGE AND ACTION

Framework

It is common to divide the world between doers and talkers: those who take action and those who don't. A film that is 'talky' is one in which not very much happens. The strong, silent type is the one who saves the day, while his more verbal sidekick provides comic relief. The fact is, however, that often talking *is* doing. In real life, talking is our primary means of persuading others, solving problems, negotiating to get what we want – it's how we effect change. One has only to watch the intense frustration of a two-year-old who doesn't yet have the words he needs to communicate what he wants, to understand how powerful language is.

When we talk about making the language in Shakespeare's plays active, we're talking about committing to making something happen, getting something done, changing hearts and minds and the very world around us through the act of speaking. And not just speaking, but speaking precisely *these* words. Contemporary acting theory posits (correctly, we believe) that the more precise and clear the actor is in his intention – what he aims to achieve – the more specific, dynamic and persuasive his actions will be. In order to achieve this in Shakespeare, the actor needs to pay very close attention to what the character is saying because it will tell him what the character is doing. Whereas in some contemporary drama one might have to dig deeper and fill in more blanks oneself to understand what a character's intention is, in Shakespeare it's right there on the page. The trick is to see it for what it is and not get too distracted by what *you* would feel or want or do in the given circumstances. Your job is first to notice line by line what the language is doing and what the character's action is: whether it is bombarding, flattering, pleading, objectifying; probing one point or ranging across many; cutting to the chase or leading down the garden path; painting pictures, playing on emotions, appealing to logic; challenging, belittling, manipulating, and so on. Whatever you discover, however, putting a label on the action is less important in the end than simply recognizing that *every word springs from a need to accomplish what only that word can accomplish.*

Exploration

Antony

As we indicated in the Introduction, in each chapter we will begin with an exploration of the opening lines from Mark Antony's famous speech from *Julius Caesar*. In this chapter we will concentrate on the first line only: 'Friends, Romans, countrymen, lend me your ears'.

Mark Antony is addressing the people of Rome over the dead body of the assassinated Julius Caesar. Antony was a close friend of Caesar's, and he is privately outraged about Caesar's murder. The conspirators who killed Caesar, however, are many and powerful, and it would be fatal for Antony to condemn them openly at this point. Many of them, in fact, wanted to kill Antony along with Caesar, but Brutus, another close friend of Caesar's who nonetheless joined the assassins, convinced them to let Antony live. He also agreed to let Antony address the crowd at Caesar's funeral under the condition that Antony would not condemn the conspirators. Brutus speaks first, giving a well-reasoned defence of his actions, which the crowd seems to find very convincing. Then Antony begins with his famous words.

- We'll investigate the first three words of his opening line in a later chapter. For now, let's look at the phrase: 'lend me your ears'. What does Antony want the crowd to do? The fact that he is asking for their ears, the organs of hearing, implies that he doesn't have them yet – that the crowd is not listening – and his intention is to get them to pay attention. Let's get more specific about those given circumstances.

- One person will be Antony, the rest will be the crowd. The crowd will gather in one part of the room, and Antony will face them.

***Working Alone*: You will have to create the crowd in your imagination. Working in the largest room you can, imagine the crowd moving where appropriate and adjust by moving in the space yourself.**

- *Crowd*: You have come to hear Brutus, and now that he's finished speaking you're ready to go home; start dispersing, even start to exit the room. *Antony*: use the line 'Friends, Romans, countrymen, lend me your ears' to try to stop the crowd from leaving. You may repeat it several times.

- Pick a new Antony. *Crowd*: Imagine that Antony is the first speaker, but it's Brutus that you're really interested in – mill around entertaining yourselves until Brutus arrives; some of you can wait outside the room. *Antony*: using the same text, try to get the crowd to come together and listen to you. Again, you can repeat yourself several times.

- Pick a new Antony. *Crowd*: You have been very agitated by what Brutus has said; actively debate with your neighbours whether or not you thought Brutus could be trusted and the assassination was justified. *Antony*: try to get the crowd to stop talking. Again, repeat the language as necessary. (Note: crowd, avoid speaking so loudly that Antony has to scream to be heard; Antony, use no more volume than you need to get their attention, and protect your voice while doing this exercise.)

- Pick a new Antony. *Crowd*: You have decided that you are completely on Brutus's side and you are glad that Caesar is dead. You know that Antony was a close friend of Caesar's and are not happy that he's being given the chance to talk; don't speak, but stare at Antony with great hostility as he begins to speak. *Antony*: try to convince the crowd with your words that you are someone they can trust. Repeat several times, trying to win over individuals in the crowd.

- Pick a new Antony. *Crowd*: In this scenario you don't trust Antony again, but you can express your disapproval vocally by booing or heckling him. Again, avoid making so much noise that he can't be heard at all. *Antony*: try to get the crowd to want to quieten down and listen (which is different from just out-shouting them).

- Discuss any discoveries you made. The lines preceding Antony's speech suggest that, in the main, the crowd is behind Brutus but some of them are willing to hear Antony out. Nevertheless, there is room for every one of the above responses in the individuals who make up the crowd, and the words that Shakespeare has written for Antony give him the tools to meet the challenges he faces.

Exercises

In order to find the action in the text and the need behind it, it helps to actively explore the language rather than sit and analyse it – to speak it and question it; to move with it, break it into chunks, change these around and put them back together again; to discover what happens when a word is left out or added; to take nothing for granted. In this chapter we will be doing just that. In the first section, 'Having an effect', we will look at how characters actively use words to try to change another character. In 'Negotiating complications', we will investigate how the action/language can change in the face of an obstacle. Finally, in 'Solving problems', we will work on finding the action in soliloquies, when characters are speaking alone onstage. This work is the foundation for all that follows. As much as the rhythm, sound patterns, imagery and style all contribute to the extraordinary power of Shakespeare's plays, none of it means anything without the deep commitment of the actor to the language in *action*.

Teaching Tip or Working Alone: You may wish to watch a video
segment that includes exercises from this chapter before you begin
practical work.

Having an effect

The first line of Antony's speech is a vivid example of how characters
often speak in order to have an effect on other people: to make them
think or feel or do something; to change them and their course of action.
In this section we'll look at how characters apply themselves to the task
of talking someone into or out of something. In each case, watch for
how the character employs a range of strategies: appealing to her
scene partner's emotions as well as his logic; engaging the partner's
imagination to get him to see a situation from a fresh perspective;
piling up evidence to prove her points. You'll find these same patterns
repeated in countless other speeches and scenes. The variations tell
us a lot about the characters and their given circumstances, but the
committed, energetic attempt to have an effect by using language
actively is the common denominator that makes these moments in
Shakespeare's plays compelling and exciting to watch.

Joan Puzel

This first passage is from Act 3 Scene 3 of *Henry VI, Part One*, a
play which chronicles, among other things, war between France
and England. Joan Puzel, known to us as Joan of Arc, is a common
country girl who has received, she says, a message from God calling
her to lead the French to victory. She manages to convince the French
prince and other military leaders to let her direct their strategy and lead
the troops. In this war, a French nobleman, the Duke of Burgundy,
has allied himself with the English soldier Talbot and has been fighting
against the French. Before a crucial battle, Joan decides that her best
strategy is to convince Burgundy to abandon Talbot and fight for the
French forces.

As we work on this speech, we will be looking at how Joan tries to get Burgundy to see certain things, feel certain things, and draw certain conclusions from evidence that she will lay out in front of him.

- Speak through the text quietly a couple of times without looking at the glosses (word definitions).

JOAN PUZEL
A
Brave Burgundy, undoubted hope of France,
Stay, let thy humble handmaid speak to thee.
(BURGUNDY
Speak on, but be not over-tedious.)

B
JOAN PUZEL
Look on thy country, look on fertile France,
And see the cities and the towns defaced   5
By wasting ruin of the cruel foe,
As looks the mother on her lowly babe
When death doth close his tender-dying eyes.
See, see the pining malady of France,
Behold the wounds, the most unnatural wounds,   10
Which thou thyself hast given her woeful breast.
O, turn thy edgèd sword another way,
Strike those that hurt, and hurt not those that help:
One drop of blood drawn from thy country's bosom
Should grieve thee more than streams of foreign gore. 15
Return thee therefore with a flood of tears
And wash away thy country's stainèd spots.
(BURGUNDY
Either she hath bewitched me with her words,
Or nature makes me suddenly relent.)

C
JOAN PUZEL
Besides, all French and France exclaims on thee,   20
Doubting thy birth and lawful progeny.

Who join'st thou with but with a lordly nation,
That will not trust thee but for profit's sake?
When Talbot hath set footing once in France
And fashioned thee that instrument of ill,   25
Who then but English Henry will be lord,
And thou be thrust out, like a fugitive?
Call we to mind – and mark but this for proof –
Was not the Duke of Orleans thy foe?
And was he not in England prisoner?   30
But when they heard he was thine enemy
They set him free without his ransom paid,
In spite of Burgundy and all his friends.
See, then, thou fight'st against thy countrymen
And join'st with them will be thy slaughter-men.   35
Come, come, return; return, thou wandering lord.
Charles and the rest will take thee in their arms.

Glosses
1, **brave** = noble, bold; 6, **wasting** = devastating; 7, **lowly** = sickly; 8,
tender-dying = dying at a tender age; 9, **pining** = consuming; **edged**
= sharpened; 17, **stained** = dishonourable; 19, **nature** = natural
feelings; 20, **exclaims on** = accuses; 21, **progeny** = parentage;
25, **fashioned** = made; 28, **mark** = notice; 35, **slaughter-men** =
murderers.

Speak

- Speak through the text quietly again, reading the glosses as
  you go, even for words you think you know.

- Next, find a place in the room where you can stand without
  looking at anyone else directly. Read the speech aloud at a
  conversational volume. Burgundy's lines are included so that
  you know what Joan is responding to; you don't have to read
  them out loud.

- Read the speech aloud again walking fairly energetically around
  the room. Change direction on every punctuation mark. This
  will make you slow down a bit on the transition from one
  phrase and sentence to the next, which is good. Remember

you're still at the speaking stage; there's no need to try to race
through the text.

Question
I *Word Order*

- Find a partner. Take turns reading **the first two lines** (section
  A) to each other.

- What's the first thing Joan tries to persuade Burgundy to do?
  ('Stay' – it's not that hard to spot.) Note that it's not the first
  thing she says. Try mixing up the order of the phrases as
  follows, taking turns. For the moment don't worry about how
  the meter of the verse changes, just try to use the words to
  make your partner stay:

  Partner A: Undoubted hope of France, brave Burgundy,
               Stay. Let thy humble handmaid speak to thee.
  Partner B: Stay, brave Burgundy, undoubted hope of France.
               Let thy humble handmaid speak to thee.
  Partner A: Stay, brave Burgundy.
               Let thy humble handmaid speak to thee.
  Partner B: Let thy humble handmaid speak to thee.
               O, undoubted hope of France, stay.

- Repeat the sequence above, and take a bit of time after each
  version to discuss it. When, as Joan, do you feel the most
  commanding and powerful? The most humble and entreating?
  When as Burgundy do you feel the most powerful and
  respected? The most bossed around?

- Go back to reading the original lines to each other. What kind of
  strategy is Joan using by phrasing her request this way? What
  does it tell us about Burgundy that he responds positively to it?

- It's interesting to note that in the first two lines Joan
  sandwiches her commands to 'stay' and 'let speak' between
  elevating Burgundy and debasing herself. In order to make
  him do something, she first tries to make him feel something –
  respected and revered. Let's look at other ways in which she

tries to persuade him to fight for France by making him feel certain things.

II *Adding Adjectives*

- Partner A, read the next section of the speech (section B) to your partner. You don't have to worry about giving a great performance; just try to make your Burgundy follow what you are saying and believe that you're telling the truth. Partner B, try doing the same.

- Get a pen, and with your partner circle the following adjectives and adjectival phrases (adjectives are words that describe or modify nouns): fertile, wasting, cruel, lowly, tender-dying, pining, most unnatural, woeful, edgèd, streams of, a flood of, stainèd.

- Now, partner A, read the speech to B again, trying to convince Burgundy that France is in terrible shape and he should stop fighting against his homeland, but omit all the adjectives you've circled. Discuss for a moment how the speech is different for the speaker and the listener without the adjectives. B, try reading it to A this way.

- Next, A and B take turns reading to each other **only** the circled adjectives and the nouns they describe (e.g. fertile fields, wasting ruin, cruel foe). Remembering that the nouns themselves are at least as important as the adjective; try to use the words to evoke an emotional response in your partner. For example, when you say 'cruel foe', try to make Burgundy feel the ugliness of a cruel enemy.

- Finally, take turns reading the speech to each other with the adjectives put back in. You don't need to lean into the adjectives quite as hard as you did in the previous step because they're not the only words you have to persuade Burgundy, but do make use of them to get what you want.

III *Repetition*

- Get a new partner and go through section B once again and underline each of the following words **the second time it**

appears: look, see, wounds (underline 'the most unnatural' too), hurt. Speak the section to each other without the underlined words. Discuss how that was different as a speaker and a listener.

- Put the underlined words back in and try to use them as battering rams to get through Burgundy's defences.

- Discuss what effect both the adjectives and repetitions have in terms of achieving Joan's intention.

IV *Handling Evidence*

- We'll move on now to section C. As a class, take a couple of minutes to circle all the adjectives and underline all the repeated words in this section. What do you notice? It seems to us that, until the last two lines, this part of the speech appeals much more to Burgundy's sense of logic than to his emotion.

- Get a new partner and half a dozen objects out of your bag, such as notebooks, pencils, phones, sunglasses – whatever you carry around – and place them on a table in front of you.

- Each of you read this part of the speech to your partner as if you were an attorney making an argument that fighting for Talbot is immoral, illegal and unwise. Use the objects in front of you as you would pieces of material evidence: anytime you bring a new element into play – say Talbot, or Henry, or Orleans' ransom – pick up something (it doesn't much matter what if you treat it like tangible proof that what you're saying is true) and show it Burgundy; force him to confront the evidence. This will slow you down significantly, which is fine. Focus on making very graphic to your partner the consequences of allying oneself with the English.

- Read this section to each other again. Don't use the physical objects, but do try to be very concrete and specific about each separate person and event you mention. Discuss any discoveries you've made.

Act

- Once you have memorized the text, take turns with your partner doing parts A and B of the speech appealing to Burgundy's sympathy. Be his best friend and impress on him how much it hurts you to see him destroying something you know means so much to him.

Teaching Tip: If students are ever unable to memorize their text, we would rather they work from the script than repeatedly call for line.

- Take turns doing part C of the speech appealing to Burgundy's sense of logic, questioning his acts and motives, and issuing him with a strong warning that he's going to get into serious trouble if he doesn't change his course of action.

- Put the two halves of the speech together and have your partner say Burgundy's line in between. This is an aside, and Joan will not be meant to hear it. Nonetheless, she can see that the balance is starting to tip in her favour and in that moment chooses to follow through with a new kind of tactic. As you do the full speech, see how much you can blend the caring best friend and the forceful attorney. One may be stronger at some moments than the other, but they are both part of Joan's moment-by-moment approach to persuading Burgundy.

- Either as a class or by yourself, reflect on anything you've discovered about the character of Joan Puzel, the structure of the speech and acting Shakespeare's language.

Lady Percy

Lady Percy is the widow of Henry (or Harry) Percy, also known as Hotspur. In *Henry IV, Part One*, Hotspur, a very accomplished and respected northern nobleman, joined a rebellion against the king. At a key moment, Hotspur's father, the Earl of Northumberland, held back his troops from his son, and Hotspur fell in battle, killed by the crown prince, Henry of Monmouth. Now, in *Henry IV, Part Two*, the rebellion continues, and Northumberland feels honour-bound to go in aid of the rebels and avenge his son's death. In this speech from Act 2 Scene 3, Lady Percy tries to persuade him not to go. Lady Percy tries to awaken Northumberland's memory, painting a vivid picture of the past to get him to make certain choices in the present. We'll also look at how she uses an accumulation of detail to bring force to her argument.

- Speak through the text quietly a couple of times without looking at the glosses.

LADY PERCY

O yet, for God's sake, go not to these wars!
The time was, father, that you broke your word
When you were more endeared to it than now;
When your own Percy, when my heart's dear Harry,
Threw many a northward look to see his father   5
Bring up his powers; but he did long in vain.
Who then persuaded you to stay at home?
There were two honours lost, yours and your son's.
For yours, the God of heaven brighten it!
For his, it stuck upon him as the sun   10
In the grey vault of heaven, and by his light
Did all the chivalry of England move
To do brave acts. He was indeed the glass
Wherein the noble youth did dress themselves.
He had no legs that practised not his gait;   15
And speaking thick, which nature made his blemish,
Became the accents of the valiant;
For those that could speak low and tardily
Would turn their own perfection to abuse,
To seem like him. So that in speech, in gait,   20
In diet, in affections of delight,
In military rules, humours of blood,
He was the mark and glass, copy and book,
That fashioned others. And him – O wondrous him!

O miracle of men! – him did you leave,   25
Second to none, unseconded by you,
To look upon the hideous god of war
In disadvantage, to abide a field
Where nothing but the sound of Hotspur's name
Did seem defensible; so you left him.   30
Never, O never, do his ghost the wrong
To hold your honour more precise and nice
With others than with him! Let them alone.

Glosses

3, **endeared** = bound in honour; 6, **powers** = armed forces, **long** =
desire; 8, **There** = at that time; 10, **stuck** = stood out; 11, **grey vault**
= blue ceiling; 12, **chivalry** = knights; 13, **glass** = mirror; 15, **legs** =
followers, **gait** = way of walking; 16, **thick** = quickly, **blemish** = failing;
17, **Became** = suited; 18, **tardily** = slowly; 19, **turn to abuse** =
corrupt; 21, **affections** = inclinations; 22, **humours** = moods, **blood**
= passion; 23, **mark** = pattern; 24, **fashioned** = formed; 26, **unsec-**
onded = unsupported; 28, **abide** = endure, **field** = battlefield; 30,
defensible = able to fight; 32, **nice** = particular.

Speak

- Speak through the text quietly again, reading the glosses as
  you go, even for words you think you know.

- Find a place where you can lie down comfortably on the floor.
  Read through the speech out loud at a conversational volume.
  Stay mostly still as you do this.

- Stand up and read through the speech aloud again, this time
  moving constantly. You can walk in spirals or circles or straight
  lines with sharp corners, etc. You can slow down or speed
  up or change direction any time you feel like it; see where the
  energy of the language takes you. Do watch out that you don't
  bump into any of your classmates.

- Discuss how the experience of speaking the text changed
  when you were moving versus when you were still.

Question
I *Launching*

- Take a look at the first line. If you had no idea what the relationship of the person saying this was to Northumberland, what would you guess? What would that person's age be? Gender? Status? How far down the list of possibilities would daughter-in-law be? What does it suggest to you about Lady Percy's character and emotional state that she begins her speech this way?

- Look at the next two lines. What changes from the first line? Why, after her initial outburst, might she choose to address Northumberland as 'father'?

- A significant change is that Lady Percy goes from using the present tense imperative, 'go not', to using the past tense: 'the time *was*'. For how many lines does Lady Percy talk about the past? We're going to investigate how she uses the past to try to persuade Northumberland to do something in the present.

II *Show and Tell*

- Get a pen and about eight notecards, large post-it notes, pieces of notepaper or just snapshot-sized pieces of scrap paper. Write each of the following phrases on a separate piece of paper:

  Harry – formal portrait
  Harry walking
  Harry speaking
  Harry eating
  Harry laughing
  Harry in uniform
  Harry's body dead on the field of war
  Other young men in England

  This may seem like a lot of prep work, but taking the time to do this will help you consider very specifically each of the things Lady Percy talks about in her rather long digression into the past.

- Place the cards in front of you on a table or desk. You are going to pretend that each one is a picture of the thing it describes, so the paper that says 'Harry walking' is actually a picture of Harry walking.

- Now grab a partner and read the speech to him/her. Every time you talk about something that appears in one of your 'pictures' or when you could use a picture to drive home your point, pick up the appropriate piece of paper and show it to your partner. So, for example, when you talk about Harry looking north for his father's army, you might hold up the paper that says 'Harry in uniform'. Or, when you talk about Harry 'in affections of delight', you could hold up the paper that says 'Harry laughing'. The paper that says 'Other young men in England' you can use every time you talk about those who wanted to copy Harry. Every time you hold up a picture, force Northumberland to remember in detail his living, breathing son; the effect he had on those around him; or his horrible fate. This will slow you down, which is fine for now.

- Switch partners and then discuss.

III *Accumulation*

- You may have noticed that Lady Percy goes on for quite some time about Hotspur. Having looked at the specific nature of the particulars from the past with which Lady Percy confronts Northumberland, let's explore the power of their accumulation.

- Partner A, using partner B as your Northumberland, read the speech from the beginning to 'but he did long in vain', then skip down to 'Never, O never do his ghost the wrong', and continue from there to the end. (You might want to put a star next to 'Never, O never' so you can find it quickly.)

- Next, partner B start at the beginning, but this time read to the next full stop (period), question mark or semi-colon before you skip to 'Never, O never ...' (So you will read through 'Who then persuaded you to stay at home?' before skipping ahead.)

- Continue switching partners, reading to the next full stop, question mark or semi-colon before skipping ahead until you have read the complete text.

- How did the nature of the encounter between speaker and listener change as this section of the speech got longer? How does the addition of more and more reminders of the past help Lady Percy persuade Northumberland not to go to battle now? How important is the idea of 'honour' to her action?

IV *Closing In*

- Try physicalizing the movement of the speech. Start quite close to Northumberland on the first line, move far away from him on the second, and then move steadily towards him again as you talk about the past until you are pushing him backwards with the present tense command, 'Never, O never do his ghost the wrong ...'

Teaching Tip: Monitor this exercise closely to ensure that the 'pushing' remains safe and within the boundaries of the exercise.

Act

- In a long speech with high stakes like this one, it's easy to get stuck on one emotional note, and more often than not that note is whiny or screechy. As you get ready to act this text (after memorizing it), add to your given circumstances that this is not the first time that Lady Percy and her father-in-law have come to loggerheads, and that she knows from bitter experience that he will completely dismiss the opinions of anyone he considers to be 'hysterical'. In order to have the effect on him you want, you will have to maintain your dignity. As you have probably noticed through your questioning of the text, after her initial outburst, her argument is very well constructed and gets its force from the accumulation of facts. Try acting the text a few times with varying degrees of letting your own fury and heartbreak seep through the language. Give each other feedback as to what is most effective.

- Either as a class or by yourself, reflect on anything you've discovered about the character of Lady Percy and about using language to have an effect on someone.

Negotiating complications

In the previous section we looked at speeches in which the characters state openly what it is that they want from the person they are talking to. They might encounter obstacles, for example, in the form of resistance from the person they are trying to persuade, but they know what they want and are able to articulate it clearly. In many other instances, however, how a character pursues his or her action is not so straightforward. There may be any number of reasons why the character does not feel able to state so baldly what he wants. He may be trying to pin down what he wants as he goes. Or she may want two things – i.e. to punish someone who has made her angry and to retain her dignity – in which case she needs to negotiate between those two objectives. In these instances, it becomes even more important to remember that characters are making up their strategies as they go along. They start with a desire or an impulse and then engage in a constant process of evaluating how close they are to achieving the desired effect and choosing what step to take next in order to get closer still. Though they are often enormously intelligent and very eloquent, Shakespeare's characters are not always perfect tacticians. They're doing the best they can, but they are subject to all the same vanities, insecurities, emotional currents and misjudgements that we all are. In this section we will focus on speeches where Shakespeare's characters have to negotiate factors that complicate the pursuit of their actions. Sometimes those factors are external and sometimes they are internal. While the journey may be complex, however, it's important that you as the actor stay active from moment to moment in playing the intentions through the language. If anything, complications push you to be more energetic in your attempts to have an effect.

Cassius

In the play *Julius Caesar*, Caesar is a senator in the Republic of Rome and also a general who has recently enjoyed a tremendously (though not universally) popular military success. There are a number of senators in Rome, of whom Cassius is one, who have come to suspect that Caesar will use his popularity to increase his power and perhaps even have himself crowned king, ending the republic and turning it into a dictatorship. These senators are hatching a plot to assassinate Caesar. In order to do so without jeopardizing their own lives, they need to persuade the powerful, honourable and universally respected Brutus to join them. If Brutus is involved, they feel, the people of Rome will accept the assassination as justified. Broaching the subject with Brutus, however, is a tricky and dangerous thing to do. Cassius can't come out and say what he wants Brutus to do the way that Joan and Lady Percy can with Burgundy and Northumberland. He can, however, work on both Brutus's emotions and sense of logic to lead Brutus to the conclusion he wants him to reach. In this speech from Act 1 Scene 2 Cassius begins by commenting to Brutus on the extravagant praise that is being heaped on Caesar at a public festival as they speak.

- Speak through the text quietly a couple of times without looking at the glosses.

CASSIUS

A

Why, man, he doth bestride the narrow world
Like a colossus, and we petty men
Walk under his huge legs and peep about
To find ourselves dishonourable graves.
Men at some time are masters of their fates.   5
The fault, dear Brutus, is not in our stars
But in ourselves, that we are underlings.

B

'Brutus' and 'Caesar': what should be in that 'Caesar'?
Why should that name be sounded more than yours?
Write them together: yours is as fair a name: 10

Sound them, it doth become the mouth as well.
Weigh them, it is as heavy: conjure with 'em,
'Brutus' will start a spirit as soon as 'Caesar'.
Now in the names of all the gods at once,
Upon what meat doth this our Caesar feed   15
That he is grown so great? Age, thou art shamed!

C
Rome, thou hast lost the breed of noble bloods!
When went there by an age, since the great flood,
But it was famed with more than with one man?
When could they say, till now, that talked of Rome,   20
That her wide walls encompassed but one man?
Now is it Rome indeed, and room enough,
When there is in it but one only man.
O, you and I have heard our fathers say
There was a Brutus once that would have brooked   25
Th' eternal devil to keep his state in Rome
As easily as a king.

Glosses
1, **bestride** = straddle; 2, **colossus** = giant; 9, **sounded** = proclaimed;
11, **become** = lend a grace to; 12, **conjure** = summon spirits; 13,
start = raise; 15, **meat** = food; 19, **famed** = made famous; 25,
brooked = endured; 26, **state** = government.

Speak

- Speak through the text quietly again, reading the glosses as you go, even for words you think you know.

- Read the text through once, whispering. Use a true whisper, which is just breath, rather than a quiet or raspy voice.

- Read the text aloud walking around the room taking big, energetic strides. Let the energy of your voice match the energy of your movement.

- Read the text aloud again while walking around the room. This time, change direction whenever there is a full stop or question mark at the end of a line – don't worry about full stops in the middle of a line for now.

Question
I *Contrasts*

- Take a look at the first sentence. What's the central idea? Whether or not one knows what a colossus is, it's not hard to gather that Cassius intends to say that Caesar has become great and mighty – outsized, even – and that other men are reduced to being small and petty. (In doing this, Cassius is using a figure of speech known as **antithesis**, which consists of the contrasting of opposites.) Does Cassius continue with this theme of contrasts? Underline all the words throughout the speech that have to do with size (like 'huge'), status (like 'master'), honour (or its opposite, shame) or comparisons (like 'more' or 'as well').

- Get a partner. Partner A will be Cassius and B will be Brutus. Draw an imaginary line down the centre of the room. Everything that is associated with being mighty and honourable lives on one side of the room. Everything that is associated with being low and petty is on the other side. A, read the speech to B, and when you get to a word having to do with greatness, take B's arm and pull her over to that side of the room. When you get to a word that has to do with smallness, pull her to that side. When you get to a comparison word, bring her to the centre line.

- B, it's your turn now to be Cassius. As you take A back and forth across the line, try to make him feel mighty every time you cross to this side and insignificant every time you cross to that side.

Working Alone: Cross the line yourself, adopting vocal and physical characteristics of greatness on one side and lowliness on the other.

- Discuss. Cassius uses a lot of antithesis. Do you think Cassius is successful in making Brutus feel the contrast between Caesar and other men? Between how men should be and how they currently are?

II *Verbs*

- You will have noticed that at the centre of the speech there is an extended comparison between Caesar's name and Brutus's name. It starts with things that apply to names, like how they look on the page and how they sound, and then proceeds to things that are beyond the power of mere names – being weighed and having the magical power to raise spirits. To investigate the progression, circle the things that Cassius suggests doing with the names: 'write, sound, weigh, conjure'. Also, circle the verb 'feed' in 'upon what meat doth this our Caesar feed'. Now everyone stand on the middle line. Read section B of the speech out loud as a group. When you come to one of the words you've just circled, stomp your foot. Try stomping it a little harder each time. Read the section again, and this time stomp not only on the circled words, but whenever else you feel a stomp is called for.

- Discuss what the energy of stomping did to this part of the speech. Does it feel like a good way to convince Brutus?

III *Saying the Unsayable*

- Having attempted to bring Brutus around to his point of view by making him feel personally frustrated not to be as renowned as Caesar, Cassius starts talking more about what is happening to Rome. In the second half of the speech, he compares Brutus not to Caesar, but to his ancestor, also named Brutus, who swore he would die before he would see a single ruler in Rome.

- Get in groups of three (if you are in a group of two or four, you can rotate through the different roles). Partner A, you will be Brutus; B, you are Cassius; and C, you are 'Shadow Cassius' and you will be saying what Cassius can only imply. Cassius, read section C. Every time you get to a full stop (period) or question mark, pause for a second. In that gap, Shadow Cassius, nudge Brutus and say, 'Someone should do something about that.' Make each one more urgent than the last. You can even embellish the phrase as you go, e.g. 'Seriously, someone should do something about that!'

- Switch around until everyone has had a chance at all three parts.

Working Alone: Speak both Cassius's lines and Shadow Cassius's suggestion, 'Someone should do something about that' to your imaginary Brutus.

- Go back to working in pairs. Partner A, read this section again, and at each full stop or question mark, leave just a microsecond for the unsaid 'Someone should do something about that' to worm its way into Brutus's consciousness. When you start speaking again, work even harder to make him see how intolerable this situation is. Switch over so that B is reading. Discuss any discoveries you've made. How does the action of repeating the phrase 'one man' help Cassius?

Act

- Perform the speech with a partner playing Brutus. Brutus, make some kind of movement every time Cassius ends a sentence (you can carry a paper and follow along to help you do this). The movement can be big, such as walking away from him, or small, such as scratching your face. Listen actively so that your movements can be in character. However, avoid doing anything elaborate – you're there to help your Cassius partner connect to the impulse behind each new thought, not to call attention to yourself. Cassius, you have to make sure that you give yourself the time (microseconds, but time nonetheless) to absorb Brutus's non-verbal reaction to what you've said and decide what to say next.

- Either as a class or by yourself, reflect on anything you've discovered about the character of Cassius and about using language strategically in the face of obstacles.

Portia

Portia from *The Merchant of Venice* is a wealthy young woman whose late father devised a test for any young man who comes to court her. Each suitor must choose between three caskets, or metal boxes, one gold, one silver and one lead. If he chooses the casket with Portia's portrait inside, he will win her hand in marriage. If, however, he chooses another casket, he must leave and swear never to marry. So far Portia has had two suitors, neither of whom she cared for much. Fortunately, they didn't find her portrait. Now Bassanio has come to her home to try his luck, and she finds that she likes him very much indeed. She desperately wants him to make the right choice, but she has sworn not to reveal to him which is the correct casket.

In this speech from Act 3 Scene 2 Portia has to contend with her desire to throw herself at Bassanio and the knowledge that to do so would be highly inappropriate; with her longing to have him pick correctly and her fear that he will not; and with her impulse to tell him which one to choose and her reluctance to break her vow to her late father.

- Speak through the text quietly a couple of times without looking at the glosses.

PORTIA
A
I pray you tarry. Pause a day or two
Before you hazard, for in choosing wrong
I lose your company; therefore, forbear awhile.
There's something tells me – but it is not love –
I would not lose you, and, you know yourself,   5
Hate counsels not in such a quality.
But, lest you should not understand me well –

And yet, a maiden hath no tongue but thought –
I would detain you here some month or two
Before you venture for me.

B

            I could teach you   10
How to choose right, but I am then forsworn.
So will I never be, so may you miss me.
But if you do, you'll make me wish a sin,
That I had been forsworn. Beshrew your eyes,
They have o'erlooked me and divided me: 15
One half of me is yours, the other half yours.
Mine own, I would say: but, if mine, then yours,
And so, all yours. O, these naughty times
Puts bars between the owners and their rights:
And so, though yours, not yours. Prove it so,   20
Let Fortune go to hell for it, not I.

Glosses
1, **tarry** = linger; 2, **hazard** = try your luck; 3, **forbear** = be patient; 6,
quality = manner, style; 7, **lest** = in case; 10, **venture** = risk your luck;
11, **forsworn** = perjured; 12, **miss** = not win; 14, **beshrew** = curse; 15,
o'erlooked = examined; 18, **naughty** = wicked; 19, **bars** = obstacles.

Speak

- Speak through the text quietly and slowly, looking at the glosses as you go.

- Walk around the room as you read the speech aloud, changing direction on each punctuation mark, or stand in a circle with your group and read it around the circle from punctuation mark to punctuation mark.

Question
I *Keep Away*

- Let's look at the first few lines of the speech from the beginning through to 'Before you venture for me' (section A).

Get a partner and a chair. One of you will be Portia, the other Bassanio.

- The first thing Portia says is, 'Pray you tarry', which implies that Bassanio is about to do something. She also asks him to 'pause a day or two' and to 'forbear awhile', which imply that he doesn't immediately respond to her first request. Bassanio, stand about three or four metres away from the chair. Let's say that you are rather interested in the chair. Before Portia starts speaking, you take a step forward to have a closer look at it. You are also, however, rather interested in Portia, so if she succeeds in distracting you, you will stop moving towards the chair. When she stops talking, or loses your attention, you can begin approaching the chair again.

- Portia, your job is to keep Bassanio as far away from the chair as possible. While you are talking you can move anywhere you like and you can even move the chair if you like. You cannot, however, touch Bassanio AND, whenever you get to a punctuation mark (a dash, a comma, a full stop, etc.), you have to freeze and stop talking for two seconds (counting 'And one and two' in your head). During those pauses, Bassanio is free to move towards the chair.

- Begin with Bassanio taking a step towards the chair and end with Portia's line, 'Before you venture for me'.

- Swap over so the partner who was Bassanio becomes Portia and repeat.

- Discuss the exercise. When you have to stop talking on the punctuation marks, what kind of energy do you have when you start speaking again? What is stopping Portia from saying everything she wants to say when she wants to say it? How hard does she have to work to get the words she can use to affect Bassanio?

Working Alone: This can be done with an imaginary Bassanio; make sure you imagine him moving while you are frozen on the punctuation marks.

II *Landmines*

- Having played with ways of postponing Bassanio's choice in order to keep him with her longer, in section B of the speech Portia entertains the possibility of just telling him which casket to pick. It's very tricky terrain for her – she desperately wants him to choose correctly, but breaking her oath to her father would be a very grave sin.

- Gather a lot of objects – books and folders, stuff from your bags, coats, scarves, shoes, etc. Scatter the objects around the floor. No two objects should be touching, but there should be at least two objects in each square metre of floor space so that to cross the room you would have to do a lot of zigging and zagging to avoid stepping on an object.

- Read the section of text out loud once. You are now going to try to hop across the room on one foot while reading the text. Take a hop every time you get to a punctuation mark, being very careful not to touch any object or any other person. If you do, you have to go back and start again. This may feel a little silly, but if you can stay focused on trying to get somewhere without losing your balance or hitting anything, you will start to get a visceral sense of how precarious Portia's position is once she starts to contemplate breaking her word and how hard it is for her to find a satisfactory answer to her dilemma.

Teaching Tip: Depending on the size of your group, you may want to have half the class do this at a time to avoid collisions.

III *Back and Forth*

- You will have noticed in the previous exercises that Portia goes back and forth quite a bit in this speech. She starts to confess her love, then backs off, then hints at it. She considers breaking her oath, then thinks better of it. She starts to say that half of herself belongs to Bassanio, then corrects herself, and then corrects herself again. This reflects her underlying quandary: she's talking so much to delay his choosing, but she knows that the only way she can really be with him is for him to make the right choice.

- When a character is contradicting herself as much as Portia does here (something that is often found in young women in Shakespeare's comedies), it's important to keep the transitions sharp. Trying to play two things at once will lead to muddy acting.

- In this exercise, you will read the whole speech as set out below. Start at one end of the room. Imagine that Bassanio is at the other end. As you speak, move towards Bassanio until you get to a slash mark; at the first slash, you must reverse direction and move away from Bassanio while you speak the next bit. When you get to the second slash, change direction and move towards him again. Continue, changing direction (either towards or away from Bassanio) on every slash mark through to the end. Move with purpose, and make the direction changes quickly and cleanly.

- If you are working with an instructor or partner, he or she can slap a table or wall with a folder on each slash so that you can react and change direction even more quickly.

    PORTIA
    I pray you tarry. Pause a day or two
    Before you hazard,/ for in choosing wrong
    I lose your company;/ therefore, forbear awhile.
    There's something tells me –/ but it is not love –/
    I would not lose you, and, you know yourself,
    Hate counsels not in such a quality./
    But, lest you should not understand me well –/

And yet, a maiden hath no tongue but thought –
I would detain you here some month or two
Before you venture for me. I could teach you
How to choose right,/ but I am then forsworn.
So will I never be,/ so may you miss me./
But if you do,/ you'll make me wish a sin,
That I had been forsworn./ Beshrew your eyes,
They have o'erlooked me and divided me:/
One half of me is yours, the other half yours./
Mine own, I would say:/ but, if mine, then yours,
And so, all yours./ O, these naughty times
Puts bars between the owners and their rights;
And so, though yours,/ not yours./ Prove it so,
Let fortune go to hell for it, not I./

- Discuss what physicalizing the action of moving towards and away from Bassanio added to your understanding of how Portia is negotiating the complications of her situation as she speaks.

Act

- Much of how this speech is played will depend on how close Bassanio is to stepping forward and picking a casket. Find a partner to be Bassanio. Play the speech once with Bassanio taking advantage of every break in Portia's language to try to step forward and pick a casket. Bassanio, don't be overly aggressive – you want to be polite and respectful, so you're not going to ignore Portia – but do try to find an opportunity to get things moving. Portia, you will have to keep your focus very tightly on Bassanio.

- Play the speech again. This time, Bassanio, you can be very patient with Portia. Though you may want to get on with it, don't make a move until you're sure that she's ready. Portia, this time you can take your focus off Bassanio whenever you feel you want to focus more on how to solve the problem for yourself. You may even find yourself pacing or effectively arguing with yourself.

> *Working Alone*: For the first step, you can try kicking a ball gently around the room as you speak, which will force you to expend energy trying to control its movements. For the second step, just place the ball on the ground where you can come back to it when you feel you want to.

- Finally, you can play the speech taking what you've learned from the previous two runs to shape it in a way that seems to work best with the text.
- Take a few minutes with your partner to discuss what you've discovered from working on this speech.
- Either as a class or by yourself, reflect on anything you've discovered about the character of Portia and Shakespeare's language.

Solving problems

So far in our investigation of actions in Shakespeare, the intention has always been directed towards another person – speaking to have a specific effect on him or her. Sometimes, though, Shakespeare's characters speak when they are alone onstage. These speeches are called soliloquies. Just because they are not directed to another character, however, does not mean that they are not active. We have found that in most instances the intention is related to solving a problem. The character speaks because there is something she is actively trying to figure out. She wants to find a solution or answer or relief from a feeling of being unsettled by an unresolved situation. This desire to achieve some kind of resolution is what motivates the character to start talking and drives him to keep going. As an actor, you need to be vigorous in pursuing that desire in order to keep soliloquies fresh, energized and forward moving rather than contrived, passive and self-reflective.

It can often be effective for the character to speak directly to the audience in a soliloquy. The number of asides and soliloquies in

Shakespeare and other Elizabethan plays strongly suggests that they did not have the same fourth-wall conventions that we do in much modern drama. In other words, the actors did not actively pretend that there was no audience, but rather regularly engaged with them as witnesses to the action. Although modern productions of Shakespeare vary in how much direct address to the audience characters use, we strongly believe that the audience can be a useful sounding board for characters who are trying to solve problems. They can test out proposed solutions and develop their ideas. While they do not seem to expect verbal responses from the audience, they can draw on its energy to propel themselves forward through the speech.

Proteus

Proteus is one of the titular *Two Gentlemen of Verona*. The other is his best friend, Valentine, who leaves Verona at the beginning of the play to make his fortune in Milan. Proteus is happy in Verona because it is also the home of the beautiful Julia, a young woman whom he wishes to court. Just as he has won her over, however, his father decides to send him to Milan. Proteus pledges his faith to Julia and follows his friend to the big city. Once there, he finds that Valentine is in love too – with the Duke's daughter, the dazzling Silvia. Proteus gets one look at his best friend's girl and is smitten. In this speech from Act 2 Scene 6 he tries to work out what to do about it.

As an acute observer of humanity, Shakespeare shows us in this speech that often what we call the process of making a decision is a process of finding a justification for what we really want to do. The conflict comes from our doubts about whether our desires really are justifiable. In this way, this speech is a great example of how soliloquies can be scenes played between the character and his better (or worse) self.

- Speak through the text quietly a couple of times without looking at the glosses.

PROTEUS
A
To leave my Julia shall I be forsworn;

To love fair Silvia shall I be forsworn;
To wrong my friend, I shall be much forsworn.
And e'en that power which gave me first my oath
Provokes me to this threefold perjury.   5
Love bade me swear, and Love bids me forswear.
O sweet-suggesting Love, if thou hast sinned,
Teach me, thy tempted subject, to excuse it.
At first I did adore a twinkling star,
But now I worship a celestial sun.   10
Unheedful vows may heedfully be broken,
And he wants wit that wants resolvèd will
To learn his wit t'exchange the bad for better.
Fie, fie, unreverent tongue, to call her bad
Whose sovereignty so oft thou hast preferred   15
With twenty thousand soul-confirming oaths.
I cannot leave to love, and yet I do;
But there I leave to love where I should love.

B

Julia I lose, and Valentine I lose;
If I keep them, I needs must lose myself.   20
If I lose them, thus find I by their loss,
For Valentine, myself, for Julia, Silvia.
I to myself am dearer than a friend,
For love is still most precious in itself,
And Silvia – witness heaven that made her fair –   25
Shows Julia but a swarthy Ethiope.
I will forget that Julia is alive,
Remembering that my love to her is dead.
And Valentine I'll hold an enemy,
Aiming at Silvia as a sweeter friend.   30

Glosses
1, **forsworn** = perjured; 4, **power** = the power of Love; 7, **sweet-suggesting** = seductive, persuasive; 11, **unheedful** = heedless, **heedfully** = consciously; 12, **wants** = lacks, **wit** = good sense, **resolved** = determined; 13, **learn** = teach; 14, **unreverent** = impudent; 15, **sovereignty** = excellence; 17, **leave to love** = stop loving.

Speak

- Read through the text out loud, slowly, looking at the glosses as you go.

- Read the speech out loud again, walking slowly around the room as you do so.

- Divide your group in half and line up facing each other. The first person in one line will read up to the first punctuation mark. The first person in the line opposite will then pick up and read to the next punctuation mark, whereupon the second person in the first line will start reading and continue to the next punctuation mark, and so forth.

- When you get to the ends of the two lines, go back to the first person and continue as above until you've read the whole speech. Try to pick up your cue quickly, particularly if you're starting in the middle of a sentence, so that the energy of the thought moves forward seamlessly.

Working Alone: Set up two chairs facing each other. Move from sitting in one chair to the other on each punctuation mark.

- What did you discover about Proteus in this speech?

Question
I *Love and Honour*

- Although we have a general sense of Proteus's dilemma, let's look at his first sentence to get a specific sense of what is bothering him:

> To leave my Julia shall I be forsworn;
> To love fair Silvia shall I be forsworn;
> To wrong my friend, I shall be much forsworn.

When a word is repeated three times in the first three lines of a speech, it's worth considering it carefully. 'Forsworn' means to be perjured, i.e. to have broken one's oath.

- Go through the entire speech and circle every word that has to do with oaths, promises or vows and breaking them. Read the speech out loud stomping your foot on every circled word until you get to the last one. Discuss anything you noticed.

- Are there any other words that are repeated several times? Let's start with 'love'. Underline 'love' and any synonyms. Read through the speech, and, in addition to stomping on every circled word, every time you say a word that's underlined, spin around in a circle. Discuss any discoveries. We'll look at another set of repeated words in section III.

II *Good Angel/Bad Angel*

- You will have found that Proteus is quite viscerally torn between what he wants to do and what he knows he should do. If some of his logic seems hard to follow, that's because he is, in fact, twisting it around quite tortuously, trying to find a justification for dumping Julia and pursuing his best friend's girl. Because his thinking and his language are so complicated, we're going to review a few of the trickier bits:

> And e'en that power which gave me first my oath
> Provokes me to this threefold perjury.
> *(Love made him want to swear fidelity to Julia, and now love*
>   *makes him want to betray her, his oath, and his friend.)*
> Love bade me swear, and Love bids me forswear.
> *(This is a restating of what he's just said.)*
> O sweet-suggesting Love, if thou hast sinned,
> Teach me, thy tempted subject, to excuse it.
> *(Now he talks directly to love and says that if it is sinning by*
>   *tempting him, he wants it to teach him how this sin can be*
>   *forgiven – which would also let Proteus off the hook.)*
> At first I did adore a twinkling star,
> But now I worship a celestial sun.

> *(The star is Julia, the sun Silvia. The implication is that he's simply progressing from a good kind of love to a better love, rather than being an ignoble two-timer.)*
> Unheedful vows may heedfully be broken,
> And he wants wit that wants resolvèd will
> To learn his wit t'exchange the bad for better.
> *(When you rush into a vow thoughtlessly, it's okay to thoughtfully break it. And you'd have to be stupid not to have the resolve to find a way to give up something bad to get something better.)*

- Once you've had a chance to look at or discuss the above, get in groups of three (if the numbers don't come out evenly, you can have a group of four with one person observing in each round). One person will be Proteus, one will be his good angel and one his bad angel.

- Good angel and bad angel, position yourselves to Proteus's right and left. Proteus, read section A of the speech to your good angel, turning your back on your bad angel. As you go, try to convince your good angel that you truly want to do what's right but there are some very strong mitigating circumstances. Note that when you talk directly to Love, you can look away from your angel, but bear in mind how he might respond to your plea. Good angel, you can respond, physically and even with one or two words (e.g. 'Really?', 'Come on', etc.). Bad angel, you can have input as well over Proteus's shoulder (e.g. 'That's right', 'Don't worry', etc.). Angels, listen carefully so that your responses are very precisely generated by what Proteus says and how convincing he is.

- Reassign roles so there's a new Proteus, good angel and bad angel in each group. Proteus, you will now face your bad angel. Try to get her to help you figure out a way that you can be with Silvia – try out your ideas on her, and make her feel your frustration when you hit obstacles. Bad angel and good angel, you can respond as in the previous step.

- The third Proteus will deliver the speech looking straight ahead with an angel on each side giving him encouragement or discouragement, as the case may be. Proteus, you can turn from one side to the other depending on which angel you feel will be the most sympathetic to what you are saying. (If you're in a group of four, two students can do this step as Proteus, one after the other.)

- Discuss in your groups any discoveries you made.

Working Alone: Do the exercise with a good angel chair to one side of you and a bad angel chair to the other. In this instance, try to cut off the imaginary angels before they can respond to you. You can add some extra words in response to what you imagine they might be about to say, e.g. 'Yes, I know', or 'Don't you see?'

III *Object Lesson*

- When you were looking for repeated words, you probably also noticed the repetition of 'lose' and words that relate to it, like 'leave', 'loss', 'keep' and 'find'. This happens around the time that Proteus stops talking about oaths and being forsworn. This calculation of what he has to gain and lose, and its relative worth, is what helps Proteus leave behind the moral calculation of what is right and what is wrong. Before proceeding to explore this part of the speech, we'd like to comment on the lines 'And Silvia – witness heaven that made her fair –/ Shows Julia but a swarthy Ethiope.' Elizabethan conventions of beauty valued pale skin over dark, and Elizabethan sensibilities saw nothing wrong in disparaging the complexions of people from Africa. This has changed, very much for the better, we believe, so these lines seem out of date and offensive, and if we were mounting a production of the play we might very well cut them. Right now, though, we want you to get a sense of how Shakespeare has built the rhythm of Proteus's (crass) argument, so we have left them in.

- Get four objects of varying degrees of desirability – so you might have a phone (very desirable), a lipstick (somewhat desirable), an umbrella (practical but kind of boring) and a pencil (very mundane). Make quick, instinctual choices, and don't worry too much about them. The most desirable object represents Silvia. The next most desirable is yourself, then Valentine, then Julia.

- Sit on the floor and put the four objects in front of you. Read section B of the speech. Whenever you talk about one of the four characters involved, pick up the object associated with that person. If you talk about losing or in any other way casting aside that person, move the object so that it is behind your back. If you talk about gaining someone, bring that object back around in front of you. If you are comparing people, hold the objects next to each other so you can see them side by side. Sometimes you may have more than one object in one hand – that's fine. Don't worry too much if you lose track of your objects for a moment – Proteus's juggling act is in fact a little precarious at this point.

Act

I

- Standing in the place in which you will perform, decide where Verona is in relation to you – is it to your left, your right or in front of you? Whenever you talk about Julia, refer to this point in space (it may help to anchor it with an object – e.g. the door is the direction to Verona/Julia). In the same way, decide where in the space you last saw Silvia and where you last saw Valentine. Now, in playing the text, whenever you talk about the other characters, refer to those points. It helps if these points are not too close together. You'll also want to find a place for Love, since you address it directly in the speech. You may find that it's useful to place it up above the horizon, where 'the gods' live. It may slow you down a bit to separate these four, which is fine. Proteus needs the time to sort through the complications of his situation.

II

- Take a look at your audience. Everyone who is wearing some red is a good angel. Everyone who is wearing more white is a bad angel. Everyone who is wearing neither red nor white is neutral (you can choose different colours if the proportions don't seem right with red and white). As you speak the soliloquy, try to engage the sympathies of all involved, knowing that some of the audience will support you as you go but some will be harder to win over.

- Either as a class or by yourself, reflect on anything you've discovered about the character of Proteus and about using language to resolve complicated situations.

Viola

In *Twelfth Night*, Viola is a young woman who was on a sea journey with her brother when a storm arose and the ship was sunk. A stranger on the shores of Illyria, she disguises herself as a young man and finds employment as a servant to the Duke, Orsino, whom she secretly falls in love with. He is in love with Olivia and sends Viola to her with his message of love. Olivia scorns Orsino, but Viola is so clever and poetic on his behalf, that Olivia, thinking Viola is a young man, falls for her. When Viola leaves, Olivia takes a ring and, pretending that Viola has left it as a love token on Orsino's behalf, asks her servant to return it as a way of reaching out to this 'young man' she is so attracted to. When Viola is given this ring, which the servant insists she left with Olivia, she is, of course, baffled.

As we saw with Proteus, in soliloquies there is sometimes something the character really wants to do, and much of his problem-solving is about finding a way to justify that course of action to the audience and, by extension, to himself. In this soliloquy from Act 2 Scene 2, Viola decides *not* to take action; to continue living in disguise so that she can be close to the Duke she loves. That too is a decision, though, and one that she needs to convince herself is justified. We'll be looking at how she does that.

- Speak through the text quietly a couple of times without looking at the glosses.

VIOLA
A
I left no ring with her. What means this lady?

Fortune forbid my outside have not charmed her.
She made good view of me, indeed so much
That methought her eyes had lost her tongue,
For she did speak in starts, distractedly.   5
She loves me sure. The cunning of her passion
Invites me in this churlish messenger.
None of my lord's ring? Why, he sent her none.
I am the man. If it be so, as 'tis,
Poor lady, she were better love a dream.   10

B

Disguise, I see thou art a wickedness,
Wherein the pregnant enemy does much.
How easy is it for the proper false
In women's waxen hearts to set their forms.
Alas, our frailty is the cause, not we,   15
For such as we are made of, such we be.

C

How will this fadge? My master loves her dearly,
And I, poor monster, fond as much on him,
And she, mistaken, seems to dote on me.
What will become of this? As I am man,   20
My state is desperate for my master's love;
As I am woman, now alas the day,
What thriftless sighs shall poor Olivia breathe?
O time, thou must untangle this, not I.
It is too hard a knot for me t'untie.   25

Glosses

2, **outside** = appearance, **charmed** = enchanted; 3, **view** = inspection;
4, **methought** = it seemed to me; 5, **in starts** = in fits and starts; 6,
cunning = craftiness; 7, **churlish** = rude; 12, **pregnant** = resourceful;
13, **proper false** = handsome deceiver; 14, **waxen** = impressionable,
forms = images; 17, **fadge** = work out; 18, **fond** = infatuated; 23,
thriftless = pointless.

Speak

- Read through the text out loud, slowly, looking at the glosses as you go.

- If you can get your hands on one, blow up a balloon. Read the speech aloud, holding the paper or book in one hand. With the other hand, keep the balloon up in the air by tapping it gently every time it starts to fall. Keep the taps relatively small and controlled or the balloon will go all over. This may slow you down a bit, and you may find yourself giving a little extra stress to the words on which you are tapping, which is fine. You may even want to do this a couple of times to find out what different tapping rhythms bring out in the speech. You can also do this with an imaginary balloon.

Question
I *Putting Together the Pieces*

- In this speech, Viola starts with one problem and ends with an even bigger one. Like Proteus, she states her first problem quite clearly in her first line: 'I left no ring with her. What means this lady?' She then considers a possible answer: 'Fortune forbid my outside have not charmed her', expressing her hope that it's not the case. To what extent Viola thinks it's a serious possibility and to what extent she thinks it's an unlikely joke is open to interpretation. What we do know is that she spends the next seven lines (section A) testing the hypothesis until she concludes that it's true.

- Get eleven scraps or pieces of paper and place them in front of you, each one further away from your starting point than the last – if you have enough space try to spread them over three to four metres. They don't have to be in a straight line, in fact it can be more fun if they zigzag a bit.

- Go back to your starting point. Read the first two lines, and then before you start the third line, pick up the first piece of paper. Every time you come to a punctuation mark, step up to the next piece of paper and pick it up. Think of the paper as a clue that's helping you piece together what happened. Then read on to the next punctuation mark. Keep holding the pieces of paper as you go so that at the end you have all eleven. When you get to 'Poor lady she were better love a dream!', you must do something to dispose of the papers. You can throw them in the air, try to hide them, tear them up – whatever impulse you have in the moment. You can stop reading after that line.

- Repeat the exercise. This time, treat 'Fortune forbid my outside have not charmed her' as a very real and undesirable possibility ('Oh no!'). Every piece of paper you pick up will then lead you closer to confirming your worst fear.

- Repeat again. This time, treat 'Fortune forbid my outside have not charmed her' as a big, unlikely joke. Each piece of paper will then lead you to the realization that, as it were, the joke is on you.

II *Question Time*

- Once Viola has solved the first problem of figuring out why Olivia has sent her a ring, she has more to contend with. Interestingly, she doesn't skip straight to 'How is this all going to work out?', but spends time on some other concerns instead. Unlike the beginning of the speech, where she comes out and says, 'This is what I'm trying to figure out', we're going to have to do some deducing to figure out what she's wrestling with next.

- Get a partner, and together look at section B. For each of the three sentences in this section, craft a couple of questions or statements which that sentence could be a response to. For example, if the sentence were, 'I think my sister is in love with John', you might come up with, 'Who is your sister in love with?' or 'Who's in love with John?' or 'Are you convinced your sister is in love with John?' You'll probably find that most of the things you are writing focus on how this situation with Olivia came to pass and where the blame lies.

> *Teaching Tip:* Depending upon your students, you may want to provide them with a list of possible questions.

- Have your partner read one of the questions/statements you've written for each sentence before you speak it. Try to respond very actively to your partner as you speak – i.e. to give a persuasive response.
- Switch over so the partner who was reading questions/ statements is now reading the text.
- Discuss what you've discovered about this section. Why do you think Viola feels the need to take time to address these issues?

> *Working Alone:* You can write some questions/statements on your own. Read them aloud and then read the answering text, as if you were having a conversation with yourself or asking yourself questions and then answering them.

III *Statues*

- The final problem that Viola tackles is 'How will this fadge?' (a great word, 'fadge' – one that reflects the preposterousness of the situation). The way that she tackles it is by working her way back through it.
- Get in groups of four (if the numbers of your group don't work out evenly, you can get in larger groups and repeat the exercise a few times so that everyone has a chance to participate). One person will be Olivia, one Orsino, one Viola and one the Speaker.

- The Speaker will read section C, going fairly slowly. Orsino, Olivia and Viola, whenever the Speaker talks about you, strike a pose that embodies what she says. So, when she says, 'My master loves her dearly', Orsino, you would make a gesture of love (or, even stronger, loving 'dearly') in Olivia's direction. Be very attentive to each detail, so that when the Speaker refers to herself as a 'poor monster' (probably because she's a mishmash of man and woman), that is reflected in Viola's physicality.

- Repeat the exercise a couple of times, changing parts. Finally, each person read this section of the speech trying to conjure the pictures in the imagination of the listeners.

Working Alone: You can 'play' all the parts, switching from one to the next as you speak. Try to always be Orsino in one place, Olivia in another and Viola in a third, so you'll be moving from place to place as you go. This will slow you down a bit, which is fine.

- Discuss any discoveries you've made. Why do you think Viola ends up handing the problem over to time in the end?

Act I

- Before performing the speech do the following exercise. In section A every time you want to emphasize a word or a point, tap your temple with your index finger (an 'Elementary my dear Watson' kind of gesture). You'll probably end up tapping once or twice per line. There are no correct answers here; just follow your impulses.

- In section B, tap your heart with your open hand every time you find yourself emphasizing a word.

- In section C, let your hand hang down by your side and tap your thigh on every stressed word, but for the last two lines, shake your fist at the heavens on the most important words.

- When you have finished, go right into performing the speech, but now let the language do the work without any physical actions.

II

- Try the speech once, and from the time you've really formulated the problem ('I am the man') through to the end of the speech, try to convince the audience that you are an innocent victim and this situation is far too complicated for you to be expected to solve it. Your choice of words will help you here ('cunning of her passion', 'churlish messenger', etc.) as will the mass of detail that you present.

- Either as a class or by yourself, reflect on anything you've learned about the character of Viola and about using language to work through mysterious or difficult circumstances.

Hamlet

Hamlet's father, the king, has died; very soon afterwards Hamlet's mother, Gertrude, married his father's brother, Claudius. Hamlet is desperately unhappy in his uncle's court and feels very isolated in his grief. He is then visited by the ghost of his father, and this spectre tells Hamlet that he was murdered by Claudius and he wants Hamlet to avenge his death. The situation is stressful, to say the least, and it forces Hamlet in this speech from Act 3 Scene 1 to examine himself and his sense of purpose in life very carefully.

This is perhaps the most famous soliloquy in the world. It's so famous, in fact, that it's easy to forget that it comes out of a very specific context and represents a very real attempt on Hamlet's part to try to work out something that is troubling him deeply. It's not poetry or philosophy or great drama to him – it's a problem to be solved. As we work on it, we'll be looking for the active steps he takes to build an explanation for himself of why human beings make the choices they do about living and dying.

- Speak through the text quietly a couple of times without looking at the glosses.

HAMLET

A

To be, or not to be – that is the question;
Whether 'tis nobler in the mind to suffer
The slings and arrows of outrageous fortune
Or to take arms against a sea of troubles
And by opposing end them;

B

               to die: to sleep –   5
No more, and by a sleep to say we end
The heartache and the thousand natural shocks
That flesh is heir to: 'tis a consummation
Devoutly to be wished – to die: to sleep –
To sleep, perchance to dream – ay, there's the rub,   10
For in that sleep of death what dreams may come
When we have shuffled off this mortal coil
Must give us pause:

C

               there's the respect
That makes calamity of so long life.
For who would bear the whips and scorns of time,   15
Th'oppressor's wrong, the proud man's contumely,
The pangs of despised love, the law's delay,
The insolence of office and the spurns
That patient merit of th'unworthy takes,
When he himself might his quietus make   20
With a bare bodkin. Who would fardels bear
To grunt and sweat under a weary life
But that the dread of something after death
(The undiscovered country from whose bourn
No traveller returns) puzzles the will   25
And makes us rather bear those ills we have
Than fly to others that we know not of.

D
Thus conscience does make cowards –
And thus the native hue of resolution
Is sicklied o'er with the pale cast of thought,   30
And enterprises of great pith and moment
With this regard their currents turn awry
And lose the name of action.

Glosses
1, **be** = live; 3, **slings and arrows** = assaults, **outrageous** = violent;
4, **arms** = weapons; 8, **consummation** = end, death; 10, **perchance**
= perhaps, **rub** = obstacle; 12, **shuffled off** = left behind, **mortal coil**
= human turmoil; 13, **respect** = consideration; 15, **scorns** = insults;
16, **contumely** = insult; 18, **office** = officialdom, **spurns** = rejections;
19, **merit** = worthiness; 20, **quietus** = release; 21, **bodkin** = dagger,
fardels = burdens; 24, **bourn** = frontier; 25, **puzzles** = bewilders; 28,
conscience = reflection; 29, **native hue** = natural colour; 30, **sicklied
o'er** = tainted, **cast** = shadow; 31, **pith** = force, **moment** = importance; 32, **regard** = consideration.

Speak

* Read through the text out loud, slowly, looking at the glosses
  as you go.

* Read through the text again; this time slow down and focus
  your attention on the movement of your lips and your tongue.
  You may even exaggerate their movement by 10 per cent so
  that you can better feel the physical shaping of the words.

Question
I *Probing*

* Hamlet states his dilemma so memorably in the first line of this
  speech, it's easy to overlook the fact that almost immediately
  he feels the need to clarify or refine his original question.

* Get a partner. Partner A will read section A of the text fairly
  slowly. Partner B, once A has finished the first line, interrupt
  and ask, 'What do you mean by that?' Partner A continue

reading, using the rest of the section to actively answer the question.

- A will read that section of the speech again. B, you can now interrupt more frequently with more detailed questions. A should always be able to answer your question by speaking the next line or going back and repeating what she has just said. For example, after 'To be, or not to be', you might ask, 'What's that?', and A would answer, 'that is the question'. Or after 'Whether 'tis nobler in the mind', you might ask, 'Whether 'tis nobler *where*?', and A would answer, 'Whether 'tis nobler in *the mind*', so as to answer your question. Aim to ask about two questions per line, making sure that your questions can always be answered with the text.

- Swap over so that B will read and A will question. Discuss any discoveries you've made.

Teaching Tip: Depending upon your students, you may want to provide them with a list of possible questions.

Working Alone: As you read the text out loud, stop before each important word (i.e. usually *not* words like 'and', 'the', 'to', etc.) and think what question that word could answer before speaking it. So the second line might go like this: 'Whether 'tis (what?) nobler (where?) in the mind to (to do what?) suffer'. This will slow you down quite a bit, and you will find that you are emphasizing a lot of words, which is fine for now.

II *Good or Bad*

- Having stated his question more exactly, Hamlet then gives closer consideration to one of the possibilities: 'to die', equating it with 'to sleep'. Sleeping is one of those things that one rarely thinks about when one is getting enough of it. It's worth noting that Hamlet says elsewhere that his sleep has been plagued by bad dreams.

- We're going to work on section B. Draw an imaginary line down the centre of the room. Every time you talk about something that is appealing from Hamlet's point of view (not necessarily your own), you will move to one side of the line. The more appealing it is, the further to that side of the room you will go. When you talk about things that are unappealing, you will cross the line and go to the other side of the room, further for the most unappealing things. The line is neutral ground, and you'll start standing on it when you say 'to die', because Hamlet hasn't made up his mind whether death is appealing or not. Bear in mind too that, while he would love to get some sleep, dreaming has been a very unpleasant experience for him lately.

- Having done the exercise once, you probably found that there were some words that very clearly sent you to one side of the room or the other but others that were harder to locate. Go back and try to find a sense in which each of those words could be positive and then a sense in which each could be negative. Read the section a couple more times, trying a few of those phrases on one side of the room and then the other.

- Discuss any discoveries you've made.

III *Pushing Through*

- Phrases that are repeated by characters are always worth close consideration. We've just looked at Hamlet's reiteration of 'to die: to sleep –'. He also repeats the words 'there's the'. It's not a terribly interesting phrase in and of itself, but when one is trying to find the answer to a problem, it marks a key moment of discovery, particularly when preceded by 'ay', as the first one is. He also repeats 'who would'.

- We're going to work on the section between 'to die: to sleep – To sleep, perchance to dream', in the middle of part B through to the end of part C and 'that we know not of'.

- Depending on the set-up of your class, there are a few ways you can do this exercise. In essence, you are going to move a heavy object around the space – it can be a chair that you push with your hand, a big bag that you move with your foot, or even a partner that you push against back to back. On the repeated phrases, 'there's the' and 'who would', put a lot of energy into moving that object a significant distance across the space (safely!). In between, give that object a smaller, but determined, push at every comma.

- You can repeat the exercise and continue on to finish the speech, giving big pushes on the repeated 'thus' as well.

IV *Stepping Stones*

- 'Thus' is a summing-up kind of word, and with it Hamlet does seem to come to a conclusion: we endure all the miseries of life because of the fear of the unknowable – death. It's important to fully inhabit the process of *coming to* this conclusion and emotionally responding to it.

- For this exercise you will need a partner and three chairs. The chairs need to be sturdy, easily able to hold your weight, and not wobbly. Set the chairs up so that, standing on them, you can step from one to the other safely. Leave enough room between them, though, that you have to reach just a bit to get from chair to chair. Your partner will stand in the middle of the three chairs and hold one of your hands lightly to help you balance. If the chairs get pushed away from each other at any point in the exercise, stop and reset them. (If there are no suitable chairs available, make three crosses on the floor with masking tape or place three objects on the floor, and move between them in the same way.)

- Read through parts A, B, and C; and every time you come to a punctuation mark that isn't a full stop (period), move from one chair to the next, going clockwise. When you get to a full stop, change directions. This will slow you down a bit, and that's fine.

- When you get to 'Thus conscience does make cowards', at the beginning of part D, step down from your chair on the comma (mark this point on your text so you don't have to worry about remembering it). From there until the end of the speech, on each punctuation mark take a step away from the chairs.

Working Alone: You can do this without a partner holding your hand; just make sure the chairs are very stable and you're not stepping quickly.

Act

I

- Try the speech once, speaking directly to individual members of the audience, and imagine that they are people you know well. When you talk about each of the pains and indignities that humans are forced to bear ('outrageous fortune', 'heartache', 'th'oppressor's wrong') address a member of the audience who might have suffered this particular misfortune as if to say, 'You know what I mean – you've had this experience too.'

II

- As a counter-balance to the gloom and doom that we usually associate with Hamlet and this speech, try it once through with a sense of amusement, taking any pleasure you can find in your own ability to figure out why it is that everyone doesn't kill themselves. Think of yourself as a detective actively solving the mystery. When you've done the speech once that way, go back and do it again, connecting more strongly to Hamlet's own given circumstances.

- Either as a class or by yourself, reflect on what you've discovered about Hamlet and soliloquies in Shakespeare.

Follow-up

- Go back through the speeches that you worked on in this chapter and examine the first thing each character says. What do those opening statements tell you about what he or she wants? What do they reveal about his relationship to the person he is talking to and his frame of mind going into the speech or scene? When is that first utterance well thought through and constructed and when is it unguarded and spontaneous? What does it tell you about what preoccupies the character and what problem he's trying to solve? Pick up another speech or scene from elsewhere in this book and take a look at the first thing the character says. Ask some of the above questions about it and then see how your answers are borne out in the rest of the speech. The first sentence is the starting block you, the actor, will push off from, and so it's worth spending time considering how it is constructed and what action it implies.

- In working on Lady Percy, we identified a large portion of the text that could have been left out and explored what happened when we added it again bit by bit. Try doing the same with Cassius: identify any repetitions or lists that could be trimmed without losing the essential point Cassius is trying to make and try doing the speech adding them back in one at a time.

- In working on Portia, we introduced slash marks where Portia seems to modify her point or change her mind. Go through Proteus's speech, and draw slash marks where he seems to do the same. As with Portia, try walking as you read the speech and changing direction sharply at each slash mark.

- Watch a video segment that includes work from this chapter. How did your exploration connect to what you see in the

video? Are there any points from the video session that did not
come up in the work you did?

Further reading

Barton, John, *Playing Shakespeare*, Methuen, London, 1984. Chapter 1: 'The
    Two Traditions'; Chapter 5: 'Set Speeches and Soliloquies'.
Berry, Cicely, *The Actor and the Text*, Virgin Publishing, London, 1992.
    Chapter 2: 'Heightened Versus Naturalistic Text'.
—*From Word to Play*, Oberon Books, London, 2008. Chapter 4: 'Group Work
    on Form and Structure: Speech Structures', pp. 92–9.
Cohen, Robert, *Acting in Shakespeare*, Mayfield Publishing Company,
    Mountain View, 1991. Lesson 2: 'Speech Acts'; Lesson 3: 'Calculated
    Effects'; Lesson 20: 'Story Telling'.
Hall, Peter, *Shakespeare's Advice to the Players*, Oberon Books, London,
    2003. 'Telling', pp. 58–61.
Houseman, Barbara, *Tackling Text [And Subtext]*, Nick Hern Books, London,
    2008. 'Phrase by Phrase', pp. 92–5; 'A Couple of Footnotes', pp. 138–42;
    'Play Objective', pp. 183–8; 'Scene Objective', p. 189; 'What's Been Going
    On Before?', pp. 191–4; 'What's Going On Now?', pp. 195–234.
Kaiser, Scott, *Mastering Shakespeare: An Acting Class in Seven Scenes*,
    Allworth Press, New York, 2003. Scene 5: 'Actions'.
Noble, Adrian, *How To Do Shakespeare*, Routledge, London, 2010. Chapter
    7: 'Vocabulary'; Chapter 8: 'Shape, Structure and Meaning'; Chapter 10:
    'Soliloquy'.
Rodenburg, Patsy, *Speaking Shakespeare*, Methuen, London, 2002. Part 2:
    'Structure, Repetition', pp. 177–9.
Weate, Catherine, *Classic Voice: Working with Actors on Vocal Style*, Oberon
    Books, London, 2009. Chapter 11: 'Demands and Challenges'.

2
LANGUAGE IN ACTION: IMAGERY, SOUND AND STORY

Framework

As you will have begun to discover in the last chapter, Shakespeare's characters are enormously creative in the range of verbal strategies they use. They are constantly making choices about how best to tackle the problem at hand through language, and among the many tools that they have at their disposal are imagery, sound and storytelling. While imagery and sound are often thought of as the stuff of poetry, in Shakespeare's hands they are very much the stuff of drama when used by characters in response to a strong need to have an impact on the listener. It's important for you as an actor to embrace the fact that language that uses a lot imagery or patterning of sound is out of the ordinary – it has a special kind of energy and edge that it would be a pity to ignore or minimize. But it's also important to remember that you need to engage with it actively and not simply lavish appreciation upon it, painting the pictures or shaping the sounds for their own sake. Similarly, when Shakespeare's characters tell stories, it is rarely with the intent of narrating events alone. The stories are constructed to bring the listener around to a particular point of view, and you will need to engage with the structure and detail of the narrative to have the desired effect.

Imagery in language is a broad category that includes description, simile and metaphor (which we will also explore in Chapter 4). Imagery evokes pictures and associations in the imagination of the listener. Even a single word can conjure a response in a listener because of what it makes him see in his mind's eye. We already began to work on specifying images and using them to influence others in the first chapter. In this chapter we will work in more detail on actively crafting images and making them vivid both for yourself and your audience.

Sound also has the power to get under the skin of the listener. The range of speech sounds used in English is quite impressive – there are sounds that have the potential to pop, to glide, to buzz, to caress, to threaten and to soothe. Furthermore, particular patterns of these sounds will catch the ear and grab the attention. In ordinary life, we often don't engage with forming speech sounds particularly energetically, nor is there much need to on an everyday basis. If you want to get a friend to join you for lunch, 'Ya wannuh getsm lunch' will usually suffice. When the stakes rise, however, we quite unconsciously use a wider range of sounds and give them greater definition so as to have greater impact. Think about how you would say 'I absolutely will not' if your intention were to end an argument once and for all. Because Shakespeare's characters are strongly committed to pursuing their actions through language, they use speech sounds energetically and with purpose. He has given them wonderfully specific words to say, formed of sounds that have the potential to be powerfully expressive and affecting.

In *stories*, imagery and sounds are often used to make the events described vivid for the listener. It can be tempting, when telling stories, to focus on the past or to try to recreate the emotions associated with the event described. The character, however, is not telling the story with the intent of re-experiencing something that is past; she's telling it to make something happen in the future. There is usually an underlying element of persuasion in storytelling. The character wants the listeners to believe her version of the events so that they will feel what she feels and, consequently, do what she wants them to do about it. Telling the story well, then – making it immediate, specific and powerful – becomes a crucial strategy for achieving your character's intention.

Exploration

Mark Antony

Let's go back to the first line of Mark Antony's speech: 'Friend, Romans, countrymen, lend me your ears'.

I

- Begin by looking at the choice of the phrase 'lend me your ears'. Instead of saying 'Listen to me' or 'Pay attention to me', Mark Antony uses a metaphorical image. In this exploration, we're going to look at why he does this.

- First, let's look at the word 'lend'. What kinds of relationships exist between people who lend things to each other? When might you ask someone to lend you a pen, your phone, some money? When would you ask someone to *give* you a pen, your phone, some money? With a partner or on your own consider the differences between lending and giving. What is the relationship between a lender and a borrower? Why do you think Shakespeare has Antony choose the word 'lend' rather than 'give'?

- Now, go back to the whole phrase, 'lend me your ears'. We cannot literally lend (or give) our ears to anyone, so what is Antony actually saying? We suggested above that it means 'listen to me' or 'pay attention to me'. You might think of some other phrases.

- As a group, choose one person to be Antony, and the rest will be the crowd. Antony will be at one end of the room, facing the crowd, who will be milling around discussing what Brutus has said. *Antony*: use any of the literal phrases ('listen to me', 'pay attention to me', or any other that you thought of) to try and get the crowd to listen to you. You can repeat it several times.

- Pick another Antony, and try the same thing with another phrase.

- Finally, choose a different Antony, and try the same thing with 'lend me your ears'. Did the crowd respond differently? If so, why? Even if they didn't, what was the difference between Antony using a metaphor and being literal? Does he present a different image of himself if he speaks literally as opposed to metaphorically? Does he have a different effect on his listeners?

II

- Find a place where you can stand or sit and work on your own. Close your eyes and make a long 'ffff' sound. What does the sound feel like on your lips? What effect does it have on you – is it soothing? Jarring? Stirring? What images does it evoke in your mind?

- Repeat the sound 'ffff', but change its dynamics in some way; for example, make it sharper, softer, fiercer, or more affectionate. What does the sound feel like on your lip? How does it affect you emotionally? What images does it evoke in your mind?

- Repeat the sound 'ffff' once more, and again change its dynamics in some way. At the same time, make a gesture or shape with your hand that matches or follows the energy of the 'ffff'.

- Now close your eyes and make a long 'rrrr' sound. What does the sound feel like on your tongue? What effect does it have on you? What images does it evoke in your mind? Again, repeat it twice, changing the dynamics in some way each time. And on the second time make a gesture or shape with your hand that goes with the 'rrrr' sound.

- Finally, close your eyes and make a 'k' sound six or seven times. What does the sound feel like in the back of your mouth? What effect does it have? What images does it evoke in your mind? Try changing the dynamics of your 'k' sound. After two or three repetitions, start moving your hand in a way that matches the energy of the 'k'.

- With your eyes still closed, say the phrase, 'Friends, Romans, countrymen'. As you do, draw out the 'f' sound of 'friends' and make a movement to match; then draw out the 'r' sound of 'Romans' and do the same; and, finally, speak the 'k' sound of 'countrymen' energetically and make a movement with your hand.

- Open your eyes. You will now address an imaginary audience with the line, 'Friends, Romans, countrymen, lend me your ears'. You don't have to gesture, or even draw out the first sounds, but be mindful of speaking them with energy, emotional commitment and intention.

- Using similarly energized sounds, say 'Countrymen, friends, Romans, lend me your ears'. Then try, 'Romans, countrymen, friends, lend me your ears'. Finally, go back to 'Friends, Romans, countrymen, lend me your ears'.

- Discuss how the energy of the sounds helps you reach out to your audience and engage them. What happened when you changed the order of the words? Is there a progression or build in sound the way Shakespeare has written the line?

Exercises

The exercises in this chapter are divided into three sections: 'Picture painting', 'Ear catching' and 'Storytelling'. In each section, we will ask you to explore two speeches.

Teaching Tip or Working Alone: You may wish to watch a video segment that includes exercises from this chapter before you begin practical work.

Picture painting

Shakespeare was writing at a time before the invention of film and television, before the use of realistic theatrical scenery, and in an era when most plays were performed outdoors in daylight. So his principal means of telling the audience where a scene was set, what time of day it was, what the weather was like, etc. was through description: imagery. This kind of informative picture painting for the audience often takes place at the beginning of a scene or occasionally at the end. However, sometimes, characters will enter into extended picture painting which is intended to have a more powerful effect on the listener: the imagery engages the imagination in a way that awakens an emotional response. As an actor, you must first make these images specific and vivid in your own imagination; if you don't see the pictures the language paints and have a response to them, neither will your scene partner nor your audience. Once you do own them as a character – that is, when you connect to them and care about them – you then need to trust the language to do the work, which will help you to avoid over-embellishing. Once you move from questioning the text to acting, your focus will shift to using those pictures to effect a change in the person or people you are talking to. The exercises in this section will help you to achieve that goal.

Chorus from Henry V

Shakespeare's use of the Chorus figure in *Henry V* is very particular. At the beginning of each act, the Chorus takes the stage to set the scene and move the story forward. Using only the power of language, the Chorus draws the audience actively into the theatrical event, engaging their imaginations through detailed descriptions of people, places and events. But the Chorus is not just there to inform the audience of facts; the imagery is also designed to arouse an emotional response: excitement, wonder, pity, fear, pride. The following chorus occurs at the beginning of Act 4, just before the famous battle of Agincourt at which Henry and his army, massively outnumbered though they were, defeated the French and paved the way for Henry to affirm his claim to the French throne and marry the French king's daughter, Katherine. The Chorus shows us, in words, the two opposing forces in their camps as they prepare for battle.

- Speak through the text quietly a couple of times without looking at the glosses.

CHORUS
Now entertain conjecture of a time

When creeping murmur and the poring dark
Fills the wide vessel of the universe.
From camp to camp through the foul womb of night
The hum of either army stilly sounds,   5
That the fixed sentinels almost receive
The secret whispers of each other's watch.
Fire answers fire, and through their paly flames
Each battle sees the other's umbered face.
Steed threatens steed, in high and boastful neighs   10
Piercing the night's dull ear; and from the tents
The armourers accomplishing the knights,
With busy hammers closing rivets up,
Give dreadful note of preparation.
The country cocks do crow, the clocks do toll,   15
And the third hour of drowsy morning name.
Proud of their numbers, and secure in soul,
The confident and over-lusty French
Do the low-rated English play at dice,
And chide the cripple tardy-gaited night   20
Who like a foul and ugly witch doth limp
So tediously away. The poor condemnèd English,
Like sacrifices, by their watchful fires
Sit patiently and inly ruminate
The morning's danger; and their gesture sad,   25
Investing lank-lean cheeks and war-worn coats,
Presenteth them unto the gazing moon
So many horrid ghosts.

Glosses
1, **entertain conjecture** = imagine the idea; 2, **poring** = peering; 5,
stilly = quietly; 6, **sentinels** = guards; 8, **paly** = pale; 9, **battle** = army,
umbered = shadowy; 12, **accomplishing** = equipping; 17, **secure
in soul** = free of anxiety; 18, **over-lusty** = overly cheerful; 19, **play**
= play for; 20, **chide** = scold, **tardy-gaited** = slow-moving; 24, **inly
ruminate** = inwardly meditate; 25, **sad** = gloomy; 26, **investing** =
accompanying, **lank-lean** = gaunt; 28, **horrid** = horrifying.

Speak

- Speak through the text quietly again, looking at the glosses as you go, even for words you think you know.

- Speak through the text again, at a more conversational volume this time, and move around the room, changing direction at every punctuation mark.

Question
I *Physicalizing the Image*

- You have probably begun to identify many of the images the Chorus uses to paint the picture. Now we want you to get even more specific. Speak the text through again; but now as you speak it, take time to find a way to physicalize or act out each image as you speak it. So if you're talking about climbing, move your arms and legs as if you were climbing. Or, more abstractly, if you're talking about shame, find a physical manifestation of that emotional response. Be sure to give each image your focus. If you need to repeat a phrase several times to find the physicalization that feels right to you, that's okay. If you're being really specific, this exercise will probably make you slow down and break up the text into smaller chunks. You might lose sight of the overall picture, but the details will begin to stand out more. This is part of the necessary process of making the language your own.

- Repeat this exercise, looking for even more detail in the text and for more definition in your physicalization. For example, the French are described as:

  'proud of their numbers'
  'secure in soul'
  'confident'
  'over-lusty'

  Make sure you give each of these phrases a different physical shape as you speak it.

II *Specifying the Image*

- In descriptive passages like this chorus, Shakespeare often uses a sequence of images that create a cinematic effect. To explore how this works in this particular speech, imagine that you are a film cameraman and the text is your shooting script. As you speak the passage, instead of physicalizing the images yourself, pretend that you're looking through the viewfinder of a camera. If this text were the voiceover, imagine what images would be appearing on the screen as you speak. Take your time and 'see' the way the shots unfold as you describe them. If necessary, repeat this exercise. What do you discover about the way Shakespeare directs the viewer?

- You probably noticed how Shakespeare begins with what might be called a wide-angle shot of the dark universe, before beginning to focus on the two camps. There is then a swift sequence of repeated or echoed images between the two armies, culminating in a focus on the armourers. The camera then cuts to a more peaceful image of the surrounding countryside before returning to examine the two camps in more detail.

- As well as visual images, Shakespeare evokes soundscapes in this description. Instead of being the cameraman, this time imagine you are the sound engineer. As you now speak the passage, pretend that you are listening through headphones to the soundtrack of the scene: the crackle of the fire; the neighing of the horses. Take your time and 'hear' the way the language engages the imagination's ear. How much of the detail of the scene is aural? How does this work on your imagination to bring the scene to life?

III *Showing the Image*

- You have almost certainly noticed that Shakespeare gives the Chorus many images which refer to the two armies: 'from camp to camp', 'either army', 'each other's watch', 'fire answers fire', etc. We're now going to explore this aspect of the imagery in more depth. Imagine your work space is the battlefield. At one end of the room is the French army, at the other end the English. Get into pairs and with your partner place yourself somewhere between these two points. Imagine you are standing in the dark no man's land that separates the two armies. Partner A, as you now speak the text, take Partner B by the arm and move between the two camps or gesture to them in order to locate each image specifically for your partner. B, if you feel you haven't been helped to see specifically enough where things are located in this space, ask A to show you again. Have you discovered anything new in this way?

- Swap over. Using the same scenario, Partner B imagine that you and A are two civilians witnessing the preparations for war. As you speak the text, use the images to create in your partner a sense of dread and anticipation of the battle.

Act

- You should now have a thorough understanding of this very descriptive text and what effect the Chorus is intending to have on the audience. In acting the speech, the challenge is to let the language do the work. To help you meet this challenge, we are going to ask you to indulge in some negative practice. Get a couple of partners. Take it in turns to act the speech for each other in the following ways:

1. Emphasizing every detail of each image.

2. Using lots of physical gestures.

3. Using lots of vocal gestures, e.g. changing pitch, whispering, imitating the sounds.

This was probably quite funny, but what else have you learned about acting this type of language?

- Over-colouring Shakespeare's language in any of these ways is likely to cause your audience to focus on how you're saying the words and not on what you're saying. Instead you need to trust your work, the language and your audience. The work you have done in speaking and questioning the text, if it has been specific and rigorous, will have enabled you to own the language, to trust that you have a connection to each image and understand its role in the bigger picture. So, your task in acting the speech is to focus actively on the Chorus's intention of inviting the audience to engage their imaginations and sympathies – 'to entertain conjecture' – and to join you in seeing these images and hearing these sounds.

• Get together with your partner again, and take it in turns to act the speech. Keep your external focus strongly on your audience and your internal focus actively in your imaginative connection to the scene, so that you are sharing the experience through the words. You cannot *make* them see or hear things by forcing the language; you have to trust that your own connection with the words in the moment will meet with an equally active receptivity in them. Try it a couple of times: *doing* less and *believing* more.

• Either as a class or by yourself reflect on anything you've discovered about the nature of the Chorus, Shakespeare's language, and the importance of 'seeing' what you are describing.

Titania

Titania is Queen of the Fairies in *A Midsummer Night's Dream*. We first see her in Act 2 Scene 1 as she and her husband, Oberon, meet each other in an angry confrontation. Oberon and Titania have been quarrelling since the beginning of summer about the custody of a little boy: he is the orphan son of one of Titania's mortal followers that Titania has promised to raise, but Oberon wants the boy for himself as his page. Moreover, their quarrelling has created disturbances in the natural world. They begin their argument by accusing each other of being unfaithful, but then Titania changes her line of attack and uses an extended description to paint a picture of just how awful the world has become as a result of their dissension.

• Speak through the text quietly a couple of times without looking at the glosses.

TITANIA

A

These are the forgeries of jealousy:
And never, since the middle summer's spring,
Met we on hill, in dale, forest or mead,
By pavèd fountain, or by rushy brook,
Or in the beachèd margent of the sea,   5
To dance our ringlets to the whistling wind,
But with thy brawls thou hast disturbed our sport.
Therefore the winds, piping to us in vain,
As in revenge have sucked up from the sea
Contagious fogs; which, falling in the land,   10
Hath every pelting river made so proud
That they have over-borne their continents.

B

The ox hath therefore stretched his yoke in vain,
The ploughman lost his sweat, and the green corn
Hath rotted ere his youth attained a beard;   15
The fold stands empty in the drownèd field,
And crows are fatted with the murrion flock;
The nine-men's-morris is filled up with mud,
And the quaint mazes in the wanton green
For lack of tread are undistinguishable.   20
The human mortals want their winter cheer:
No night is now with hymn or carol blest.
Therefore the moon, the governess of floods,
Pale in her anger, washes all the air,
That rheumatic diseases do abound.   25

C

And thorough this distemperature we see
The seasons alter: hoary headed frosts
Fall in the fresh lap of the crimson rose;
And on old Hiems' thin and icy crown,
An odorous chaplet of sweet summer buds   30
Is, as in mockery, set; the spring, the summer,
The childing autumn, angry winter, change

Their wonted liveries; and the mazèd world,
By their increase, now knows not which is which.
And this same progeny of evils comes   35
From our debate, from our dissension;
We are their parents and original.

Glosses

1, **forgeries** = inventions; 2, **spring** = beginning; 3, **mead** = meadow;
5, **beached margent of the sea** = seashore; 6, **ringlets** = circle
dances; 7, **sport** = amusement; 10, **contagious** = harmful; 11, **pelting**
= petty, **proud** = swollen; 12, **over-borne** = overflowed, **continents**
= banks; 16, **fold** = sheep-pen; 17, **murrion** = diseased; 18, **nine-
men's-morris** = area for playing this game; 19, **quaint** = intricate,
wanton = lush, **green** = greenery; 20, **undistinguishable** = unrec-
ognizable; 21, **want** = lack; 24, **washes** = moistens; 25, **rheumatic**
= phlegmy; 26, **thorough** = through, **distemperature** = disorder;
27, **hoary** = white; 29, **Hiems** = Winter; 30, **chaplet** = garland; 32,
childing = fruitful; 33, **wonted** = usual, **liveries** = costumes, **mazed**
= confused; 34, **increase** = enhancement; 35, **progeny** = family; 36,
debate = quarrel; 37, **original** = source.

Speak

- Speak through the text quietly again, looking at the glosses as
  you go, even for words you think you know.

- Speak through the text again, at a more conversational volume
  this time, and move around the room, changing direction at the
  end of every verse line.

Question

I *Visualizing*

- Although Titania is very passionate and explicit about the
  effects of their quarrel on nature, she presents her argument
  to Oberon quite logically. The speech develops from an
  opening section which points the finger of blame at Oberon
  and his followers for disturbing the fairies' sport and so for
  being responsible for the winds, fogs and floods that have

afflicted the countryside. She then proceeds to give a thorough description of the consequences for the natural world and human society, before detailing the larger confusion of the seasons. She finishes with an acknowledgement of their joint responsibility for this 'progeny of evils'.

- Read through section A again, and notice all the specific images of landscape and weather that Titania draws upon. Set the text aside for a moment and begin to let these images work on your imagination. Conjure up in your own mind a landscape where there are hills and dales, rivers and brooks, forests and meadows – take time to be specific, try to see yourself in the middle of this world (perhaps at the top of one of the hills) rather than looking at a painting. Where are the 'pavèd fountains', where is the sea? Now, think about the weather – imagine yourself on a pleasant country walk in some beautiful early summer sunshine. Let yourself move through your imagined landscape, enjoying the sights and sounds of nature. All of a sudden the gentle breeze that's been blowing through the leaves starts to toss the branches back and forth; dark clouds roll swiftly in, bringing a cold, dank fog; and then it begins to pour with rain, torrential rain. What can you see of your landscape? What does it look like? If this rain persists, how soon will the countryside be flooded all around? How does it make you feel?

Teaching Tip: This guided visualization is intended to be led by the teacher. You can use our own descriptions, or adapt them to the specific needs and culture of your group.

Working Alone: You might like to record the instructions for the guided visualization, so that you don't have to keep opening your eyes and reading our instructions.

- Now, pick up the text again and, as you speak it through, let the words paint this inner landscape of imagery and emotional response to the natural world that you've just explored. Take your time, and see yourself in the middle of this world as you speak. If you need to, speak it through several times.

- What effect did this visualization exercise have on your speaking? What discoveries have you made about Titania and her world?

II *Reporting*

- Now let's move on to the next section. Read through part B again, and notice all the specific images that Titania chooses to focus on. How are these images different from the ones in the previous section?

- Instead of imagery of the countryside and weather – images from nature – Titania focuses on agricultural scenes and village life – images from human society. The pictures she evokes would have been very familiar to Shakespeare and his audience: ploughing fields, growing corn and grazing sheep were much more part of people's experience than they are today; village mazes and nine men's morris were as common as modern football pitches and BMX parks. These activities also might normally have connotations of growth, health and enjoyment, but Titania paints a gloomy picture of decay and sickness. Speak this text out loud now, and take time to explore the separate images in turn. You can either physicalize or visualize them, but make sure you create a clear picture for yourself of what each one describes: see the ox labouring in vain, the ploughman's futile sweat, the overgrown mazes.

- In groups of four or five, choose one of your number to be a TV journalist. The rest of you will be villagers, explaining the results of some recent severe flooding and bad harvests in order to get support from the government and city viewers. You can show the journalist animals and crops, or take him to film parts of your village. Use the text of this section to describe things to the viewers, repeating phrases as necessary. Remember, this is a major emergency.

Working Alone: Imagine you're one of the few survivors of this catastrophe and you're streaming a webcast in the hope of getting government aid.

- What effect did this improvisation exercise have on your speaking? What discoveries have you made about Titania and her intentions?

III *Crossing the Line*

- Finally, look at the remainder of the speech. Read though section C again, and notice the specific images that Titania chooses to focus on this time. As you'll realize, the imagery in this section is mainly concerned with the seasons and how confused they've become. More specifically, however, the seasons become personified in Titania's imagination: they have heads, laps, clothes; they can be angry or give birth. What human age do you think each season would be? What gender? How are they dressed?

- Draw an imaginary line down the centre of the room. Read section C aloud, and every time you talk about something that evokes spring or summer – growth or warmth – move to one side of the line. Every time you talk about something that evokes autumn or winter – coldness or decline – move to the other.

- If you're in a group, grab a couple of partners. Make one of them summer/spring and have her stand on that side of the line. Make the other winter/autumn and have him stand on the other side. Read the text again, and when you talk about wintery things happening to summer/spring, physically pull her across the line. Summer/spring, you can resist a bit without turning the exercise into an all-out tug-of-war. When you talk about spring-like things happening to winter/autumn, pull him across the line. When you talk about the seasons changing places try to push them back to where they belong. You'll have to take the text quite slowly – don't worry if you lose your place on the page – what's important is that you are physically engaging with the image of everything being in the wrong place.

Working Alone: If you're in a space with furniture, try shoving it back and forth across the centre line as you speak.

- What effect did this improvisation exercise have on your speaking? What discoveries have you made about Titania and her use of imagery?

IV *Putting It All Together*

- When there is a long story or description like this, it's important to break the speech down into its component parts, but now it's time to put the whole text back together again as a unified whole. Try this exercise to help you build one part of Titania's argument upon the one before.

- Working individually, speak through the whole text with a focus on discovering the progression of the images from the landscape through the agricultural scenes to the seasons. As you do so, explore Titania's personal connection to what she's describing – this is a landscape, a community and a natural world that matters to her.

- Still working individually, write down a phrase or sentence that could lead you from section A to section B and one that could lead you from B to C. Perhaps something like 'Not only that, but also …' or 'Because of that, this is happening …' or 'And do you know what's even worse …' Speak through the whole text again, inserting the phrases you've written. Then repeat the speech once more without them, but following the logical progression that holds Titania's argument together. You may need to do this a couple of times to find your ownership of this aspect of the speech.

Act

- Building on the previous exercises, get together with a partner. One of you will be Oberon, the other Titania. Titania, as you act the speech, let your emotional connection to the world of nature and humanity be the driving force behind your argument. You may be trying to make Oberon feel guilty; you may want him to recognize the passionate woman he's been missing in consorting with other women; you may be demonstrating your moral superiority. Whatever over-riding action you choose, use the images and your feelings for them to realize this. Oberon, feel free to react in any non-verbal way you feel is in character.

- Change over, so that the partner who was Oberon is now Titania. This time, Titania, your intention is to convince Oberon to give up the quarrel, and this detailed description of both the natural and human world is your vehicle for doing so. However, you know from past experience that Oberon will dismiss any argument that is over-emotional, and so you have to keep a tight rein on your feelings – they are your obstacle. Oberon, if at any point you suspect that Titania is being too emotional, make a dismissive gesture or vocalization.

- What was the effect of acting the speech in these two ways? Which did you prefer? Which Oberon was more engaged in the argument? Is it possible for Titania to use her personal connection to the images to work on both Oberon's emotions and his intellect and convince him to give up the feud?

- Either as a class or by yourself reflect on anything you've discovered about Titania and the uses of extended imagery.

Ear catching

Just as characters use imagery to awaken the imaginations of their listeners and, ultimately, have a specific effect on them, so they can use the sounds of words to catch their listeners' ears and focus their attention in a particular way. You will find this in many of the *Henry V* choruses. For example, in describing the English and French armies' preparation for battle in the chorus we looked at earlier, Shakespeare uses the word 'steed' where he could have used 'horse'. The hiss of the initial 's', the punch of the plosives 't' and 'd', and the strength of the long vowel 'ee' have a particular effect that is in keeping with the militaristic scene he is setting. Think, also, of the way Shakespeare uses the hiss of the 's' sounds in the lines 'That the fixed sentinels almost receive/ The secret whispers of each other's watch' to recreate the soldiers' whispers. In the same speech is the line 'Each battle sees the other's umbered face'. It would have been much more straightforward to say 'Each army sees the other's shadowed face'. To what extent Shakespeare consciously thought 'I'll use "battle" because the sound of it has more punch than "army", and "umbered" sounds spookier than "shadowed"' is ultimately irrelevant. What's important is that the words you are given often present you with sounds that you can use to further your intention, to get under your listener's skin and have an effect on him.

The chapter on sound in our book *The Verbal Arts Workbook* has several exercises for exploring the qualities of different speech sounds that would make a good warm-up for the work we will do here. It also has an introduction to different sound patterns that are commonly used in dramatic writing. There are two in particular that we will work with in this section: **alliteration**, which is the grouping together of words that begin with the same sound ('*same sound*' is an example); and **rhyme**, which happens when the final vowel sound and any consonant sounds after it are the same in two words ('w*ords*' and 'b*irds*' rhyme).

Lady Macbeth

Macbeth has shared with his wife the witches' prediction that he will become king, and together they have hatched a plan to kill the present king, but Macbeth is now having second thoughts. When Lady Macbeth accuses him in Act 1 Scene 7 of being a coward, he insists that he is bold enough to do anything that it is proper for a man to do. She replies by demanding to know if it was a beast then that plotted with her, and tries to persuade him to go through with it.

Lady Macbeth is very good with words – she can use them to bully, to seduce, to hypnotize, to castigate, and so on. We'll explore in particular how you can use the sounds that make up the words and the alliteration that Shakespeare peppers her speech with to help bring those actions to life and give them force and dimension.

- Speak through the text quietly a couple of times without looking at the glosses.

(MACBETH
I dare do all that may become a man;
Who dares do more, is none.)
LADY MACBETH
        What beast was't then,
That made you break this enterprise to me?
When you durst do it, then you were a man;
And, to be more than what you were, you would   5
Be so much more the man. Nor time, nor place,
Did then adhere, and yet you would make both:
They have made themselves, and that their fitness now
Does unmake you. I have given suck, and know
How tender 'tis to love the babe that milks me: 10
I would, while it was smiling in my face,
Have plucked my nipple from his boneless gums,
And dashed the brains out, had I so sworn
As you have done to this.
(MACBETH
        If we should fail?)
LADY MACBETH

We fail?   15
But screw your courage to the sticking-place,
And we'll not fail. When Duncan is asleep
(Whereto the rather shall his day's hard journey
Soundly invite him), his two chamberlains
Will I with wine and wassail so convince,   20
That memory, the warder of the brain,
Shall be a fume, and the receipt of reason
A limbeck only: when in swinish sleep
Their drenchèd natures lie, as in a death,
What cannot you and I perform upon   25
Th'unguarded Duncan? what not put upon
His spongy officers, who shall bear the guilt
Of our great quell?

Glosses

1, **become** = befit; 3, **break** = reveal; 4, **durst** = dared; 7, **adhere** = agree, **you would make both** = you wished to make the opportunity; 9, **unmake** = undo; 19, **chamberlains** = attendants; 20, **wassail** = spiced ale, **convince** = overpower; 21, **warder** = guardian; 22, **fume** = mist, **receipt** = receptacle; 23, **limbeck** = distilling glass; 24, **drenched** = drunken; 26, **put upon** = attribute to; 27, **spongy** = drunken; 28, **quell** = murder.

Speak

I

- Read through the text out loud, slowly, looking at the glosses as you go.

- Sitting in a chair or lying down, read the speech in a whisper. Don't use any voice, just breath. Notice how you have to use a little more energy in your lips and tongue when you are whispering. This may slow you down a bit, which is fine.

II

- Lie on your back in a comfortable position. Hold your paper in one hand. Read through the speech out loud at a conversational volume fairly slowly. As you do, hold your

other hand up and keep it in constant motion. Let what you
are saying influence how you gesture. Sometimes your hand
may mirror what you are saying, so if you were to talk about
slapping someone, you would make a slapping motion with
your hand. Sometimes you may simply jab with your hand
to emphasize an important point or wave it in time with the
rhythm of the speech. Don't think too hard about it – just let
your impulses flow freely and boldly through your arm.

Question
I *Repeating Sounds*

- **Alliteration** is the name given to the repetition of the same
  consonant sound, particularly at the beginning of words. Speak
  the text aloud again, and any time you feel two or more words in
  the same line starting with the same *sound*, underline them. Note
  that not all words that begin with the same letter begin with the
  same sound; for example 'thin' and 'try' both begin with a 't', but
  they start with different sounds. And while 'fish' and 'philosophy'
  have different first letters, they start with the same sound.

- Reading the speech aloud (skipping Macbeth's lines), whenever
  you come to a word that is underlined, stomp your foot as you
  say the line.

- Read through the speech again, and whenever you come to
  a word that is underlined, make a flicking motion with your
  hand.

- Read through the speech once more, and whenever you come
  to a word that is underlined, push to one side or the other with
  your shoulder.

- Discuss. Did some of the underlined words work better with
  one action than another? Why do you think this was the case?

- Go through the speech and mix and match actions with
  alliterative words depending on both the sound that is repeated
  and what Lady Macbeth is saying. So if she is chastising
  Macbeth and using explosive sounds, you may choose to
  stomp your foot. Or if she is reassuring him and using softer

sounds, you might push with your shoulder. You can bring in new actions too if you are so inspired, such as pounding a fist or making a stroking motion with your hand; just use the same action for each of the paired words.

II *Words in Action*

- We're going to look now at the expressive quality of individual words. If you are working with an instructor, she will read a list of words to you one at a time. If you are working alone, read a word from the list that follows, do the exercise, and then read the next word.

- If you are in a group, find a place in the room where you can work by yourself without directly looking at anyone else. Whether you are in a group or on your own, you may want to work with your eyes closed to help you stay focused.

- First whisper the word to yourself, exaggerating the movements of your lips and tongue ever so slightly.

- Next, say the word out loud and make whatever movement the word suggests to you. For example, if the word were punch, you would probably make a punching motion with your fist as you said the word. If the word were 'flame', you might make a flickering motion like a flame.

- Repeat the word again, and make your movements bigger – so you might throw more of your weight into your 'punch' or let the 'flame' flicker throughout your body. As you do so, shape the word so that it too reflects the meaning of the word. For example, you might explode the 'p' and 'ch' sounds in 'punch' very strongly. Or you might make the 'fl' sounds of 'flame' very quickly and strongly to capture its incendiary nature. The words will start to become more clusters of sound than spoken language, which is fine for now.

- Repeat a fourth time, and let your body be still but continue to shape the sounds very strongly and vividly.

    Love
    Smiling

Pluck

Dash (as in to break apart)

Courage

Stick (as in adhere to)

Fume

Limbeck (flask)

Swinish (like a swine or pig)

Drenched

Death

Spongy

Quell (slaughter)

Teaching Tip: Read the definitions in parentheses as well.

- Now pick up the speech and read it out loud from 'I have given suck' (skipping Macbeth's line). When you get to one of the words that you've been exploring, don't shy away from filling it with some of the energy and specific qualities you found in the exercise.

Act

- Get a partner to be your Macbeth, or if you are working alone, read each of his lines silently to yourself before you begin speaking. Perform the speech three times in a row without stopping to talk about it or reflect. The first time lean into the words and sounds that you explored in the questioning section a bit more than you might ordinarily. The second time be mindful of them, but don't lean into them – let the alliteration and expressive sounds sit as lightly as possible. The third time, think only of actively using the language to get Macbeth to go ahead with the murder.

- Discuss at which points you felt the sound work supported your intention best.

Helena

Helena, from *A Midsummer Night's Dream*, is in a love quadrangle. She is in love with Demetrius, who used to love her but then fell for Hermia. Hermia is not interested in Demetrius because she and Lysander are in love. When Hermia and Lysander sneak into the woods outside of town to elope, Demetrius follows them, and Helena follows him. Once in the woods, Demetrius and Lysander both fall under the magic spell of fairies, which causes them to fall madly in love with Helena. When they profess their love in Act 3 Scene 2, Helena thinks that they are making fun of her, and she rebukes them.

In *A Midsummer Night's Dream* much of these four lovers' language is in rhyming couplets, where pairs of subsequent lines end with rhyming words. *Love's Labour's Lost* is another play with a lot of rhyming dialogue, and couplets appear in many of the plays. Rhymes catch the ear very strongly, and it can be easy to either overplay them, so that the audience is distracted from the meaning of the words by the rhyme, or to underplay them, which means that you as the actor are not entirely fulfilling the potential of the language. Rhyming is a choice, and when Shakespeare chooses it, it's worth investigating what it can add to the scene and what it says about the effect the character wants to have on his listener.

- Speak through the text quietly a couple of times without looking at the glosses.

HELENA
A
O spite! O hell! I see you all are bent
To set against me for your merriment.
If you were civil, and knew courtesy,
You would not do me thus much injury.
Can you not hate me, as I know you do,   5
But you must join in souls to mock me too?
If you were men, as men you are in show,
You would not use a gentle lady so:
To vow, and swear, and superpraise my parts,
When I am sure you hate me with your hearts.   10

You both are rivals, and love Hermia;
And now both rivals to mock Helena.

B
A trim exploit, a manly enterprise,
To conjure tears up in a poor maid's eyes
With your derision! None of noble sort   15
Would so offend a virgin, and extort
A poor soul's patience, all to make you sport.

Glosses
1, **bent** = determined; 2, **set against** = attack; 3, **courtesy** = good
manners; 4, **injury** = insult; 9, **parts** = qualities; 13, **trim** = fine; 16,
extort = abuse; 17, **sport** = entertainment.

Speak

- Read through the text out loud, slowly, looking at the glosses
  as you go.

- If you're working in a group, scatter yourselves around the
  room so that you're at least two metres away from anyone
  else. Pick one person to start. That person will read the first
  line while walking around the room. When he gets to the last
  word of the line, he will tag the person nearest to him. That
  person will then read the next line while walking towards
  someone else, whom he will tag on the last word of the line,
  and so forth.

Working Alone: As you read the speech, walk around the room and
touch a different object on the last word of every line.

Question

I *Couplets and Triangles*

- We'll work with just section A in this exercise.

- Get in groups of three (if the numbers don't come out evenly, one or two groups can have an observer who swaps in). One person will be Helena, one Demetrius and one Lysander.

- Stand in a triangle with at least three metres between each person. Helena, you will speak the first pair of rhyming lines to Demetrius. When you finish, wait a second to see if he will respond (which he won't because he's too dumbstruck with love). When he doesn't respond, turn to Lysander and speak the next pair of rhyming lines to him and wait a second for a response. Then everyone take one step forward.

- Repeat speaking two lines first to Demetrius then to Lysander then taking a step forward until the end of the section.

- Swap roles so that there's a new Helena, a new Demetrius and a new Lysander. This time, start about a metre away from each other and take a step backwards after Helena has delivered one couplet to Demetrius and one to Lysander.

- Swap roles again. This time, Helena, swap between talking to Demetrius and Lysander at the end of each line. So, for example, you might give the first line of the couplet to Demetrius, and the second to Lysander.

- Discuss. How did getting closer and further away change the dynamics of the speech? How did delivering a complete couplet to each partner compare to splitting the couplet between the two?

Working Alone: Set up two chairs to be your Demetrius and Lysander. Move closer to the chairs in the first step and further away in the second.

II *Tap the Balloon*

- If you can get your hands on one, blow up a balloon. If not, use an imaginary balloon.

- Stand up and read the speech aloud. On the last word of every line, gently tap the balloon up into the air. Try to use just enough force to keep it in the air long enough for you to say the next line, and then tap it again on the last word. Note that a tap with your fingertips is much more effective than a slap with your whole hand.

- Read through the speech again, and this time instead of tapping the balloon, stomp your foot on the last word of every line.

- Read through the speech once more. This time you can *either* tap the balloon (use an imaginary one so you don't have to worry about it sinking too quickly) *or* stomp at the end of every line. Don't think too hard about which one you will do – just follow your instincts.

Act

- On the basis of the work you did in the questioning section, decide which parts of the speech you want to direct to Demetrius and which to Lysander. Decide as well where you want to give them a chance to respond. Perform the speech and lean into the rhyming words a little bit to try to get a response from them. Perform it again immediately without thinking about the rhyming words.

Storytelling

One of the most common forms of monologue in many plays, both classical and contemporary, is the narrative – a character tells a story about something that has happened. In telling the story, many characters often paint pictures and try to catch their listeners' ears. As you work on the speeches in this section, look for places where you can use what you've already learned in this chapter to bring the stories to life.

Benvolio

Benvolio is the cousin and great friend of Romeo of *Romeo and Juliet* fame. Last night, Benvolio, Romeo and their friend Mercutio donned masks and crashed a party thrown by the Capulets, the great enemies of Romeo and Benvolio's family, the Montagues. Romeo was spotted at this party by the hot-headed Tybalt, but Lord Capulet persuaded Tybalt not to confront him at the party. Tybalt then sent Romeo a challenge to a duel, despite the fact that the Prince of Verona has expressly forbidden public fighting on pain of death. Tybalt finds Benvolio and Mercutio in the public square and begins trading insults with Mercutio. When Romeo arrives, though, he refuses to fight with Tybalt. What none of these other young men know is that Romeo has just secretly married Juliet, Tybalt's cousin. Disgusted by Romeo's passivity, Mercutio draws his sword and fights with Tybalt. Romeo tries to part them, but Tybalt thrusts his sword under Romeo's outstretched arm and kills Mercutio. Maddened with grief and rage, Romeo then kills Tybalt and flees. Benvolio is left in Act 3 Scene 1 to tell the Prince and other onlookers what happened.

- Read through the text once silently without looking at the glosses.

(PRINCE
Where are the vile beginners of this fray?)
BENVOLIO
A
O noble Prince, I can discover all
The unlucky manage of this fatal brawl.
There lies the man, slain by young Romeo,
That slew thy kinsman, brave Mercutio.   5
(CAPULET'S WIFE
Tybalt, my cousin, O my brother's child!
O prince, O cousin, husband, O, the blood is spilled
O my dear kinsman! Prince, as thou art true,
For blood of ours shed blood of Montague.
O cousin, cousin!   10
PRINCE

Benvolio, who began this bloody fray?)
BENVOLIO

B
Tybalt, here slain, whom Romeo's hand did slay,
Romeo, that spoke him fair, bid him bethink
How nice the quarrel was, and urged withal
Your high displeasure. All this, uttered   15
With gentle breath, calm look, knees humbly bowed,
Could not take truce with the unruly spleen
Of Tybalt deaf to peace, but that he tilts
With piercing steel at bold Mercutio's breast,
Who, all as hot, turns deadly point to point   20
And, with a martial scorn, with one hand beats
Cold death aside, and with the other sends
It back to Tybalt, whose dexterity
Retorts it. Romeo, he cries aloud
'Hold, friends, friends, part!', and swifter than his tongue   25
His agile arm beats down their fatal points,
And 'twixt them rushes; underneath whose arm
An envious thrust from Tybalt hit the life
Of stout Mercutio, and then Tybalt fled.
But by and by comes back to Romeo,   30
Who had but newly entertained revenge,
And to't they go like lightning, for, ere I
Could draw to part them was stout Tybalt slain,
And as he fell did Romeo turn and fly.
This is the truth, or let Benvolio die.   35

Glosses
2, **discover** = reveal; 3, **manage** = conduct; 13, **spoke him fair** = spoke courteously to him, **bethink** = think about; 14, **nice** = trivial, **withal** = besides; 17, **spleen** = temper; 18, **tilts** = thrusts; 20, **hot** = angry, **point** = sword point; 21, **martial** = war-like; 23, **dexterity** = skill; 24, **Retorts** = returns; 28, **envious** = malicious; 30, **by and by** = immediately; 31, **entertained** = conceived; 32, **ere** = before.

Speak

I

- Speak through the text quietly again, looking at the glosses as you go, even for words you think you know. You will not be speaking the Prince and Lady Capulet's lines; they are there so that you know what Benvolio is responding to.

- Stand in a circle with the rest of your group. Choose one person to read to the first punctuation mark (after 'O, noble Prince') where the person next to him or her will pick up and read to the next punctuation mark (after 'fatal brawl'), and so forth around the circle until you've completed the text. Try to carry on the energy of the thought from the person before you and pass it on to the person after you so that it still makes sense even though it's being spoken by many voices.

Working Alone: Skip this step, and instead of the next step place five or six chairs or other large objects around the room. Start at one of the chairs, and when you get to a punctuation mark, pause – without dropping the energy of the thought – and walk to another chair before you begin speaking again. As in the group exercise, strive to carry forward the momentum of the thought even when you're pausing to move from chair to chair.

II

- Remember who spoke before you in the circle and scatter around the room. The first person will again speak to the first punctuation mark where the next person (who is no longer standing next to the first person – this is why you have to remember who spoke before you) will pick up, and so on. When it's your turn, try to grab the attention of everyone in the room immediately. If you want to, you can move as you speak.

- Discuss any discoveries you've made.

Question

I *Proceed with Caution*

- Take a moment to consider Benvolio's given circumstances. Under the Prince's decree, his cousin and dear friend Romeo would be condemned to death for fighting, let alone killing, Tybalt. Telling the story in such a way that Romeo appears to be justified without incurring the displeasure of the Prince by seeming to make excuses or challenge the justness of the decree is literally a matter of life and death for Benvolio.

- Let's look at section A. What is the first thing Benvolio does? The use of the adjective 'noble' in addressing the Prince is a wise move. As we've seen with Mark Antony and Joan Puzel, an effective way to get your listeners to behave in a certain way is to ascribe that attribute to them. In other words, flattery is a useful tactic. What other adjectives does Benvolio use in his first four lines of text (through 'brave Mercutio')? Discuss how each adjective might help Benvolio influence the Prince even before he starts telling the story of what happened. Note that Mercutio was in fact kin to the Prince and how Benvolio reminds him of that fact before he even says Mercutio's name.

- Find some space where you can work on your own. We'll be working on Benvolio's first four lines of text. For this exercise, we're going to slow down time. Benvolio is in the same given circumstances, under the same tremendous pressure with his heart pounding and his mind racing, but we're going to give him the chance to pause at each punctuation mark to think before he speaks again. In one way this is a luxury, but in another it means he has the time to consider how extremely important it is that he say the right thing and to feel the resulting anxiety about getting it wrong. Your instructor will begin by reading the Prince's first line. Take a second after he does to breathe and consider how you should respond to his question, then speak Benvolio's text up to the first punctuation mark (after 'Prince'). Pause here again and try to think of what would be the most effective thing you could say to get the Prince to listen to you and sympathize with your version of the story before speaking to the next punctuation mark. Continue speaking through to the next punctuation mark and then pause again to consider the best way to proceed.

- Discuss what you learned about the text. Does Benvolio answer the Prince's question right away? Why does he start with other information? Why do you think Benvolio doesn't name Tybalt? What information does he give about Tybalt instead of his name? Why do you think Benvolio admits right up front that Romeo killed Tybalt instead of trying to hide it? Repeat the exercise again trying to recreate the thought processes that lead Benvolio to say exactly what he says.

- Now we're going to speed up time again. Benvolio still has to think and still has to be careful about what he chooses to say, but he has to do it fast. Your instructor will read out the Prince's line again, and this time you must respond immediately. As you continue the text, rather than pausing at each punctuation mark, tap your hand against your thigh.

- Repeat once more. This time you won't tap your hand at each punctuation mark, but remember that little pulse of energy that comes with having to think very quickly about what you're going to say next.

II *See What I See*

- Having looked at Benvolio's first four lines, in which he does a rather good job of starting his story, read over Lady Capulet's response. What effect do you think she might have on the Prince? On the crowd? On Benvolio? With her calling for Romeo's blood, it suddenly becomes even more important for Benvolio to communicate his version of the events.

- As a group, read out loud the text from 'Tybalt, here slain' through to the end.

- If you are working in a small group, it's worth each student doing the following exercise in front of the rest of the group. If there are more than six, break into groups of three to five and have each person in the smaller group do the exercise with the others watching.

- As you read the text, act out the story you are telling. So when you talk about Tybalt, act out whatever you are describing Tybalt doing. This will slow down your reading of the text, which is fine. As you act out the story, try to portray each person in it *as you want the Prince to perceive him*. This will influence how you use your body and your voice. For example, as you talk about Tybalt, you will probably take on bullying qualities.

- Once everyone has had a go, discuss the exercise. What words did you find yourself really lifting? At what points did you feel like you were in control of the story? At what points did you feel like you were jumping around having to become someone new every couple of words? Notice the care that Benvolio takes with 'all this – uttered /With gentle breath, calm look, knees humbly bowed – /Could not take truce ...', so interjecting into his story about how gentle Romeo was an even more detailed description of his gentleness ('uttered with gentle breath, etc.').

III *Team Spirit*

- Working as a group, assign one person to be Benvolio, one to be the Prince, one to be Lady Capulet, and one to be Lord Montague (Romeo's father). About a third of the group who are left, go stand by the Prince and join his 'team'. Another third go with Lady Capulet and the final third with Lord Montague. You will play the scene with the Prince and Lady Capulet speaking their lines.

- Benvolio will deliver the speech, and while he does, everyone else respond according to what your point of view is about what he's just said. So if you are on Lady Capulet's 'team', you will be very sceptical about anything good he says about Romeo, whereas Lord Montague's team will be very supportive. This is very much an exercise in listening and sensing where the rhythm of the text creates room for a response and where it doesn't. If you feel there is space for a gasp, an outraged 'No!', a sympathetic 'oh', even a challenging 'He lies' or encouraging

''Tis so', get it in there. There won't be room for any more than one or two words at a time, and remember your job isn't to shout down Benvolio; it's to feel the give and take between him and his audience. Benvolio, your job is to try to stay in control of the narrative. Don't let your audience form responses that you don't want; stay one step ahead of them. Note – you'll need to be energetic to do this, but simply racing as fast as you can won't get the job done.

- You can repeat this exercise with different students in the roles.

Working Alone: Sit and simply read the speech out loud once. Wherever you feel there is space for a response from someone like Lady Capulet or Lord Montague, draw a little star. Stand up to speak the speech, and when you come to a star tap your thigh to help yourself register that moment of vulnerability where it could all spin out of control if you're not careful.

Act

- This speech will be performed with two classmates playing the Prince and Lady Capulet and speaking their text.

Working Alone: Read the Prince and Lady Capulet's lines silently to yourself when you come to them to remind yourself of the kind of pressure you are facing as you tell this story.

- Before you begin, take a minute to stand in the space and visualize the fight. Make sure you establish for yourself exactly where you and Mercutio were when Tybalt first entered;

where you all were when Romeo arrived; where Tybalt and Mercutio first started exchanging blows; where Romeo was standing when he pleaded with them to stop; where they all were when Romeo came between them; where Tybalt exited; where Mercutio fell; where he was taken; where Tybalt re-entered; where they fought; where Tybalt lies now and where Romeo exited. Whenever you tell a story, it's important that you have a concrete sense of where things happened in space.

- As you play the scene, neither the Prince nor Lady Capulet will interrupt you, but as Benvolio, you don't know that. You need to be as clear and precise and persuasive as you can, and you have no idea how much time you'll be given, so make every word count.

- Either as a class or by yourself reflect on anything you've discovered about Benvolio and the action of storytelling.

Hotspur

This speech is from Act 1 Scene 3 of *Henry IV, Part One*. Harry Percy, also known as Hotspur, is a brave and bold soldier who has been fighting for the king of England against the Scots. In the course of battle he has taken several noble prisoners. According to the conventions of the time, Hotspur should give these prisoners to the king. The king can then demand a ransom for their return. Hotspur has, however, held back the prisoners because the king has refused to pay the ransom for Percy's brother-in-law who was captured while fighting the Welsh. As much as he might like to, however, Hotspur cannot directly challenge the king. When the king comes to confront him, he has to tell the story of refusing to turn over the captives so that it seems like he was reacting to the snobby, unmilitary demeanour of the messenger who came for them rather than being wilfully disobedient to the king. The speech is full of storytelling challenges for the actor, as Hotspur switches between past and present events and between direct and reported speech. (Note: we've taken a small cut in this speech because it is quite long. Please refer to any edition of the play if you'd like to put it back in.)

- Speak through the text quietly a couple of times without looking at the glosses.

HOTSPUR

A

My liege, I did deny no prisoners.
But I remember, when the fight was done,
When I was dry with rage and extreme toil,
Breathless and faint, leaning upon my sword,
Came there a certain lord, neat and trimly dressed,   5
Fresh as a bridegroom, and his chin, new reaped,
Showed like a stubble-land at harvest-home.
He was perfumèd like a milliner,
And, as the soldiers bore dead bodies by,
He called them 'untaught knaves', 'unmannerly'   10
To bring a slovenly unhandsome corpse
Betwixt the wind and his nobility.
With many holiday and lady terms
He questioned me, amongst the rest demanded
My prisoners in your majesty's behalf.   15
I then, all smarting with my wounds being cold,
To be so pestered with a popinjay,
Out of my grief and my impatience
Answered neglectingly, I know not what –
He should or he should not – for he made me mad   20
To see him shine so brisk, and smell so sweet
And talk so like a waiting gentlewoman
Of guns, and drums, and wounds, God save the mark!

B

And telling me 'the sovereignest thing on earth'
Was 'parmaceti' for an inward bruise,   25
And that it was great pity, so it was,
This 'villainous saltpetre' should be digged
Out of the bowels of the harmless earth,
Which many a good tall fellow had destroyed
So cowardly, and but for these 'vile guns'   30
He would himself have been a soldier.

This bald, unjointed chat of his, my lord,
I answered indirectly, as I said,
And I beseech you, let not his report
Come current for an accusation   35
Betwixt my love and your high majesty.

Glosses

6, **reaped** = shaven; 7, **harvest-home** = end of harvest; 8, **milliner** = hat-maker; 10, **unmannerly** = lacking good manners; 11, **slovenly** = nasty; 13, **holiday** = refined, **lady** = lady-like; 14, **questioned** = talked at; 16, **smarting** = hurting; 17, **popinjay** = a parrot, a chatterer; 18, **grief** = distress; 19, **neglectingly** = carelessly; 21, **brisk** = smartly; 24, **sovereignest** = finest; 25, **parmaceti** = whale oil; 27, **saltpetre** = mineral source of gunpowder; 29, **tall** = brave; 32, **bald** = foolish, **unjointed** = confused; 33, **indirectly** = distractedly; 35, **come current** = be accepted.

Speak

- Find a place where you can work on your own and read the text out loud once, looking at the glosses for words you don't know.

- Find a partner. Take turns reading to a punctuation mark (so the first person will read to 'liege', the second to 'prisoners', and so forth). As you do this speak about 10–15 per cent more slowly than you did the first time.

Working Alone: Read the speech again and, as well as speaking more slowly, take about 10–15 per cent more time at each punctuation mark. Instead of the next step, go back over the speech to make sure you understand every word and phrase.

- Come together as a group and discuss what you've noticed about the speech. Work together to analyse any words or phrases that may be unclear.

Question
I *Modelling*

- Get into groups of three (if the numbers don't work, get into groups of four and one person can play the King to whom Hotspur is speaking). There are two main characters in this story, Hotspur himself and the messenger who came to collect the prisoners, and Hotspur spends much of the speech describing them. For this exercise, one person in your group will be the Hotspur who is speaking in the present and the other two will be the Messenger and the Hotspur in the story, or Past Hotspur.

- Present Hotspur, you are going to read section A. Take it at the slower speed you were using in the Speak section. Messenger, whenever Hotspur talks about you, you are going to demonstrate physically whatever he says about you. So, for example, when he says your chin was freshly shaved, you might stroke it proudly to show off how smooth it is. Past Hotspur, you will do the same whenever Present Hotspur talks about you. So when he says he was 'breathless and faint', you will assume the appropriate physicality. It will be easy to get rather theatrical with this; some of Hotspur's language does paint a somewhat cartoonish picture. Your challenge is to reflect the language as accurately as possible and not add more. In other words, you want to serve what Hotspur is saying, not make it funnier than it is or call attention to yourself. When Hotspur is not talking about how you looked or what you were doing, you should simply freeze.

- Hotspur, as you go through the speech, use your 'models' to help tell your story and help the king understand what kind of condition you were in and why you would not have wanted to give your prisoners up to this particular messenger. Walk around them; point at them; you can even show them what pose or expression you want them to assume.

- Switch roles and repeat the exercise until everyone has had a chance to be Present Hotspur.

> *Working Alone:* Get two chairs; one will be the Messenger and the
> other Past Hotspur. When you describe Past Hotspur, stand in front
> of that chair and adopt the physical persona you are describing.
> Move to the other chair when you talk about the Messenger. Do
> the speech again, and this time simply refer to the chairs as if they
> were those two characters.

II *I Said, He Said*

- As well as describing the messenger and himself, Hotspur
  also recounts the conversation they had. On your own or with
  a partner, starting with 'And as the soldiers bore dead bodies
  by', try to identify everything Hotspur reports the messenger
  saying and underline it. Even though the text doesn't use
  quotation marks, you are likely to find direct quotations after
  words like 'called' and 'telling'.

- Now look in the same section for anything Hotspur reports
  himself as having said. You'll notice there's much less. In fact,
  he rather deliberately avoids being specific: 'I know not what –
  He should or he should not –'.

- For the purposes of the exercise, we're going to explore
  making the contrast between how Hotspur and the messenger
  use language and their voices differently (at least in Hotspur's
  version of events). Starting with 'And as the soldiers bore dead
  bodies by', read the rest of section A and all of section B and
  explore using the deeper, more matter-of-fact part of your
  voice when you speak as Hotspur. When you begin quoting
  the messenger, directly or indirectly, allow yourself to use more
  pitch range and expressivity. There will be a temptation to use
  a voice that is stereotypically effete, and Hotspur certainly is
  doing his best to make the messenger out to be a total fop.
  Nonetheless, see how much vocal variety you can find within
  that characterization.

- Repeat the text. This time you can let the vocal characterizations become more subtle, but every time you use a word that in some way refers to the military or war (e.g. 'sword', 'soldiers' – if you're in doubt, include it), stomp your foot as you say it. Hotspur's sense of his military identity is very important, and the contrast between himself as someone who truly understands war and the messenger as someone who doesn't is a key part of the story.

III *Carry the Bag*

- There's a particular momentum to this speech which we'll explore in this exercise. Everyone in the group grab a relatively heavy bag (or if you don't have one, a shoe or a coat will do). Scatter the objects around the room.

- Each person stand by a bag. As you speak the first word of the speech, bend down and pick up that bag with one hand. Carry it high above your head – don't let your energy flag – and walk and read until you get to a punctuation mark. If that punctuation mark is not a full stop (period), change the direction you are walking in. If it is a full stop, put the bag down onto the floor as you say the last word of the sentence, NOT BEFORE AND NOT AFTER. Then move to a new bag and pick it up on the first word of the next sentence.

- Discuss any discoveries you made. Were there places where you felt you wanted to let the bag drop before the full stop? What happened to the story when you kept driving through? Where were the most changes of direction? What did it feel like to then have a long, straight passage?

Act

- Perform the speech once, giving yourself complete freedom to follow any movement impulse. If you are working in a group, half the group can do this exercise at once while the other half observes from the side of the room.

- This time, each person will perform the speech for the rest of the group. Before you do, take a moment to assume a military posture – one that will impress the king. Plant your feet on the floor, your weight evenly distributed on them; keep your tailbone neatly tucked under your spine without thrusting your pelvis forward; imagine the crown of your head lifting up a quarter-inch, lengthening your entire spine. Keep your hands still at your sides. You do not need to thrust either your chest or your chin forward to convince the king that you are a serious and disciplined soldier. As you perform the speech, you will feel impulses to move; you can experiment with how much you want to give in to them and how much you want to resist and maintain your stance. Each time you breathe, however, use the breath to help you come back to your strong, confident military centre.

- Either as a class or by yourself reflect on anything you've discovered about Hotspur and how one can use a story to convey a point of view.

Follow-up

- Watch a video segment that includes work from this chapter. How did your exploration connect to what you see in the video? Are there any points from the video session that did not come up in the work you did?

- Try 'filming' what you are describing with Benvolio's and Titania's speeches from this chapter and Cassius's from Chapter 1 as you did in working on the Chorus from *Henry V*.

- In working on Benvolio, we tried 'slowing down time' in the first section of the speech, giving you the chance to really consider what your next step should be and the consequences of getting it wrong. Try doing this with the first section of Joan Puzel's speech in Chapter 1.

- Try doing the exercise from the Hotspur speech in which you carried bags the length of sentences and changed direction on internal punctuation marks with Lady Macbeth and Helena and with Lady Percy from Chapter 1.

- In working on Lady Macbeth, we identified repeated sounds and explored emphasizing those sounds in a variety of ways to discover how their qualities could be used to further the character's action. Do the same with the Chorus from *Henry V* and Joan Puzel from Chapter 1.

- Also with Lady Macbeth, we picked words that had particularly strong evocative power or 'juicy' combinations of sounds and tried exaggerating the sound quality while physically expressing the meaning of the word. Do the same with a dozen or so words from Hamlet's speech in Chapter 1 and then go back and act it again, observing how a deeper exploration of those particular words might enrich the overall commitment to solving the problem of the speech.

- In working on Joan Puzel in Chapter 1, we tried taking all of the adjectives (words that describe or modify things) out of the speech and then putting them back in. You can do the same with any speech in this chapter.

Further reading

Barton, John, *Playing Shakespeare*, Methuen, London, 1984. Chapter 3: 'Language and Character'.

Berry, Cicely, *The Actor and the Text*, Virgin Publishing, London, 1992. Chapter 4 Part 3: 'Substance of the Word', pp. 95–104; Chapter 4 Part 5: 'Nature of the Image', pp. 110–15; Chapter 5 Part 6: 'Sounds: Vowels and Consonants', pp. 143–8.

—*From Word to Play*, Oberon Books, London, 2008. Chapter 2: 'Group Work on Form and Structure: Language Textures', pp. 90–2.

Block, Giles, *Speaking the Speech: An Actor's Guide to Shakespeare*, Nick Hern Books, London, 2013. Chapter 11: 'Rhyming Verse'; Chapter 12: 'To Rhyme or Not to Rhyme'; Chapter 13: 'Trusting Rhyme'.

Carey, David and Rebecca Clark Carey, *The Verbal Arts Workbook: A Practical Course for Speaking Text*, Methuen, London, 2010. Chapter 1: 'Sound'; Chapter 2: 'Image'.

Hall, Peter, *Shakespeare's Advice to the Players*, Oberon Books, London, 2003. 'Rhyme', pp. 40–2; 'Alliteration', pp. 49–50; 'Assonance and Onomatopoeia', p. 50.

Houseman, Barbara, *Tackling Text [And Subtext]*, Nick Hern Books, London, 2008. 'Handling Classical Text: Patterns of Sound', pp. 104–19;

'Connecting With the Words and Images', pp. 120–4; 'Internal Geography', pp. 125–7.

Kaiser, Scott, *Mastering Shakespeare: An Acting Class in Seven Scenes*, Allworth Press, New York, 2003. Scene 3: 'Images'.

Linklater, Kristin, *Freeing Shakespeare's Voice: The Actor's Guide to Talking the Text*, Theatre Communications Group, New York, 1992. Chapter 1: 'Vowels and Consonants'; Chapter 2: 'Words and Images'; Chapter 3: 'Words Into Phrases'; Chapter 5: 'Figures of Speech: Alliteration, Assonance, Onomatopoeia', pp. 80–2; Chapter 7: 'Rhyme'.

Noble, Adrian, *How To Do Shakespeare*, Routledge, London, 2010. Chapter 3: 'Metaphor'.

Rodenburg, Patsy, *Speaking Shakespeare*, Methuen, London, 2002. Part 2: 'Structure: Alliteration, Assonance, Onomatopoeia', pp. 78–83; 'Rhyme', pp. 126–54.

Weate, Catherine, *Classic Voice: Working with Actors on Vocal Style*, Oberon Books, London, 2009. Chapter 2: 'Sound'; Chapter 3: 'Word'.

3
RHYTHM AND METER

Framework

> Friends, Romans, countrymen, lend me your ears:
> I come to bury Caesar, not to praise him.
> The evil that men do lives after them:
> The good is oft interrèd with their bones.

It may seem obvious to say that these first lines of Mark Antony's famous speech are verse, distinct from prose you're reading now. But actually, how would it be if we instead had set these prose lines out like this:

> It may seem obvious to say that these
> First lines of Mark Antony's famous speech
> Are verse, distinct from prose you're reading now.
> But actually, how would it be if we
> Instead had set these prose lines out like this?

How does this affect the way you read them? How would it affect the way you spoke them? What does this tell you about any differences between verse and prose? And any similarities?

There is rhythm in both verse and prose – a rhythm that is created by regularly occurring patterns of stressed and unstressed syllables. (See our book, *The Verbal Arts Workbook*, for a fuller discussion of this.) But only writers of verse will structure that rhythm into **meter**, in which a particular stress pattern is repeated for a specific number of times in each verse line. Rhythm in prose, on the other hand, is much less regular and more fluid in its patterns, but those patterns are still likely to be there, and they help make the writing varied and engaging. In both verse and prose, rhythm can help give shape and expression to thought and feeling. The repetition of a rhythmic pattern can give drive and energy to speech and sweep up both speaker and listener in the flow of the language. The fulfilment of a rhythmic phrase can be enormously satisfying and help a point to land with authority and finality. The disruption of a rhythmic pattern, on the other hand, can be disarming, even disturbing. It can make us catch our breath and perk up our ears to listen even more carefully. Shakespeare makes great use of rhythmic regularity and irregularity in verse and also in prose to heighten the impact of the language in his plays.

Although some of Shakespeare's plays are written mainly in verse or prose, all of his plays include at least some of both. This was the fashion of his time. Whereas today verse plays are the exception to the rule, in Shakespeare's day it was the prose play that was the rarity. English dramatists of the time inherited a tradition of playwriting in verse that went back many centuries. However, they had only recently started writing in what is known as **blank verse**, and they found it to be the perfect vehicle for the heroic, tragic, romantic and comic stories they wanted to tell and their audiences wanted to hear. One playwright in particular, Christopher Marlowe (1564–93), was greatly admired for his mighty lines of verse in service of extravagant stories of tyrants, murderers, magicians and mythical lovers. Plays such as Marlowe's *Tamburlaine the Great* helped establish the dramatic potential of blank verse and paved the way for Shakespeare to develop it further as he introduced more subtlety and psychological realism into his plays and characters.

But what are the characteristics of blank verse that Shakespeare inherited? Blank verse was composed of unrhymed lines in the meter known as **iambic pentameter**. This term, which has come down to us from the poetry of classical Greece, tells us that the metrical structure of each line is based on a rhythmic unit (or **foot**) composed of a syllable of weak stress followed by a syllable of stronger stress; for example, the word 'composed' would make such a rhythmic unit because the first syllable (com) is relatively weak or unstressed, while the second syllable (posed) is more strongly stressed This type of foot is called an **iamb** (from the use of this rhythm in Greek satirical poems called *iambi*) and it occurs five times (*penta*, from the Greek for 'five') in a line of iambic pentameter.

Take a look at this line from Marlowe's *Tamburlaine the Great, Part Two* (Act 3 Scene 2):

I'll have you learn to sleep upon the ground

Speak it out loud and notice how the writer has arranged it into a pattern of five iambic feet (the vertical line is used to show the foot divisions):

I'll **have**| you **learn**| to **sleep**| u-**pon**| the **ground**

We call this a regular iambic pentameter line, because the pattern of a relatively weak syllable followed by a more strongly stressed syllable is kept constant over the five feet. But notice that not all the stressed syllables have the same weight: if you say the line quite naturally, it's likely that *learn, sleep* and *ground* have more stress than *have* and *-pon*. Similarly, the unstressed syllables are not all equally weak: it's likely that *I'll* and *you* are more strongly stressed than *to, u-*, and *the*. This is because words with more semantic content (or significance) normally take more stress in English than words with little or no semantic content. So, the iambic pattern exists in the *relative* strength of the syllables *in each foot* rather than across the whole line. This makes it remarkably flexible and is one reason why it appealed to Elizabethan playwrights.

However, while the regular ten-syllable iambic line is very flexible, by Shakespeare's time poets and playwrights had established a number of variations on the pattern which give it even more dramatic and expressive potential and prevent it from sounding too repetitive. One common feature is a shift in focus/sense at a point in the middle of the line. For example, look at this line from Act 1 Scene 2 of Shakespeare's *The Two Gentlemen of Verona*:

O hateful hands, to tear such loving words!

Julia, a young woman of Verona, has just torn up a letter from her boyfriend, Proteus, and is now regretting it. As you speak the line aloud, you'll find that it's a regular iambic line, even though some of the foot boundaries occur in the middle of words:

O **hate**|-ful **hands**| to **tear**| such **lov**|-ing **words**

But now speak it again, and notice how Julia's focus shifts from cursing her hands to what they have done to the letter. The point where this focus-shift happens in this instance is represented by a comma on the page; but when we speak the line, it might cause us to pause, take a breath or change the vocal dynamic in some way. However we choose to speak it, there will be a change in the energy of the line at this point which breaks it into two parts of different length and emotional energy:

O hateful hands,   to tear such loving words!

This breaking point is known as a **caesura** (Latin for 'a cut' and related to our word 'scissor'). In iambic pentameter this cut usually happens after the second or third foot, but it can also occur at other points. For example, look at these opening lines from *Romeo and Juliet*:

Two households, both alike in dignity,
In fair Verona, where we lay our scene

They are both regular iambic lines with a focus-shifting caesura in the middle of the line, but notice how the caesura in each case occurs in the middle of a foot:

Two **house**|-holds   **both**| a-**like**| in **dig**|-ni-**ty**
In **fair**| Ve-**ron**|-a   **where**| we **lay**| our **scene**

As you speak these lines, feel how the shifting of the caesura breaks up the regularity of the iambic pulse. In musical terms, we start to get a more syncopated rhythm that is also closer to how we normally speak. Two other standard variations also help to create this sense of syncopation and so give the playwright more rhythmic possibilities for expressing the thoughts and feelings of his dramatic characters.

The first of these involves the possibility of reversing the stress pattern of a foot so that a stressed syllable is followed by an unstressed syllable. This can happen in any foot in the line apart from the last, but it happens most often in the first foot. For example, the first line of Shakespeare's *King Richard III* reads:

Now is the winter of our discontent
Now is| the **win**|-ter **of**| our **dis**|-con-**tent**

And this line, spoken by the King in Act 3 Scene 1 of *Henry VI, Part Two*:

Looking the way her harmless young one went
Look-ing| the **way**| her **harm**|-less **young**| one **went**

The reversal of the stress pattern at the beginning of the line gives a lot of potential expressive energy to the words 'now' and 'looking'. This reversed foot is sometimes referred to as a **trochee**, which is the name for this type of rhythmic unit in classical Greek verse. Classical Greek verse made use of various other types of rhythmic unit, such as spondees (units of two stressed syllables) and dactyls (units composed of a stressed syllable followed by two unstressed ones), and some of these have occasionally been identified by scholars in Shakespeare's verse. However, since what we are offering here is an *introduction* to Shakespeare's use of meter, we feel a more simplified approach is helpful at this stage. We refer you to the Further reading section of this chapter if you wish to go deeper into the subject.

The other standard variation on regular iambic pentameter is the addition of an unstressed syllable at the end of the verse line. For example, in Julia's speech in 'Two Gents', she has these lines:

Be calm, good wind, blow not a word away
Till I have found each letter in the letter,
Except mine own name. That, some whirlwind bear
Unto a ragged, fearful, hanging rock

Which in regular iambic pentameter would be:

Be **calm**| good **wind**| blow **not**| a **word**| a-**way**
Till **I**| have **found**| each **let**|-ter **in**| the **let**-ter
Ex-**cept**| mine **own**| name   **That**| some **whirl**|-wind **bear**
Un-**to**| a **ragg**|-ed **fear**|-ful **hang**|-ing **rock**

Although most of the lines have the regular five feet of iambic pentameter, the eleventh unstressed syllable at the end of the second line creates a type of foot known as an **amphibrach** rather than an iamb. This is a metrical unit in which a strong syllable has a weak syllable on either side of it, and takes its name from a Greek word meaning 'with two branches'. When an amphibrach occurs at the end of a line like this it creates what is usually called a **feminine ending**, and it helps to give a more natural feel to the verse, making it fuller and less regular. This happens quite frequently in Shakespeare's later plays, but occurs more sparingly in his earlier works.

While we're looking at this passage, there are some other interesting features of the verse to notice. There are the strong caesuras in the first and third lines, which correspond to Julia's energetic shifts in focus. Additionally, there is the opportunity for a slight caesura in the second line after the word 'found', representing perhaps Julia's discovery of her need for 'each letter':

> Till I have found   each letter in the letter

There is also the possibility of a reversed foot after the caesura in the first line, depending upon the actor's interpretation:

> Be **calm|** good **wind|**   **blow** not| a **word|** a-**way**

As you can begin to appreciate, there is room for a lot of variation within iambic pentameter, and so the rhythm of each line can be open to interpretation by the actor to some extent. This interpretation will, of course, depend upon the actor's understanding of the meaning of the line. So, as well as considering lines as rhythmic units, it's also important to look at how they behave as units of sense. In Shakespeare's earliest plays, such as *The Two Gentlemen of Verona*, the sense often fits neatly into the ten syllables of the line; for example, here is Julia again:

> O hateful hands, to tear such loving words!
> Injurious wasps, to feed on such sweet honey
> And kill the bees that yield it with your stings!
> I'll kiss each several paper for amends.

Speak the lines through for yourself. Even though Julia is quite worked up, notice how each of her thoughts is contained within the line. You could pause at the end of each line, and the whole thing would still make sense. When this happens, the line is said to be **end-stopped**. However, sometimes the sense continues beyond the end of the line and overflows into the next, producing what's called a **run-on** line, as you can see in these lines of the King in Act 3 Scene 1 of *Henry VI, Part Two*:

> Ah, uncle Humphrey, in thy face I see
> The map of honour, truth and loyalty.

Again, speak the lines through for yourself. The King's meaning only becomes clear when the thought is completed in the second line. It doesn't make much sense if you pause at the end of the first line: rather, the first line has to run on into the second, which is then end-stopped. This sharing of the sense across two lines is also known as **enjambment**. Shakespeare's use of enjambment, like his use of feminine endings, became much more frequent in his later plays, enabling his writing to be richer, more flexible and more fluid. The play between the underlying pattern dictated by the meter and these rhythmic variations that break its boundaries makes for a very dynamic tension. If you as an actor have a strong feel for both the meter of the verse and the rhythm of the thought, you can use their convergences and clashes to make the language do what your character needs it to do in any given moment.

Before we finish this exploration of Shakespeare's rhythm and meter, we want to draw your attention to a few important points of Elizabethan pronunciation which can affect the rhythm when spoken in modern English. Here is Julia in the same scene from *The Two Gentlemen of Verona*. This time, she is talking to her maid, who is trying to pick up scraps of the letter that Julia is tearing up:

> This babble shall not henceforth trouble me;
> Here is a coil with protestation.   *coil = disturbance*
> Go, get you gone, and let the papers lie.
> You would be fingering them to anger me.

Speak the lines through for yourself a couple of times, focusing on the rhythm of each line. You may have noticed as you spoke these end-stopped lines that some of them felt a bit odd. Speak the second line through again. Not only does it start with a reversed foot, but it may also feel like a short line of nine syllables:

Here is| a **coil**| with **pro**|-tes-**ta**-tion

However, in Shakespeare's day, a word like 'protestation' with its '-tion' ending could have been pronounced with five syllables not four, giving us instead a normal ten-syllable line:

Here is| a **coil**| with **pro**|-tes-**ta**|-ti-**on**

Some actors like to honour Shakespeare's meter by pronouncing such words with their full complement of syllables. But others feel that this **expansion** of the word is too archaic for a modern audience and prefer to let the extra syllable quietly disappear into history.

Now, speak the fourth line through again. This time it might feel as if there's an extra eleventh syllable and a reversed foot disturbing the rhythm:

You **would**| be **fing**|-er-**ing**| them **to**| **ang-**er me

While that is possible, it makes much more sense if we pronounce 'fingering' as a two-syllable word 'fing'ring', as it often is today in informal speech and as it appears in the original Folio printing of the text:

You **would**| be **fing**|-ring **them**| to **ang**|-er **me**

Speak it through, and you can probably feel how much easier and more natural it sounds like that with the **contraction** of the syllable. (This process of contraction is also known as **elision**.) On the other hand, some actors might prefer to use the full three syllables for a dramatic purpose, breaking the rhythm in an expressive way. So, there's a choice – to expand or contract.

With the past tense '-ed' ending for verbs, as in the word 'changed', Elizabethans also had a choice of expanding or contracting. The older way of saying 'changed' involved pronouncing the '-ed' ending, making it an expanded two syllables: 'chang-ed'. But many speakers had begun to compress the '-ed' syllable, so making the word 'chang'd', as it is today. Shakespeare makes liberal use of both '-ed' possibilities depending on the rhythm of the line. Thus, in the opening speech from *King Richard III*, Gloucester says:

Our stern alarums changed to   *alarums = call to arms*
merry meetings

In the original Folio edition of the play, 'changed' was written as 'chang'd', so we know that the contracted form is used here, keeping the rhythm regular. On the other hand, in Act 2 Scene 2 of *Hamlet*, the Queen says to Rosencrantz and Guildenstern:

And I beseech you instantly to visit
My too much changed son.

Here, the Folio has 'changed', indicating the expanded form which fits the iambic rhythm. Many modern texts follow this printing convention of using the full spelling for the expanded form and an apostrophe to represent the contracted one. However, some editors prefer to use the normal spelling for the compressed form and to represent the expanded form with '-èd' or '-éd', which is what we have chosen to do. More recently, some editors have chosen to print all '-ed' words in the normal way, while noting the expanded forms in a footnote. You soon get used to each convention, but it can get slightly confusing if you're using different editions of the plays, which is why we mention it here.

The process of analysing the verse to find where words might need to be contracted or expanded to fit the iambic weak-strong rhythm; looking for possible caesuras, reversed feet and feminine endings; and identifying other irregularities in the meter is called **scansion**. Scanning the verse helps you to become more aware of how Shakespeare uses rhythm in ways both subtle and powerful to convey the character's thoughts, experiences and intentions with great specificity. It will also make you more aware of acting choices that the language offers you and the ramifications of the rhythmic choices you make. This discussion has of necessity been rather technical but, as you will discover, we take quite a physical approach to scansion in the exercises that follow.

Exploration

Mark Antony

To help you get the feeling of the verse in your body, let's return to those lines of Mark Antony's that we quoted at the beginning of this chapter:

Friends, Romans, countrymen, lend me your ears:
I come to bury Caesar, not to praise him.
The evil that men do lives after them:
The good is oft interrèd with their bones. *interred = buried*

|

- Speak them through a few times, getting a sense of their meaning and how you want to say them. Notice the expanded '-ed' in the word 'interred'. Now, stand up with your feet about hip-width apart, and step forward onto your left foot. Keeping your left foot forward, let your weight settle back onto your right leg.

- In this position, speak the text through again and, as you do so, rock forward slightly onto your left foot on the syllables you want to emphasize and shift your weight back onto your right foot on the unstressed syllables. Do this a few times until you're really committing to the impulse to move forward on the stressed syllables. Sometimes those stressed syllables will be whole words, but at other times they will just be one (or perhaps two) of the syllables in a word, so take time to connect to the *syllables* you want to emphasize. (Feel free to switch the position of your feet when your legs get tired.)

- You probably found that this exercise brought out the three or four strongest syllables in each line – the ones with most semantic content – but you may also have begun to feel the iambic alternation of strong/weak stressing at some points. To feel this underlying meter more powerfully, read the lines out loud again, but this time lean forward on every second syllable. This might alter the way you say some of the lines and may even feel awkward in places; make a mental note of these changes, but strive to stay connected to the regular iambic beat for the time being. Take each line one at a time so that you can feel the shape of the five-beat pentameter line. (There are no lines where the sense runs on into the next, so this should be quite straightforward.) Do this a few times until you really feel the iambic rhythm of the syllables in your body and in the language. (Again, feel free to switch the position of your feet when your legs get tired.)

II

- You've probably become aware of the feminine ending in the second line, with its unstressed final 'him', but otherwise the lines can be spoken quite regularly. However, you may have found yourself stressing some syllables and words differently when you were leaning forward with the iambic rhythm, particularly in the first line. We'll come back to this point in a moment, but first we're going to examine the lines for any caesuras. Remember that the caesura is a point in the line where the character's focus shifts. Not every line of Shakespeare has a caesura, and sometimes the focus-shift is quite subtle, but it's worth exploring.

- To investigate this, simply speak the lines through once, focusing on their meaning. Then, as you did earlier in Section I, stand with your feet about hip-width apart, and step forward onto your left foot. Keeping your left foot forward, let your weight settle back onto your right leg.

- In this position, speak the text through again and, as you do so, rock forward slightly onto your left foot when you feel a point where the focus of Antony's language changes in the middle of the line. Rock back onto your right foot after you reach the end of the verse line, so that you're ready to rock forward again when the focus shifts in the middle of the next line. This focus-shift might correspond to a punctuation mark, but more often it might feel like a tipping point or fulcrum where there's a slight shift in intention. Notice where this happens in each line and, as you become more confident with the exercise, exaggerate the focus-shift by pausing slightly at the caesura. Greg Doran, Artistic Director of the Royal Shakespeare Company, speaks of the caesura being a *poise* not a pause, and likens it to a springboard into the second half of the line. So go back to speaking the text focusing on your action, but see if you can keep alive that sense of a tipping point or springboard within the line.

- Here's one possible outcome of the exercise that you can experiment with:

  Friends, Romans, countrymen,   lend me your ears:
  I come to bury Caesar,   not to praise him.
  The evil that men do   lives after them:
  The good   is oft interrèd with their bones.

- Notice how the caesuras in this example don't all occur in the same place. How does this affect the way you say the lines? What does it bring out in the language? What does it tell us about Antony? What effect does it have on the listeners?

III

- Finally, let's look at that famous first line again. Often, when actors speak this line, we hear it stressed like this:

  Friends, Rom|-ans, **coun**|-try-**men**| **lend** me| your **ears**

This may well have been the way you spoke it at first, with two relatively equal stresses at the beginning and a reversed foot after the caesura. But when you spoke it with a regular iambic rhythm, you would have stressed it like this:

  Friends, **Rom**|-ans, **coun**|-try-**men**| lend **me**| your **ears**

This might have felt strange: to make 'friends' unstressed and to emphasize 'me'. However, if we remember that iambic stress is relative, then 'friends' can be quite strong as long as the 'Rom' of 'Romans' is stronger. This choice would make sense if we think of Antony having to call more and more loudly on his audience to attract their attention, which is what the scene suggests. Antony is trying to speak to the Roman people after Brutus has won them over to his cause, and it takes him a few attempts to get them to listen to him.

- Trying to get the attention of the crowd even though they're already cheering Brutus might also be a reason for Antony to emphasize 'me' more strongly than 'lend': Antony could be asking the people to listen to *him* as well as *Brutus*. Try it both ways: stressing 'lend' and then stressing 'me'. This is an instance where scanning calls your attention to a choice you may not have considered.

Exercises

The exercises in this chapter are organized into three sections: 'Finding the Rhythm', 'Mastering the Rhythm' and 'Breaking the Rhythm'. We suggest that you work through them in this order, not only because you will develop your own skill and understanding more organically, but also because we explore a different period of Shakespeare's writing in each one. In 'Finding the Rhythm', we begin where Shakespeare began, with the less complex forms of iambic pentameter; in 'Mastering the Rhythm', we explore in more detail some of the variations and irregularities that Shakespeare used to dramatic effect in his middle period; and in 'Breaking the Rhythm', we delve into the more complex verse forms that Shakespeare used in his later plays. In the first two sections we will also look at the particular rhythms in a prose passage from the period, while in the last section we include an additional verse dialogue.

Teaching Tip or Working Alone: You may wish to watch a video segment that includes exercises from this chapter before you begin practical work.

Finding the rhythm

The following exercises are designed to extend your understanding of how scansion of iambic pentameter can contribute to your understanding of a character and highlight the subtle shifts of thought and feeling in the language. We also look at some basic prose rhythms. We begin with the full text of the speech from Act 1 Scene 2 of *The Two Gentlemen of Verona* which we referenced in the Framework. Most critics agree that this is a fairly early play of Shakespeare's, and certainly the relative simplicity of the verse suggests this. Nevertheless, this is a challenging speech for the actor.

Teaching Tip: We pack a lot into the questioning sections of both the following verse speeches, and you can structure your investigation of rhythm in these speeches in a number of ways. For example, you may want to spend a session focusing just on leaning into the iambic rhythm to find possible expansions and contractions in both speeches, and then look at caesuras in both in the next session. You might choose to focus primarily on how reversed feet give drive and energy to one or the other and then move to acting the speech. With some groups it will be more appropriate to go into a very detailed analysis of all the rhythmic features.

Julia

Julia is a young noblewoman of Verona, who has just received a letter from Proteus, the young man she is in love with and one of the two gentlemen of the play's title. However, she does not want her maid, Lucetta, to know how interested she is in Proteus, and so she tears the letter up in a fit of mock anger. Lucetta, of course, can see through Julia's pretence and leaves her alone with the scraps of paper. Julia then proceeds to regret her actions.

- Speak through the text quietly a couple of times without looking at the glosses.

JULIA

A

O hateful hands, to tear such loving words!
Injurious wasps, to feed on such sweet honey
And kill the bees that yield it with your stings!
I'll kiss each several paper for amends.
Look, here is writ *kind Julia*. Unkind Julia!   5
As in revenge of thy ingratitude,
I throw thy name against the bruising stones,
Trampling contemptuously on thy disdain.
And here is writ *love-wounded Proteus*.
Poor wounded name, my bosom as a bed   10
Shall lodge thee till thy wound be throughly healed;
And thus I search it with a sovereign kiss.
But twice or thrice was *Proteus* written down.

B

Be calm, good wind, blow not a word away
Till I have found each letter in the letter,   15
Except mine own name. That, some whirlwind bear
Unto a ragged, fearful, hanging rock,
And throw it thence into the raging sea.
Lo, here in one line is his name twice writ,
Poor forlorn Proteus, passionate Proteus,   20
To the sweet Julia – that I'll tear away;
And yet I will not, sith so prettily
He couples it to his complaining names.
Thus will I fold them, one upon another;
Now kiss, embrace, contend, do what you will.   25

Glosses
2, **injurious** = harmful; 3, **yield** = produce; 4, **several** = separate; 11, **throughly** = thoroughly; 12, **search** = examine, **sovereign** = healing; 17, **ragged** = rugged; 20, **forlorn** = unhappy; 22, **sith** = since; 23, **complaining** = plaintive; 25, **contend** = quarrel.

Speak

- Speak through the text quietly again, looking at the glosses as you go, even for words you think you know.

- Speak it through a few more times, so you get a clear sense of the meaning.

- Now, speak through the text again, at a more conversational volume this time, and begin to lean into the regular iambic rhythm of each line as you did in the Exploration section.

Question
I *Expanding and Contracting*

- You've probably discovered a number of places where the rhythm doesn't feel quite right. So, first of all, ask yourself whether there are any possible expansions or contractions that would make the lines flow more naturally. Speak the text through slowly, and lean into the iambic stress of each line. Stop whenever you feel the rhythm becomes unnatural; for example, if you find yourself stressing words or syllables we don't normally emphasize in everyday speech, or if you realize that there are more or less than five full feet in each line. These are often signs that there is an expansion or contraction to be found in the vicinity. The first contracted word you're likely to come across is 'injurious'. Today, we often pronounce this formally as 'in-jur-i-ous' with four syllables, but if we want it to fit into the iambic rhythm of the line we need to say 'in-jur-yus' with three syllables in the more informal way that's open to us, as it was to Shakespeare. Work through section A by yourself and see where you can identify other contractions (or expansions).

- Now get a partner, if one is available to you, and compare notes.

- You've probably found several other contractions, but no expansions. What does this tell you about Julia and how she's using language to solve her problem in this speech? The word 'contemptuously', which we are likely to say with five syllables, needs here to be 'con-temp-tyous-ly' with four, and 'sovereign', which we might be tempted to expand into three syllables, is its usual two.

- The other contractions in the text concern the names, Julia and Proteus. Just as today we have the option of saying 'Ju-li-a' or 'Ju-lya', so did Shakespeare. Similarly, Proteus might be 'Pro-te-us' or 'Pro-tyus'. In this section, Julia is always 'Jul-ya', but Shakespeare uses both forms of Proteus: 'Pro-te-us' the first time it occurs and 'Pro-tyus' the second.

- Read through this section once to your partner (if you have one) speaking all the syllables in 'injurious', 'Julia', 'contemptuously', 'Proteus' (both times), and 'sovereign'. Read through it again compressing each of those words so they fit the rhythm – except the first Proteus, which rhythmically needs to be three syllables. In that instance, really savour all the sounds in his name. What kind of force does it give to Julia's language when she does not take the time to be formal and precise with these words? What happens when she slows down and says 'Pro-te-us' where it would usually be compressed in everyday speech?

- As time permits, look for possible compressions and expansions in the second half of the speech and explore the effect of keeping to or breaking the iambic rhythm on those words.

II *Reversals*

- As well as discovering the contractions in the speech, you've almost certainly noticed where there are some reversed feet. If not, speak the text again, feeling where the beat gets a little syncopated, particularly paying attention to the beginning of the lines. Where do you *have to* begin a line with a strongly stressed syllable in order to make sense, and where might there be a choice? Are there any possible reversed feet in the middle of a line? Compare notes with a partner, if you have one.

- There are a couple of obligatory reversed feet at the beginning of lines as well as several optional ones. The obligatory ones are:

> **Tramp**-ling| contemptuously
> **To** the| sweet Julia

- Although these are both reversed feet, they feel quite different. 'Trampling' has a lot of semantic content, making it a strong reversed foot; 'to the' has very little semantic content, making it weak. Speak these particular lines again, and feel how the rhythm of the words reflects Julia's action. In the first line, the strong reversed foot of 'trampling' suggests the vigour with which Julia is behaving physically. In the second line, the relatively weak reversed foot of 'to the' catapults the speaker into the emotionally resonant phrase 'sweet Julia'. It's almost as if the weak first foot lends its energy to the strong second – a pattern that Shakespeare uses fairly frequently.

- The optional reversed feet we've identified (although you may find others, depending on your own interpretation) are:

> **Look**, here| is writ
> **Poor** woun|-ded name
> **Till** I| have found
> **Lo**, here| in one line
> **Poor** for|-lorn Proteus
> **Thus** will| I fold

In each of the optional cases, there is a possibility that the second syllable in the foot might be more strongly stressed, depending on interpretation. Note the word 'forlorn' – today, it is only pronounced with the stress on the second syllable; but, for Shakespeare, it could also be pronounced with stress on the first syllable, giving the option:

> Poor **for**|-lorn Proteus

Try these options out for yourself, and see how they feel in your mouth and how they sound to your ear. If you have a partner, how do these options sound when spoken by someone else?

- We've also identified a potential mid-line reversed foot in the following line:

Lo, here in one line is his name twice writ

Here are the two possibilities, using a reversed foot at the beginning of the line as well:

Lo here| in **one**| line **is**| his **name**| twice **writ**
Lo here| in **one**| **line** is| his **name**| twice **writ**

Try them both. Which do you prefer? Why? In which version is Julia's delight stronger at finding Proteus's name twice?

- Speak the whole speech through again, stomping your foot on the stressed first word/syllable in each reversed foot (trochee). How does this syncopation of the rhythm change or enhance the energy of the speech?

III *The Tipping Point*

- There are very few feminine line endings: *honey*, *Julia*, *letter* and *another* are the ones we've identified. However, there is a substantial number of potential caesuras. We've already drawn your attention to some of them in the Framework. Here, we're going to look at part B of the speech. As you did with the Mark Antony speech earlier, stand with your feet about hip-width apart, and step forward onto your left foot. Keeping your left foot forward, let your weight settle back onto your right leg.

- In this position, speak each line in that section several times on its own. As you do so, rock forward slightly onto your left foot whenever you feel there's a definite point where the focus of Julia's language changes in the middle of the line. Rock back onto your right foot after you reach the end of the verse line, so that you're ready to rock forward again when the focus shifts in the middle of the next line. This might correspond to a punctuation mark, but more often it might feel like a tipping point or fulcrum where there's a shift in intention or energy. Not every line will have a definite caesura. But where there is one, notice where it occurs in the line and, as you become more confident with the exercise, rock further onto each foot and exaggerate the focus-shift by pausing slightly at the caesura.

- We'd like to focus now on these few lines:

  Lo, here in one line is his name twice writ,
  Poor forlorn Proteus, passionate Proteus,
  To the sweet Julia – that I'll tear away;
  And yet I will not, sith so prettily
  He couples it to his complaining names.

  Here is one possible way of scanning these lines:

  Lo, here| in **one| line**   is| his **name|** twice **writ**
  *Poor for|-lorn **Pro|**-tyus*   ***pash|**-nate **Pro|**-te-**us***
  *To the| sweet **Jul|**-ya*   **that|** I'll **tear|** a-**way**
  And **yet|** I **will|** not   **sith|** so **pre|**-tti-**ly**
  He **cou|**-ples **it|**   to **his|** com-**plain|**-ing **names**

- With this scansion, not only are there several reversed feet in this passage but all of the caesuras except the last occur in the middle of the third foot. This may just be coincidence, or it may be an example of Shakespeare marrying the character's emotional intensity to a rhythmic intensity in the verse.

- Get two chairs and place them about nine or ten feet away from each other. On the first half of the first line, walk from one chair to the other, and when you get to the caesura we've marked, change direction and walk back to the first chair. Repeat with the following lines. Your rhythm and pace walking from chair to chair may vary depending on how the line scans, which is fine.

- Contrast that with an alternative scansion. Stay standing at the first chair on the two lines where we've taken out the caesura, and keep the rhythm very regular:

  Lo, **here|** in **one|** line **is|** his **name|** twice **writ**
  *Poor **for|**-lorn **Pro|**-tyus   **pash|**-nate **Pro|**-te-**us***
  *To the| sweet **Jul|**-ya*   **that|** I'll **tear|** a-**way**
  And **yet|** I **will|** not   **sith|** so **pre|**-tti-**ly**
  He **cou|**-ples **it|** to **his|** com-**plain|**-ing **names**

What does smoothing out the rhythm and the caesuras do in this section of the speech?

- Go through the whole speech and find where you feel there's a shift in focus in the middle of the line. Rock forward and back or move between chairs on all the caesuras, then read the speech again and simply tap your thigh with your fingers when you come to one. You don't need to pause on that tap – just feel that there's a little change in energy there that springs you into the second half of the line.

Act

- Take a piece of paper, tear it into at least eight pieces and throw them on the floor.

- Practise the speech once picking up pieces of paper whenever the text indicates. You will imagine that certain phrases are written on some of them (e.g. 'kind Julia').

- Now take a moment to put yourself in Julia's position. She is in love with Proteus, and has just received a letter from him. However, before she could read it in private, she tore it up because she didn't want her maid to know how interested in Proteus she is. Her maid has just left her alone, and this is the first opportunity she has to gather the pieces of the letter together. She is torn between punishing herself for ripping up the letter and relishing the contents of the letter, particularly any mention of Proteus.

- After you perform it for the first time, consciously review all the discoveries you made as a result of your work on the rhythm; then perform the speech again. The aim is not to demonstrate your intellectual understanding of these elements but rather to allow your experience of them to shape and support your performance in the moment, marrying character choice with the form of the verse.

Richard

The title character of *King Richard III* begins the play as Richard, Duke of Gloucester. Gloucester and his older brothers in the House of York, Edward and Clarence, have just defeated their rivals for the English throne, the House of Lancaster, in a civil war known as the War of the Roses. Richard had a 'good war' – he relishes fighting and killing – but, as a despised hunchback, he finds peace difficult to bear. Edward is now king, but Richard is not satisfied with just being the king's brother. He wants the crown for himself. Act 1 Scene 1 opens with the following speech. (Please note that this is not the entire speech, as we have cut the last ten lines.)

- Speak through the text quietly a couple of times without looking at the glosses.

RICHARD
A
Now is the winter of our discontent
Made glorious summer by this sun of York,
And all the clouds that loured upon our house
In the deep bosom of the ocean buried.
Now are our brows bound with victorious wreaths,   5
Our bruisèd arms hung up for monuments,
Our stern alarums changed to merry meetings,
Our dreadful marches to delightful measures.
Grim-visaged War hath smoothed his wrinkled front;
And now, instead of mounting barbèd steeds   10
To fright the souls of fearful adversaries,
He capers nimbly in a lady's chamber
To the lascivious pleasing of a lute.

B
But I, that am not shaped for sportive tricks,
Nor made to court an amorous looking-glass;   15
I, that am rudely stamped, and want love's majesty
To strut before a wanton ambling nymph;
I, that am curtailed of this fair proportion,

Cheated of feature by dissembling Nature,
Deformed, unfinished, sent before my time   20
Into this breathing world, scarce half made up,
And that so lamely and unfashionable
That dogs bark at me as I halt by them –
Why, I, in this weak piping time of peace,
Have no delight to pass away the time,   25
Unless to see my shadow in the sun
And descant on mine own deformity.

C
And therefore, since I cannot prove a lover
To entertain these fair well-spoken days,
I am determinèd to prove a villain   30
And hate the idle pleasures of these days.

Glosses
3, **loured** = frowned; 6, **arms** = armour, **monuments** = memorials;
7, **alarums** = call to arms; 8, **measures** = dances; 9, **grim-visaged**
= stern-faced, **wrinkled front** = furrowed brows; 10, **barbed** = fitted
with barbs; 12, **capers** = dances; 14, **sportive** = amorous; 16, **rudely
stamped** = roughly marked, **want** = lack; 17, **wanton** = lascivious,
ambling = walking suggestively; 18, **curtailed** = cut short, **proportion**
= figure, shape; 19, **feature** = good looks, **dissembling** = deceitful;
21, **scarce** = scarcely; 22, **lamely** = imperfectly; 23, **halt** = limp; 27,
descant = comment; 29, **well-spoken** = courteous; 30, **determined**
= resolved; 31, **idle** = frivolous.

Speak

- Speak through the text quietly again, looking at the glosses as
  you go, even for words you think you know.

- Speak it through a few more times, so you get a clear sense of
  the meaning.

- Now, speak through the text again, at a more conversational
  volume this time, and begin to lean into the regular iambic
  meter of each line as you did with Julia's speech. This may
  mean that you stress words you wouldn't ordinarily stress or

pronounce words strangely to fit the meter, which is fine for now.

Question
I *Expanding and Contracting*

- *Richard III* is usually thought of as a relatively early play, but Gloucester is a more complex character than Julia, and his rhythm gets quite rocky in this speech. Some of this syncopation is deliberate but, as with the previous speech, begin by asking whether there are any possible expansions or contractions that would make the lines flow more naturally. Work slowly through the whole speech by yourself, leaning into the iambic stress. Stop whenever you feel the rhythm becomes unnatural, and check for any expansions or contractions in the line.

- The first contracted word you're likely to come across is 'glorious'. We sometimes pronounce this formally as 'glor-i-ous' with three syllables, but if we want it to fit into the iambic rhythm we need to say 'glor-yus' with two syllables in a more informal way. There are two words with a similar pattern in this speech – 'victorious' and 'lascivious' – and they need to be treated the same: so, 'vic-tor-yus' and 'la-sciv-yus'. Something similar happens with the word 'amorous'. Instead of the three syllables of 'am-or-ous', it becomes 'am-rous'.

- There are two possible expansions. The first depends on how you pronounced the word 'alarums'. Although this is the old form of our two-syllable word 'alarms', it was usually pronounced in Shakespeare's time with three: 'a-lar-ums'. The second potential expansion involves the word 'proportion', which Elizabethans could pronounce as either 'pro-por-shun' or 'pro-por-shi-un'. Whether to pronounce the word with three or four syllables raises another rhythmic issue, which we'd now like to turn to.

II *Six Feet*

- Although the normal blank verse line is an iambic pentameter of five feet, occasionally Shakespeare and other dramatists would break the rhythm with a line of six feet, a variation known as an iambic hexameter (from 'hex', the Greek for 'six'). There is already one line in this speech that is possibly an iambic hexameter, and if 'proportion' were four syllables it would make another. Here are the two lines together, with the six feet marked off:

> I, that| am rude|-ly stamped| and want| love's ma|-jes-ty
> I, that| am cur|-tailed of| this fair| pro-por|-ti-on

Try the two lines for yourself, and notice how similar they are. They both begin with the same three words, and they both express Richard's shame and anger at his physical condition. It is this similarity which makes us think that 'proportion' might be four syllables here rather than create a feminine ending with three. If so, we would suggest that Shakespeare was using these hexameters to express the strength of Richard's emotion, which couldn't be contained within the normal pentameter: the deformity of his body and mind is mirrored by the deformity of the lines.

III *Tracking Trochees*

- Let's look at section B of the speech, in which these lines appear, more closely.

- Read this section aloud once, leaning into the iambic rhythm (making those two lines hexameters). Now read it again to a partner fairly slowly, trying to make him understand the points you are making. Together go back and look for places where you felt like you needed to stress the first syllable in a line instead of the second to make your point.

- There are a number of places where you may have wanted to begin with a reversed foot. The following seem fairly inevitable to us:

> **I**, that| am rudely stamp'd and want love's majesty
> **I,** that| am curtail'd of this fair proportion
> **Cheat**-ed| of feature by dissembling Nature
> **In**-to| this breathing world scarce half made up

Grab a partner and have her hold up her hand in front of her. Speak each of these lines stressing the first syllable, and punch your partner's hand (lightly!) as you say it. Now go back, speak each line stressing the second syllable and punching your partner's hand on it.

Working Alone: Punch a pillow. In each case, which felt like it served Richard's intention to convince the audience that he is justified in disrupting this newly established peace? What do these tell you about how Richard uses (or can use) rhythm and language to command attention?

Teaching Tip: If it does not seem appropriate to have your students punch each other's hands, they can punch one of their own hands with the other.

- Reverse feet can also appear in the middle of a line, often occurring in conjunction with a caesura. A potential one is:

  In-to| this **breath**|-ing **world**| **scarce** half| made **up**

  Here's another possible example:

  I, that am curtailed   of this fair proportion

  Our modern pronunciation of 'curtailed' stresses the second syllable. Assuming that Elizabethan pronunciation was the same and coupling it with the potential hexameter would create this scansion for the line:

  I, that| am **cur**|-tailed   of| this **fair**| pro-**por**|-ti-**on**

In this case, the reversed foot is split by the caesura, making a very unusual line.

This is another tricky line:

That dogs bark at me, as I halt by them

There's clearly a caesura here:

That dogs bark at me,   as I halt by them

Speak it quite naturally for yourself a couple of times, and see where the sense stresses want to fall. Now, compare your reading of the line with the way the iambic rhythm might suggest you stress it:

That **dogs**| bark **at**| me,   **as**| I **halt**| by **them**

It's certainly possible to say it this way, but depending upon interpretation, there are a couple of potential reversed feet here, and only one of them occurs at the caesura. Here they are together:

That **dogs**| **bark** at| me,   **as**| I **halt**| by **them**

Even in that last foot, 'by' could be almost as strong as 'them', if not a bit stronger, which is a very unusual way to end a line.

- Go through your copy of the speech, and underline the stressed word or syllable in each of the potential reversed feet we've identified in part B.

- Sit at a table and read this section aloud to a partner if you have one. As you do, pound or slap your hand on the table (not too hard!) *any time* you want to stress a word. Be generous with your pounding – there are a lot of strong, juicy words in here, and the accumulation of them will do a lot to make sure that you succeed in pummelling your listeners into acceptance of your evil plans. The only words you MUST slap or pound the table on, however, are those that you have underlined.

- Where in the speech did your slapping feel the most regular and controlled? Where did it feel the most sporadic, frenzied and/or urgent? Which images were most vivid for you and your partner? What effect did the alternation between regular and more unpredictable slapping have? Swap over and repeat.

- You can go back and use these exercises to find and explore reversed feet in part A as well.

IV *Feminine Endings*

- Shakespeare gives a good number of Gloucester's lines feminine endings. You've probably noticed them already, so here are the particular instances as a reminder:

  ... the ocean **bur**-ied
  ... to merry **meet**-ings
  ... to delightful **mea**-sures
  ... fearful ad-ver-**sa**-ries
  ... lady's **cham**-ber
  ... this fair pro-**por**-tion (if spoken as 'pro-por-shun')
  ... dissembling **Na**-ture
  ... prove a **lov**-er
  ... prove a **vill**-ain

  The last word in any verse line can be significant for a character, but several of these feminine endings occur quite closely together: 'meetings' and 'measures'; 'adversaries' and 'chamber'; 'proportion' and 'Nature'; 'lover' and 'villain'. That this is not purely accidental is suggested by the fact that in a number of these cases, Shakespeare could have chosen to write another word which would have eliminated the feminine ending; for example, instead of 'buried' he could have written 'drowned', or instead of 'adversaries' and 'chamber' he could have written 'enemies' and 'room'. There may be other reasons why he instinctively chose the former words, but let's look at the effect of these clusters of weak line endings.

- Take the first pair:

Our stern alarums changed to merry meetings,
Our dreadful marches to delightful measures

Speak these lines through, leaning into the iambic rhythm, but
when you reach the end of each line, make a sweeping gesture
with your arm on the last word.

- On the following lines, pound your fist on something as you
  say the last word when the line ends with a strong stress, and
  make a sweeping gesture whenever there's a feminine ending:

  And now, instead of mounting barbèd steeds
  To fright the souls of fearful adversaries,
  He capers nimbly in a lady's chamber

  Again, what happens to the energy of the thoughts? What
  choices does this offer the actor? Try pounding on the feminine
  ending and waving when the line ends with a strong stress.
  Does this fit rhythmically?

- Do the same with:

  And therefore, since I cannot prove a lover
  To entertain these fair well-spoken days,
  I am determinèd to prove a villain,
  And hate the idle pleasures of these days.

  This pair of feminine endings is bound up with a pair of
  rhyming lines, and the four lines together have a strong parallel
  structure. With a partner or on your own, reflect on how these
  elements give a sense of inevitability to Richard's conclusion
  that the best thing he can do is be a villain.

- Now, go back to speaking the whole text quite easily, but with
  this awareness of the feminine endings in your mind. Has this
  changed your understanding of the speech at all?

V *The Final Word*

- Finally, we'll take some time to explore Shakespeare's use of
  end-stopped and run-on lines in part A of this speech. Speak

the text through quite easily and, as you do so, take a small breath in at the end of every line. Do this a couple of times, and notice where taking a breath pause seems to break up the sense of what you're saying.

- Many of Richard's lines are end-stopped; but some only appear to be end-stopped. This is particularly true of the famous first line, which can make complete sense as a thought on its own: 'This time we live in now is like the coldest and unhappiest winter'. But the thought is only fully realized by the addition of the following line: 'The awful winter of civil war that we endured has now become a wonderful peaceful summer thanks to the son (note the pun on 'sun') of the House of York (Richard's brother, the new king).' Sir Anthony Sher writes of making just this mistake and subsequent discovery in his book, *The Year of the King* (Sher, 1985). There are a number of places like this, where the thought seems like it could end but then develops further. It's as if Richard is thinking on his feet, in the moment, and discovers the turns or developments in his thought as he speaks.

- Set up two chairs about twenty feet away from each other – or as far apart as the room will allow. Start at one chair and walk towards the other as you speak the first line, aiming to get to it as you finish the line. If there is a full stop (period), question mark or exclamation point at the end of this line, sit in the second chair when you get to the last word, pause there for a moment, then get up and walk back to the first chair on the next line. If there is no full stop, turn right around on the last word of the line and walk back to the other chair on the second line. Continue through to the end of the speech – sitting in the chair if there is a full stop at the end of the line and turning away from the chair if there isn't. Breathe whenever it feels right to do so.

- What you may have discovered is that the end of the verse line often reflects a very energized choice in the development of Richard's argument. To bring this into greater focus, speak part A of the speech through again, and on the last stressed word of each line make a strong physical gesture in response to that

word. You can literally 'act out' the word, or simply make a
movement to punctuate it. How important are these final words
to Richard? What does this tell you about how he builds an
argument?

Teaching Tip or Working Alone: We explore run-on lines in more
detail in the 'Breaking the Rhythm' section of this chapter.

Act

- As part of your personal preparation, go through the speech
  once, investigating the use of caesuras, as you did with Julia's
  speech.

- Though Richard may be physically deformed, his intellect is
  extremely sharp and vigorous. There are great energy and
  determination in both the content and the rhythm of this
  opening speech. There are also great charm and wit, which he
  will need to pursue his ambitions.

- Take the speech through once and really show off your
  mastery of the verse form – drive the meter when it is regular,
  committing strongly to the beat of that iambic rhythm – let it
  carry you through the clever and complex images rather than
  lingering on them. When there are rhythmic variations (like
  feminine endings, lines of hexameter, reversed feet) be bold in
  showing your audience how masterfully you can use them to
  surprise, belittle, assault, entertain, etc.

- Identify where you found that a strong commitment to the
  rhythmic features of this speech was particularly useful to help
  you land specific points on your listeners. Perform the speech
  once again without feeling that you need to focus quite so
  much on the rhythm, but using it where you can to make the
  most of the variety and power in the writing.

Teaching Tip or Working Alone: Before moving on you may like to review the work of this section with other verse speeches from Shakespeare's early comedies and history plays, for example, *The Taming of the Shrew* and the *Henry VI* plays. Here is a summary of how to proceed:

1. Speak the text with a regular iambic beat.
2. Feel where any irregularities occur.
3. Look for expansions and contractions.
4. Consider the effects of keeping or breaking the rhythm.
5. Look for reversed feet, both obligatory and optional, and where they occur.
6. Consider why the reversed foot is there.
7. Consider feminine endings and why they are there.
8. Look for caesuras and what they might contribute to the line.
9. Look for end-stopped and enjambed lines and consider how they affect the speech.
10. Physicalize the last stressed word of each verse line and consider their significance for the character.

Grumio

We finish this section of exercises with a short piece of prose from Act 4 Scene 1 of *The Taming of the Shrew*. This comedy is another early play and centres on the madcap Petruccio's wooing and wedding of Katherina, the bad-tempered daughter of Baptista. Grumio is Petruccio's personal servant and, as such, has had to accompany his master and new mistress home from their wedding in Padua to their house in the country. It has been a cold and muddy journey, and Grumio has been beaten a lot. He has now been sent on ahead to get a fire ready. He is a small man.

- Speak through the text quietly a couple of times without looking at the glosses.

GRUMIO

Fie, fie on all tired jades, on all mad masters, and all foul ways! Was ever man so beaten? Was ever man so rayed? Was ever man so weary? I am sent before to make a fire, and they are coming after to warm them. Now were not I a little pot and soon hot, my very lips might freeze to my teeth, my tongue to the roof of my mouth, my heart in my belly, ere I should   5 come by a fire to thaw me; but I with blowing the fire shall warm myself, for considering the weather, a taller man than I will take cold.

Glosses
1, **jades** = old horses, **foul ways** = muddy trails; 2, **rayed** = dirtied; 4, **a little pot** = a small man; 5, **ere** = before; 6, **come by** = get.

Speak

- Speak through the text quietly again, looking at the glosses as you go, even for words you think you know.
- Speak it through about 30 per cent more slowly than you did at first. Speak it again about 30 per cent more quickly.

Question
I *Triplets*

- We said at the outset that both verse and prose make use of the rhythm that is created by regular occurring patterns of stressed and unstressed syllables. But rhythm in prose is much less regular and more fluid in its patterns than verse. To explore some of the prose patterns Shakespeare employs, speak the speech again and, this time, move about the room as if you're trying to keep yourself warm. Whenever you come to a punctuation mark, stop and change direction. Do this a couple of times.
- You've probably noticed one of the main patterns that Shakespeare uses to create a comic rhythm here: repetition of phrases. More specifically, the same type of phrase is said three times, and this triple pattern is used three times.

The group-of-three pattern is very common throughout Shakespeare and many other writers, but Grumio seems addicted to it.

- Mark the three groups of three in the speech. Take it again, still moving with the punctuation marks. But now, when you get to each of the triplets, speak the first iteration of the phrase as if it's the only time you're going to use this phrase, and then find that you just can't resist going on to a second iteration, and then actually need a third before you're satisfied that you've made your point. Don't let this slow you down too much – it doesn't take you but a microsecond to realize you have one more thing to add. What does this reveal to the audience about Grumio's character and state of mind?

- In the middle of these groups of three is another pattern, which might be seen more easily if we set it out like this, using different fonts to highlight it:

  I am **sent before** TO MAKE A FIRE, and
  they are **coming after** TO WARM THEM

  In this case, there is a parallel structure rather than a simple repetition. Stylistically, it varies the pulse of Grumio's speech while at the same time maintaining a rhythmic quality. Speak these two lines, and as you do take one big step in one direction on each of the three parts of the first line and then one big step in the other direction on each of the three parts of the second line.

  In addition, you might have noticed that another type of group of three follows this parallel structure – a group of three rhymes: *not*, *pot*, *hot*. Just for fun, read that part of the speech and hop on each of these rhyming words.

- Speak the speech once more, relishing the rhythmic repetitions and variations these patterns produce.

Act

- We'd like you to work with a partner for this speech, but if you don't have one you can easily envisage one. Imagine how cold and tired you are, how sore from all the beatings, and how patient you've had to be to endure this (and note this group of three that we instinctively used to describe Grumio's situation). You've just arrived at your house and you're greeted by a fellow servant. You take this opportunity to let off a bit of steam about your lot in life. Your only consolation is that, because you're small, you can get warmer more quickly than a tall person can.

* Swap places with your partner, and then discuss anything you discovered about Grumio and his use of prose rhythms.

Mastering the rhythm

The following exercises look in more detail at the variations and irregularities in iambic pentameter and how they contribute to character development and argument, concentrating on examples from Shakespeare's middle period, when he had gained mastery of the form. We also look further at prose rhythms. We start with a speech from Act 1 Scene 3 of *The Merchant of Venice*.

Shylock

Shylock is a Jewish moneylender in the Christian city of Venice at a time when it was common for Jews to be despised and mistreated by society. He has been approached by a wealthy merchant, Antonio, who is in need of a loan in support of his friend Bassanio. In the past, Antonio has behaved badly towards Shylock and other Jews in the city. This speech is part of Shylock's response to Antonio's request for money.

* Speak through the text quietly a couple of times without looking at the glosses.

SHYLOCK
A
Signior Antonio, many a time and oft
In the Rialto you have rated me
About my moneys and my usances.
Still have I borne it with a patient shrug,

For sufferance is the badge of all our tribe.   5
You call me misbeliever, cut-throat dog,
And spit upon my Jewish gaberdine,
And all for use of that which is mine own.
Well, then, it now appears you need my help.
Go to, then, you come to me, and you say,   10
'Shylock, we would have moneys.' You say so.
You, that did void your rheum upon my beard
And foot me as you spurn a stranger cur
Over your threshold, moneys is your suit.

B

What should I say to you? Should I not say,   15
'Hath a dog money? Is it possible
A cur should lend three thousand ducats?' Or
Shall I bend low and in a bondman's key,
With bated breath and whispering humbleness,
Say this: 'Fair sir, you spat on me on Wednesday last,   20
You spurned me such a day; another time,
You called me dog: and, for these courtesies,
I'll lend you thus much moneys.'

Glosses
1, **oft** = often; 2, **rated** = rebuked; 3, **usances** = interest payments; 4,
still = always; 5, **sufferance** = endurance; 7, **gabardine** = cloak; 12,
void your rheum = spit; 13, **foot** = kick, **spurn** = strike, **cur** = dog;
14, **suit** = petition; 17, **ducats** = gold coins; 18, **bondman's key** =
slave's tone of voice; 19, **bated** = reduced.

Speak

- Speak through the text quietly again, looking at the glosses as
  you go, even for words you think you know.

- Speak it through a few more times, so you get a clear sense of
  the meaning.

- Now, speak through the text again, at a more conversational
  volume this time, and begin to lean into the regular iambic
  rhythm of each line.

Question
I *Rockier Rhythms*

- Taking each line on its own, this is a pretty regular speech. If you explore it for contractions, you will find very few: 'Antonio' needs to be 'Antone-yo'; 'sufferance' is 'suff-rance'; 'whispering' is 'whisp-ring'; and 'Wednesday' is 'Wens-day' – all standard in modern spoken English. There are no feminine endings to the lines and, except for a number of obligatory and optional reversed feet at the beginning of lines, most lines maintain a strict iambic rhythm. However, add to those reversed feet the amount of run-on lines and strong caesuras, not to mention the hexameter in the middle and a short line at the end, and the speech takes on a more complex and intriguing rhythm.

- Look at the reversed feet first of all. Speak the speech again, once more leaning into the iambic rhythm, but this time focus on identifying any reversed feet either at the beginning, in the middle, or at the end of a line. For the initial reverses, notice which ones are semantically rich and which have little semantic content.

- There are several obligatory reversed feet, as well as quite a few optional ones. The obligatory ones in our opinion are:

> **Sign**-ior| Antonio (if we assume the English-language pronunciation of 'Signior')
> **In** the| Rialto
> **Shy**-lock| we would
> **You** that| did void
> **O**-ver| your threshold
> **Hath** a| dog money

We consider 'In the', 'Over' and 'Hath a' quite weak, propelling the speaker into the next foot and so emphasizing 'Rialto', 'your threshold' and 'dog money'. Read each phrase rocking onto your front foot lightly on that first word or syllable and then strongly when you get to the stressed syllable in the second foot. Notice how the weak first foot thrusts you towards the second.

- The remaining three have much more semantic content – 'Signior', 'Shylock', 'You that' – and so the reversed foot helps to highlight words that have to do with their personal identities. Speak each of them for yourself, leaning into the first syllable physically. Why might Shylock want to draw attention to the personal aspect of their relationship?

- The optional initial reversed feet we've identified are:

  Still have| I borne it
  Well then| it not
  What should| I say
  Shall I| bend low

  Again, in each case, it would be possible to put more emphasis on the second syllable, depending on interpretation. But try these lines out for yourself, and see how they feel in your mouth and how they sound to your ear. If you have a partner, how do these options sound when spoken by someone else? Which feel like weak reversed feet, and which like strong?

- There are two potential mid-line reversed feet, in consecutive lines. Here are the lines scanned with a regular iambic:

  Go **to,**| then, **you**| come **to**| me, **and**| you **say,**
  '**Shy**-lock,| we **would**| have **mon**|-eys.' **You**| say **so.**

  And now with the reversed feet:

  Go **to,**| then, **you**| **come** to| me, **and**| you **say,**
  '**Shy**-lock,| **we** would| have **mon**|-eys.' **You**| say **so.**

  You might also feel that there could be a reversed foot at the end of the second line, with the emphasis on 'say' rather than 'so'. Try all these options for yourself, and with a partner if you have one, and see how they feel. Why might the rhythm be getting very rocky for Shylock at this point?

II *The Tipping Point*

- Now explore the speech for where the caesuras occur. Return to saying the lines focusing on their meaning. As you did with the earlier speeches, speak the speech through several times and, as you do so, begin to shift your weight from back foot to front foot whenever you feel there's a definite point where the focus of Shylock's language shifts in the middle of a line. Not every line will have a definite caesura, *and you may feel that some lines have more than one*. But where there is one, notice where it occurs in the line and exaggerate the focus-shift by pausing slightly at the caesura.

- Notice how the caesuras get stronger as the speech progresses, often occurring near the beginning or end of the line. Go through the speech once more and let your back-and-forth movement become bigger as the speech progresses – so you may start by shifting your weight and end by taking several steps in either direction. What effect does this have on the flow of the speech? Notice also that in those two consecutive rocky lines we identified above there could be two caesuras, and that several of the other caesuras are coupled with run-on lines and extended thoughts. How do these rhythmic elements help you connect to Shylock's given circumstances?

- Now, go back to speaking the text without moving or pausing on the caesuras, but see if you can keep that sense of there being dynamic tipping points present throughout the speech.

III *Tapping*

- You can probably appreciate how much more rhythmic variation Shakespeare has begun to find in iambic pentameter, and how much more muscular and flexible this makes it as a medium for dramatic characterization. Before we ask you to perform the text, however, let's look at that long hexameter and the short, four-foot line in part B of the speech. (This short line is technically an iambic tetrameter, from the Greek for the number 'four'.)

Get a partner. Read through part B, and on every strong stress, tap your partner's breastbone with your index finger. With the exception of the reversed foot at 'Hath a dog money', you'll be tapping in an iambic rhythm. Start by speaking fairly slowly and tapping quite lightly; you're likely to find that there's a momentum that will make you want to speed up and tap more vigorously as you go on.

Teaching Tip: You may want to assign same sex partners for this exercise. If tapping on the breastbone doesn't feel appropriate for your group, you can substitute tapping on the shoulder.

Working Alone: You can tap your finger on a table for this step.

- Switch partners. The new Shylock will need to have part B of the speech memorized, or his partner will have to hold it up so he can read from it. Shylock, speak part B again, keeping a strong sense of the iambic beat that you and your partner found in the previous step, and when you get to the last word of each line, clap your hands. You can clap with varying degrees of intensity and closeness to your partner depending on what the language suggests to you. Do use the claps, though, to reinforce the point you are trying to make to Antonio.

- What do the hexameter and the short tetrameter contribute to Shylock's energy or purpose here? The short line at the end perhaps allows for a silent moment of confrontation between Shylock and Antonio, or allows for a physical movement. Or, perhaps, we should allow Shakespeare some metrical licence

here, recognizing that, taken together, the hexameter and the
tetrameter make up two pentameters!

Act

- Earlier in this scene Shylock has spoken privately of an 'ancient
  grudge' that he bears Antonio, not only for being a Christian
  who hates Jews but also for being a man who lends out
  money for no interest and so disrupts Shylock's own business.
  When Antonio and Bassanio come to him for a loan, he sees
  a chance to get his revenge on Antonio (to 'catch him upon
  the hip', as he puts it). In performing the speech, therefore,
  the actor has a choice between allowing Shylock's hatred to
  come to the surface and covering it with a veneer of deceitful
  politeness. So, get a partner, if one is available to you, and
  take it in turns to act the scene: first, with Shylock barely
  able to contain his emotion; and second, with Shylock coolly
  presenting a logical and reasonable argument.

- Which feels more in tune with the rhythm of the text? Perhaps
  they both do to some extent. Perhaps Shylock begins by
  presenting a reasonable front but, as the rhythm becomes
  more turbulent, increasingly his emotion surfaces. Try
  performing it this way.

- Take some time to reflect on how the rhythms in the text have
  informed and supported your interpretation.

Portia and Lucius

Portia is the wife of Brutus in *Julius Caesar*. Brutus has been conspiring
with several other senators in Rome to assassinate Julius Caesar. Here
we explore a short piece of dialogue from Act 2 Scene 4 that she
shares with their servant boy as she waits to hear the outcome of their
attempt on Caesar's life. You will find it useful to work with a partner for
this text, but it isn't essential.

Teaching Tip: When working on dialogues, feel free to assign roles to students without respect to gender. We would also encourage you to have pairs of students swap roles frequently as they work on the scene. This is because one character will often have more language than the other, and it also serves to encourage the students to approach the scene as text they are exploring together rather than get attached to performing one of the characters.

Working Alone: When working on dialogues, you should generally read both parts. It may help you to move to a different spot when you change characters.

- Speak through the text together quietly a couple of times without looking at the glosses.

PORTIA
I prithee, boy, run to the Senate House.
Stay not to answer me, but get thee gone.
Why dost thou stay?
LUCIUS
                            To know my errand, madam.
PORTIA
I would have had thee there and here again
Ere I can tell thee what thou shouldst do there.   5
O constancy, be strong upon my side:
Set a huge mountain 'tween my heart and tongue.
I have a man's mind, but a woman's might.
How hard it is for women to keep counsel.
Art thou here yet?

LUCIUS
              Madam, what should I do?   10
Run to the Capitol, and nothing else?
And so return to you, and nothing else?
PORTIA
Yes, bring me word, boy, if thy lord look well,
For he went sickly forth; and take good note
What Caesar doth, what suitors press to him.   15

Glosses
5, **Ere** = before; 6, **constancy** = self-control; 9, **keep counsel** = keep
a secret; 15, **suitors** = petitioners, **press** = push forward.

Speak

- Speak through the text quietly again, looking at the glosses as
  you go, even for words you think you know. If you are working
  on your own, speak both parts.

- If you are working with a partner, sit back to back and read
  through the text a couple of times this way. Be aware of
  communicating with your partner even though you can't see
  her.

- Now, speak through the text again, facing each other, and lean
  into the regular iambic rhythm of each line.

Question
I *Sharing Lines*

- Take some time to explore the text with your partner (or by
  yourself) for expansions or contractions, feminine endings and
  potential reversed feet.

- As with Shylock, the rhythm of this dialogue is quite regular,
  apart from a number of possible reversed feet. There are
  no expansions or contractions to trip you up, and only two
  relatively insignificant feminine endings: 'madam' and 'counsel'.

- Although the reversed feet are important to Portia's state of
  mind, we wish to focus more on the nature of the line. You'll

have noticed that there are two lines that are split between the speakers. In the Folio, these are simply printed as short lines, but where two characters' sequential short lines together add up to ten (or eleven with a feminine ending) syllables, most contemporary editors lay them out on the page so as to help the reader see that there is a potential rhythmic connection – that the characters might be sharing the line.

- Take the dialogue again, and this time speak it as if each line of verse is a separate unit of thought. Breathe in at the end of each line and find the impulse for the next line as you do so. Think of each of the split lines as a unit of thought that you share with your partner; so Lucius, don't pause before you begin speaking in the middle of the line, and breathe together at the ends of lines throughout the dialogue. If you need to, repeat this several times, changing roles, until you feel yourselves working together without rushing. Are the lines end-stopped or run-on? How does it feel to share a line? And what do you discover about Portia's thoughts and Lucius's relationship to his mistress in the process?

Working Alone: Speak both Portia's and Lucius's lines. When a line is shared, wait to breathe until you have completed the line.

- Most of the lines are quite heavily end-stopped. Shakespeare was certainly capable of using run-on lines, but he chooses not to here. Take the exchange one more time. This time, you don't have to breathe at the end of every line, but when you do, really use that breath to launch yourself into the next line. How does the stop/start rhythm of this passage help to create tension?

Act

- As part of your personal preparation, spend some time exploring the caesuras in the dialogue.

- This scene comes immediately before the assassination of Caesar in the Roman Senate by Brutus and his fellow conspirators. Portia, who knows of the plot, is anxious to know what is happening and has come out of her house with Lucius to send him to the Senate to find out. She can't let Lucius know what's afoot or he might betray them, but her need to know the outcome is clearly driving her to distraction. The stakes, which for her are high, are relatively low for the boy. She must find a reason that will explain her anxiety and make him hurry.

- Prepare to act the scene with your partner. In particular, review the end-stopped lines and the shared lines for indications of physical actions. For example, Portia's first two lines both end with a full stop – they are both instructions to the boy which he doesn't obey. What might each character be doing at the end of each line?

Working Alone: Play Portia, but as part of your preparation decide what Lucius is doing at each point in the scene.

- Perform the scene, and then review how your awareness of these rhythmic factors contributed to your performance.

Falstaff

Falstaff is one of the great speakers of prose in the Shakespeare canon. A braggart, rogue and coward, he is also a philosopher and pragmatist, and we come to see him as all too human. In this short scene from Act 5 Scene 1 of *King Henry IV, Part One*, Falstaff and Prince Henry exchange a brief farewell before going into battle against a rebel army at Shrewsbury. Falstaff then debates with himself the relative merits of honour as a reason to die.

- Speak through the text quietly a couple of times without looking at the glosses.

(FALSTAFF
I would 'twere bed-time, Hal, and all well.
PRINCE HENRY
Why, thou owest God a death.

Exit PRINCE HENRY)

FALSTAFF
'Tis not due yet. I would be loath to pay him before his day. What need I be so forward with him that calls not on me? Well, 'tis no matter; honour pricks me on. Yea, but how if honour prick me off when I come on? How then?   5
Can honour set to a leg? No. Or an arm? No. Or take away the grief of a wound? No. Honour hath no skill in surgery, then? No. What is honour? A word. What is in that word 'honour'? What is that 'honour'? Air. A trim reckoning. Who hath it? He that died o'Wednesday. Doth he feel it? No. Doth he hear it? No. 'Tis insensible, then? Yea, to the dead. But will it not live with the living?   10
No. Why? Detraction will not suffer it. Therefore I'll none of it. Honour is a mere scutcheon. And so ends my catechism.

Glosses
3, **be loath** = hate; 4, **forward** = willing, **pricks** = urges; 5, **prick me off** = stab me; 6, **set to a leg** = mend a broken leg, **grief** = pain; 8, **trim** = fine; 10, **insensible** = imperceptible; 11, **Detraction** = slander, **suffer** = tolerate; 12, **scutcheon** = painted shield, **catechism** = set of questions and answers.

Speak

- Speak through the text quietly again, looking at the glosses as you go, even for words you think you know.
- Lie down on your back and speak the text through once. Try to keep energy in your voice even though your body is still.
- Stand up and read the text again moving freely through the room as you do so.

Question
I *Drum kit*

- You will certainly have noticed the rhythmic question-and-answer structure here, even if Falstaff didn't draw attention to it with his reference to a 'catechism'. But how does Shakespeare prevent this repetitive structure from becoming boring? As you did with Grumio, speak the speech again, moving about the room. Whenever you come to a major punctuation mark (period, question mark or exclamation mark), stop and change direction. Do this a couple of times.

- When you were walking around, you probably noticed that there's a lot of syncopation in the rhythm – the length of phrase between punctuation marks varies quite a bit. You might even call it jazzy. We're going to play a little with that jazzy rhythm.

- Lay four or five books in front of you on a table. You're going to pretend that they are your drum set. One book you will hit every time you say the word 'no'; you'll hit another every time you say the word 'honour'. You can hit any of the other books on any other word or syllable you want to stress. Don't be stingy with your drum hits – this is your solo! Speak it with relish!

- One of the elements that Shakespeare varies is simply the length of question or answer: from one word up to an average of six. But take a look also at the type of questions. Once he starts on his catechism, Falstaff employs all the standard ways of asking a question: beginning with an interrogative word ('how ...', 'what ...', 'who ...', and 'why ...'); turning statements into questions with a questioning 'then?'; and by reversing the subject and verb ('doth he ...', 'can honour ...'). Play through the speech on your 'drum kit' again, this time hitting one of the books on every question word we've mentioned (and any others you spot) as well as hitting your 'no' and 'honour' drums.

> *Teaching Tip:* It can get a little chaotic to have a large group all doing this at once, so you may want to set up three or four stations in the room where one student at a time can do the exercise while others watch and wait their turn.

II *Parallels*

- Falstaff's prose is much more complex than Grumio's, but there are still groups of three, and parallelism. Go through the speech looking for sentences that are built of parallel phrases.

- The catechism begins with a parallel phrase:

  honour pricks me *on*
  honour pricks me *off*

  And there is a pair of parallel questions:

  Doth he *feel it*
  Doth he *hear it*

- Get two partners. Together, go through the speech and underline all the parallels you can – that's any place where something is repeated with a variation in the repetition. If you're unsure of a possible parallelism, just underline it and the exercise will help you figure out if it's useful to play those two phrases off each other. Read the speech and deliver the first of any two parallel phrases to one partner and the second to the other.

> *Working Alone:* You can use chairs to stand in for partners.

- Discuss or reflect on any discoveries you've made about how Falstaff works his way through this question of whether or not it's worth it to die for honour. Do you find his argument persuasive? How do you think he uses rhythm to win his listeners over to his point of view?

Act

- Falstaff's fear of death makes him question what he's doing on the battlefield. He then interrogates his answer – Honour – and finds it wanting! As you act the text, play with the various rhythms of Falstaff's questions and answers. If you feel yourself becoming too remote and rhetorical, imagine speaking this to an audience and actively asking them the questions before supplying the answer.

Breaking the rhythm

Once an artist has learned his trade and gained mastery of his chosen medium, he is likely to experiment with new ways of doing things. Shakespeare was certainly this kind of artist, and in his later plays he experimented not only with dramatic forms but also with the medium of iambic pentameter, as he made greater use of rhythmic variations to represent the variety and intensity of human communication. To explore this, we begin with a speech from Act 1 Scene 2 of *King Lear*.

Edmund

Edmund is the bastard son of the Earl of Gloucester, one of King Lear's senior courtiers. Gloucester has a legitimate son, Edgar, who is a year older than Edmund. Edmund has just returned to court after a long absence, and he is determined to get Edgar's inheritance by whatever means he can. In this speech, he reveals his motives and his plans.

- Speak through the text quietly a couple of times without looking at the glosses.

EDMUND

A

Thou, Nature, art my goddess; to thy law
My services are bound. Wherefore should I
Stand in the plague of custom, and permit
The curiosity of nations to deprive me?
For that I am some twelve or fourteen moonshines   5
Lag of a brother? Why bastard? Wherefore base?
When my dimensions are as well compact,
My mind as generous and my shape as true
As honest madam's issue? Why brand they us
With base? With baseness, bastardy? Base, base?   10
Who in the lusty stealth of nature take
More composition and fierce quality
Than doth within a dull stale tirèd bed
Go to the creating of a whole tribe of fops
Got 'tween a sleep and wake.

B

                                     Well, then,   15
Legitimate Edgar, I must have your land.
Our father's love is to the bastard Edmund
As to the legitimate. Fine word, 'legitimate'!
Well, my legitimate, if this letter speed
And my invention thrive, Edmund the base   20
Shall top the legitimate. I grow, I prosper:
Now gods, stand up for bastards!

Glosses
2, **bound** = engaged; 3, **Stand** = remain, **plague** = torment; 4,
curiosity = moral delicacy, **deprive** = dispossess; 5, **moonshines**
= months; 6, **Lag of** = behind, **base** = illegitimate; 7, **dimensions** =
bodily parts, **compact** = composed; 8, **generous** = noble; 9, **honest**
= virtuous, **issue** = children; 12, **fierce quality** = passionate nature;
14, **fops** = fools; 15, **got** = conceived, **wake** = waking; 19, **speed** =
succeed; 20, **invention** = plot, plan; 21, **top** = rise above.

Speak

- Speak through the text quietly again, looking at the glosses as you go, even for words you think you know.

- Speak it through a few more times, so you get a clear sense of the meaning.

- Now, speak through the text again at a more conversational volume, and lean into the iambic rhythm of each line as far as possible.

Question
I *Syllables and Action*

- You probably experienced a lot of turbulence in this speech, and very little of it is created by expansions or contractions. Modern actors often treat the expansion 'tirèd' as if it were a two-syllable elongation of our own 'tie-erd' pronunciation. Try it both ways, and see what you prefer.

- Apart from variations on the word 'legitimate', the only contraction we can find is 'generous', which needs to be 'gen-rous' to fit the rhythm of the line. However, the word 'legitimate' may have caused you to stumble over the rhythm each time it occurred. Of course, from Edmund's point of view, his legitimate brother is quite literally a stumbling-block to him. But let's look more closely at the word and the various lines concerned.

- 'Legitimate' is normally a four-syllable word, 'le-gi-ti-mate'. However, it is possible to contract it into three syllables: 'le-git-mate', and this seems to be what is happening the first time it occurs:

  Legitimate Edgar, I must have your land
  Le-**git**|-mate **Ed**|-gar **I**| must **have**| your **land**

  How does it feel to say the word this way? Does it give the word a particular spin?

  'Legitimate' appears twice in the same line next time we hear it:

As to th' legitimate. Fine word, 'legitimate'.

There are two possible scansions here. Pronouncing 'legitimate' as a four-syllable word both times produces an iambic hexameter with three feet either side of the caesura:

As to| th'le-**gi**|-ti-**mate**| Fine **word**| le-**gi**|-ti-**mate**

Or one of the pronunciations might be a three-syllable one. If it were the second one, it would produce a feminine ending:

As to| th'le-**gi**|-ti-**mate**   Fine **word**| le-**git**-mate

If it were the first one, however, we would be looking at what's known as an **epic (or feminine) caesura**; for just as an additional weak syllable can occur at the end of the line, so it can also appear before the caesura, creating an eleven-syllable line:

As to| th'le-**git**-mate| Fine **word**| le-**git**|-i-**mate**

Try them out for yourself and see which one you prefer. That Edmund is perhaps savouring the word might suggest that the hexameter is the better choice, but it is really a matter of interpretation and taste. (Contracting the phrase 'the legitimate' into 'th'legitimate' may feel awkward at first, but with a little practice you'll find it comes quite naturally.)

The word appears again in the very next line:

Well, my legitimate, if this letter speed

Once again, it needs to be three syllables for the iambic rhythm to be maintained:

Well, my| le-**git**|-mate,   **if**| this **let**|-ter **speed**

The last time it appears, however, it needs to be four syllables again:

Shall **top**| th'le-**gi**|-ti-**mate**| I **grow**| I **pros**-per

- Go through part B of the speech: circle the word 'legitimate' every time the meter requires or you have chosen to pronounce it with four syllables. Underline it every time you're using three syllables.

- Get a partner. Read part B and every time you get to an underlined (three-syllable) 'legit'mate', walk around to your partner's back and give him a little shove as you say it. Every time you come to a circled (four-syllable) 'legitimate', walk around to your partner's front and do something annoying to him – ruffle his hair, or untie his shoelace, or just get in his face – as you say the word. You'll need to be pretty familiar with the text for this to work.

Teaching Tip: If it feels inappropriate to have your students touch each other in this way, simply have them speak the three-syllable 'legitimates' with the intention to intimidate a partner and the four-syllable ones with the intention to tease.

Working Alone: As explained in the teaching tip, you can also use non-physical intentions with an imaginary partner.

- Discuss what you've learned about how Edmund might use the rhythmic variations on this word to specify the kind of attack he's making on his brother's status from moment to moment.

II *Long and Short*

- Having made your choices concerning 'legitimate', take the speech again and lean into the rhythm. Where else do you feel some turbulence in the regular pentameter? In addition to the possible hexameter we suggested above, are there any other long or short lines?

- The following line scans as a hexameter in our modern pronunciation, and we suspect it did for Shakespeare too:

    The **cu**|-ri-**o**|-si-**ty**| of **na**|-tions **to**| de-**prive** me

    There's also a feminine ending here, which makes it a very long line indeed. Why might Shakespeare have given Edmund a long line at this point? What is Edmund's focus here?

- Then there is the short tetrameter at the end of the speech. This line is immediately followed by Gloucester's entrance, and Shakespeare sometimes writes a short line when it precedes a physical action. However, the action might be Edmund's upon finishing his prayer or on seeing Gloucester. Alternatively, is there anything in Edmund's intention with the line which might suggest you expand the speaking of it, making it equivalent to a pentameter? It is always worth exploring various possibilities when a short line occurs, so try them out for yourself and see what choices work well here.

III *In and Out of Step*

- Exploring the caesuras and enjambments will also provide you with specific insights and choices. In particular, we mentioned above the possibility of an epic caesura, where an additional unstressed syllable can occur before the caesura. There are two further epic caesuras in part A of this speech:

    Lag of| a **bro**-ther?| Why '**ba**|-stard'? **Where**|-fore '**base**'?

And

    As **ho**|-nest **ma**|-dam's **is**-sue?| Why **brand**| they **us**

Notice that in each case the caesura occurs before the word 'why'.

- As much as the first part of this speech is about Edmund's bastardy and the second is about Edgar's legitimacy, the first part is also about posing questions and the second is about Edmund's response to the lack of answers. It seems to be no coincidence that Shakespeare gives Edmund a very particular rhythmic launch into these two questions.

- Walk around the room energetically (If you walk as if you have some place to go it will help you talk as if you have something to say!); and as you walk, read the first two lines of part A. Walk and read to a steady beat: if you can, try to land your foot on each of the strong iambic stresses. Do these first two lines several times until you have a good rhythm going. Notice how the first question, 'Wherefore should I', starts right on the meter.

- Once you've got your rhythm established, read the first two lines again and then continue with the rest of part A. There will be a few places where what you are saying will fall out of step, as it were. Notice how long it takes you to get back in synch and how off balance each rhythmic shift makes you feel.

- Repeat once more and try to adjust your walk to accommodate the epic caesuras that take you into the second two questions.

- This time walk rhythmically through the whole speech and change direction sharply whenever you have the impulse to do so.

- Repeat and change direction only on the last word of every line.

- You'll feel that there is a very sophisticated interplay between thoughts, feelings, meter, caesuras and line endings throughout this speech. They mirror a very complicated intellectual and emotional process that Edmund is going through in response to the problem posed by his bastardy.

Teaching Tip: If you have a largish group, it can be very interesting for some students to watch while others do the exercise and then swap.

Act

- As part of your personal preparation, scan the speech for reversed feet. You'll find quite a few at the beginnings of lines and after caesuras. You'll also find some in other feet. Look particularly for weak reversed feet that propel you into the next foot. Spend some time physically exploring these rhythmic variations by stomping or otherwise moving on the strong syllables in and around the reversed feet. You'll find the rhythm is rocky but strong at many points.

- Edmund plans to undermine his father's love for his legitimate brother, Edgar. To do this, he has forged a letter in Edgar's handwriting which suggests that Edgar cannot wait for their father to die and is planning to kill him. Edmund seems very committed to his plan to show this letter to his father. But why, then, does he need to talk so much before he does it? And why isn't his rhythm more controlled if he's simply reporting on something that's already settled? Try convincing the goddess Nature that this is an action she should support – maybe you doubt she's on your side. Try also to convince your audience that it is *outrageous* that you be barred from inheritance. See how you can use the rhythm to add real force and bite to your argument.

- What have you learned about Shakespeare's mature verse and the challenges it presents?

Hermione

In *The Winter's Tale*, Hermione is the wife of Leontes, the king of Sicilia. They have a son, Mamillius, and Hermione has just given birth to a daughter. However, Leontes has grown jealous. He believes that

Hermione has had an affair with his best friend, Polixenes, the king of Bohemia, and that the baby is therefore a bastard. He has accused his wife of treason, and she is now on trial for her life. The following text from Act 3 Scene 2 is the first three quarters of the speech in which she begins her defence.

- Speak through the text quietly a couple of times without looking at the glosses.

HERMIONE

Since what I am to say must be but that
Which contradicts my accusation, and
The testimony on my part no other
But what comes from myself, it shall scarce boot me
To say 'Not guilty'. Mine integrity   5
Being counted falsehood shall, as I express it,
Be so received. But thus: if powers divine
Behold our human actions – as they do –
I doubt not then but innocence shall make
False accusation blush and tyranny   10
Tremble at patience. You, my lord, best know,
Whom least will seem to do so, my past life
Hath been as continent, as chaste, as true
As I am now unhappy; which is more
Than history can pattern, though devised   15
And played to take spectators. For behold me,
A fellow of the royal bed, which owe
A moiety of the throne; a great king's daughter,
The mother to a hopeful prince, here standing
To prate and talk for life and honour, 'fore   20
Who please to come and hear. For life, I prize it
As I weigh grief, which I would spare. For honour,
'Tis a derivative from me to mine,
And only that I stand for.

Glosses
4, **boot** = benefit; 13, **continent** = restrained; 15, **history** = stage play, **pattern** = show; 16, **take** = delight; 17, **owe** = own; 18, **moiety** =

half; 20, **prate** = prattle, chatter; 22, **weigh** = consider, **spare** = avoid; 23, **derivative** = something transmitted by descent; 24, **stand for** = fight for.

Speak

- Speak through the text quietly again, looking at the glosses as you go, even for words you think you know.

- Stand with your back resting against a wall; walk your feet forward about half a metre (eighteen inches), and bend your knees a bit, keeping your back against the wall, so it's like you're sitting on a high chair. Speak the text through once in this position.

- Now, speak through the text again while standing and lean into the iambic rhythm of each line as far as possible.

Question

I *Possibilities*

- You have probably found that, in terms of the iambic pentameter, the speech is quite regular. It may appear that there is a short line at the end, but this is because of where we chose to end the extract. There are only two contractions required for the rhythm: 'Being' needs to be a monosyllable instead of 'be-ing', and 'moiety' should be 'moi-ty' rather than 'moi-e-ty'. There are relatively few feminine endings, and remarkably few reversed feet. In fact, we can find only two obligatory reversed feet:

  Trem-ble| at patience
  'Tis a| derivative

  The first of these is clearly strong, while the second is quite weak, throwing the emphasis onto 'derivative'. Most of the optional reverses are quite weak also, but there is one strong one:

  False acc|-usation

Since this line comes immediately before the 'Tremble' line, there might be dramatic and emotional value in having both lines begin with reversed feet. Explore the various possibilities for yourself. Depending on your interpretation, the falsehood of the accusation may be more galling to Hermione than the accusation itself.

II *Exploring Enjambment*

- What makes this speech distinct, however, as an example of Shakespeare's mature writing, is the way he uses caesuras and enjambment. It is noticeable that practically every line has a strong caesura, where there is a major focus-shift in Hermione's argument somewhere in the middle of the line; and practically every line is a run-on (enjambed) line, so that the new focus is usually extended into the next line. As before, speak the lines through one at a time and, as you do so, shift your weight from back foot to front foot whenever you feel there's a definite tipping point where the focus of Hermione's argument shifts in the middle of the line. Exaggerate the focus-shift by pausing slightly at each caesura.

- Repeat the exercise, but this time shift your weight without pausing at any of the caesuras, AND take an in-breath at the end of every line. This is going to chop up the text in some strange ways, which is fine for now; there's a tension between the verse form and the sense of the language that we're exploring deliberately. Do notice where taking a breath pause seems to break up the sense of what you're saying and where the breath coincides with the end of a phrase or sentence. What discoveries do you make by doing the speech this way? Does it give you any insight into the obstacles that Hermione is facing in these circumstances and how she is negotiating them? What might she gain by not leaving room for a response at the ends of her sentences and mostly pausing mid-phrase?

- In asking these questions, we're raising an issue that can arouse fierce opinions among actors, directors and voice and text specialists: namely, what is the right way to speak a run-on line? We have left this question unstated up to this point, while quietly exploring a number of options. Hermione's speech, however, asks us to investigate this quite openly. We would argue that there are so many run-on lines in this text that it can't be coincidental, that Shakespeare must have been trying to capture something in the writing here. The first option is the one we've just asked you to explore: to breathe at the end of every verse line. This choice is often mistakenly attributed to Sir Peter Hall in his book, *Shakespeare's Advice to the Players*. In fact, while Sir Peter says that the end of the line 'is always the place to breathe' (Hall, 2003, p. 29), *he does not say that one should always breathe at the end of the line*. However, it is an interesting option to explore, particularly with this speech. In doing this exercise, you may have discovered a sense of difficulty in Hermione's expression of her thoughts. This might be attributed to her anger at being put on trial or to her physical weakness after just giving birth.

- The second option is to follow the thought of the run-on line into the next line, breathing appropriately at the ends of phrases and sentences with no particular awareness of the end of the line or the caesuras. Try this for yourself. You'll probably find that the speech ends up sounding like very good prose. Hermione's argument becomes very clear, even logical, but perhaps now it lacks tension or dramatic shape. Shakespeare was perfectly capable of making this a prose speech, but that's not the choice he made.

- So, a third option is to conduct a mindful exploration of how the form and the content play off each other. By rocking but not pausing at caesuras and breathing at the end of every verse line, you've started to do this.

- To find more variety and subtlety, stand behind a chair with its back to you – give yourself at least a foot in front of you. Read through the speech. On each caesura, you will shift your weight, but you can play with how sudden or slow, big or small that shift is. In addition, tap the chair on the last word of each line before you shift your weight back. In this exercise, you can breathe wherever it makes sense to you.

- Other things you can try:

  Walk around the room as you read the speech and rise up on your toes at every caesura; then do it again and rise up on your toes on the last word of every line. You can simply lift up onto your toes without breaking your stride, or you can linger there depending on what rhythm works best to communicate your thought clearly.

  Walk around the room and change direction on the last word of every line.

  If you are working with a group, have everyone stand in a circle around one student, who will be Hermione; the circle is the court. Hermione, shift your focus to a new person at each caesura. Pick a new Hermione who will shift her focus to a new person on the first word of each new line. See what happens if you only breathe as you are shifting your focus before the first word of a new line – you don't have to breathe every time you do it, but you can only breathe in those moments of shifting focus between lines. Have a few students try it this way – it can take a few rounds to get the hang of shifting focus and breathing with the new line.

Working Alone: Stand in the middle of the room and work with an imaginary court. Setting up chairs or other pieces of furniture in a circle around you to help you be specific in your focus-shifts might be useful.

- Reflect, as a group or on your own, on what acting choices were suggested by your investigation into the caesuras and line endings. Why do you think Shakespeare chose to use so many run-on lines? What kind of emotional, intellectual or tactical complexity do they bring to Hermione's pursuit of her intention here?

Act

- Having made your own decisions with regard to the choices presented by Hermione's verse lines, think again about the regularity of the iambic pentameter and the relatively few reversed feet. Consider what this might suggest about Hermione's character, her temperament, or her intention. Remember her sense of status and honour, her given circumstances, and her concern for her children. Now explore in performance how the rhythm and verse support your characterization.

- What have you learned about Shakespeare's mature verse and the challenges it presents?

Antony and Cleopatra

We finish this consideration of Shakespeare's rhythm and verse with a short extract from Act 4 Scene 15 of *Antony and Cleopatra*. Antony has been defeated by Octavius Caesar in battle and, believing Cleopatra to be dead, has attempted suicide rather than be humiliated by Caesar. However, hearing that Cleopatra is alive, he has had himself carried to the monument in which she has locked herself. You will find it useful to work with a partner for this text, but it isn't essential.

ANTONY
I am dying, Egypt, dying.
Give me some wine and let me speak a little –
CLEOPATRA
No, let me speak, and let me rail so high
That the false huswife Fortune break her wheel,
Provoked by my offence –
ANTONY
                    One word, sweet queen: 5
Of Caesar seek your honour with your safety. Oh!
CLEOPATRA
They do not go together.
ANTONY
                  Gentle, hear me.
None about Caesar trust but Proculeius.

CLEOPATRA

My resolution and my hands I'll trust;

None about Caesar.   10

ANTONY

The miserable change now at my end,

Lament nor sorrow at, but please your thoughts

In feeding them with those my former fortunes

Wherein I lived the greatest prince o'th' world,

The noblest; and do now not basely die,   15

Not cowardly put off my helmet to

My countryman; a Roman by a Roman

Valiantly vanquished. Now my spirit is going;

I can no more.

CLEOPATRA

                    Noblest of men, woo't die?

Hast thou no care of me? Shall I abide   20

In this dull world, which in thy absence is

No better than a sty? O see, my women,

The crown o'th' earth doth melt. My lord!

                                        [Antony dies.]

O withered is the garland of the war,

The soldier's pole is fallen; young boys and girls   25

Are level now with men; the odds is gone

And there is nothing left remarkable

Beneath the visiting moon.

Glosses

3, **rail** = rage; 4, **huswife** = hussy; 5, **offence** = anger; 7, **gentle** = dearest; 8, **none about** = no one surrounding; 15, **basely** = shamefully; 19, **woo't** = wouldst; 22, **sty** = pig-sty; 24, **garland** = emblem of glory; 25, **pole** = standard; 26, **odds** = advantage; 27, **remarkable** = exceptional; 28, **visiting** = watching.

Speak

* Speak through the text quietly again, looking at the glosses as you go, even for words you think you know.

- Speak it through a few more times, so you get a clear sense of the meaning. If you're working with a partner, take it in turns to be Antony and Cleopatra.

- Now, speak through the text again at a more conversational volume, and lean into the regular iambic rhythm of each line.

Question
I *Fine Tuning*

- Take some time to explore the text with your partner for expansions or contractions, feminine endings and potential reversed feet.

- We expect that you found this quite an irregular piece of dialogue. However, there aren't many contractions or expansions. 'I am dying' should be pronounced as 'I'm dying', 'miserable' needs to be said with four syllables (mis-er-ab-le), 'spirit' with one (spirt) and 'visiting' with two (vis-ting) for the sake of the iambic (though pronouncing it with three does give a very interesting syncopation to the concluding line – try it both ways).

  There are several feminine endings, mainly spoken by the dying Antony, and some notable reversed feet. The obligatory ones seem to us to be:

  > **Give** me| some wine
  > **No**, let| me speak
  > **That** the| false huswife
  > **None** a|-bout Caesar (twice)
  > **Val**-iant|-ly vanquished
  > … **No**-blest| of men

  And there are optional ones at:

  > … **One** word,| sweet queen
  > … **now** at| my end
  > … **put** off| my helmet
  > **In** this| dull world

The repetition of the obligatory 'None about Caesar' makes this phrase rhythmically very strong. The following line is open to two possibilities, both intriguing:

Hast **thou|** no **care|** of **me?|** Shall **I|** a-**bide**
Hast thou| no **care|** of **me?| Shall I|** a-**bide**

In the first, the iambic stress falls on the pronouns 'thou', 'me' and 'I', which would be a strong emotional choice; in the second, the two reversed feet place more emphasis on the questions.

Take a moment to review all these small irregularities, and consider what effect they have on the energy of the thought and the line. How do they contribute to the tension of the dialogue?

‖ *Putting It All Together*

- While these small irregularities help to create an underlying sense of emotional tension, this is amplified by the variation in line length, the use of run-on lines and the way the mid-line caesura works to create shared lines and individual patterns.

- You have probably noticed the two short lines:

  I am dying, Egypt, dying.
  None about Caesar.

  (What looks like a short line at the end of the extract is actually a shared line with another character.) With your partner, take the text again and, where there is a shared line, remember to breathe together to help you find a shared rhythm. But where there is a short line, look for a physical action to fill out the line in some way. How do the shared lines and short lines affect the energy of the scene?

- There is a long hexameter in the line:

  Of Caesar seek your honour with your safety. Oh!

  This 'Oh!' is probably an expression of Antony's anguish, and shows how painful it is for him to speak. This pain also seems to be suggested by the way the caesuras break up the thought in Antony's speech beginning 'The miserable change ...'

- Take time now to explore the caesuras and line endings throughout the text, as with earlier speeches. How do these contribute to the dramatic situation the characters are in?

- Now, work through the text a few times, putting all these factors together and trying different possibilities. Reflect on how the fractured rhythm of the scene and the rhythmic choices you make can help raise the stakes in this short scene.

Act

- Take some time to review the text with your partner, making choices with regard to physical action and character intention.

- This is, of course, a scene of tremendous pain and grief, and both characters fight being overwhelmed by it. Play through the scene once, and try consciously to establish and maintain a strong iambic meter as a means of keeping control. Of course, the rhythm will periodically become uneven – always try to get back on track when it does.

- Play through the scene again giving a little less conscious attention to the rhythm but using it when and where you can to have an impact on your partner.

- Discuss with your partner what you have discovered about Shakespeare's mature verse and how it contributes to dramatic tension.

Follow-up

- Watch a video segment that includes work from this chapter. How did your exploration connect to what you see in the video? Are there any points from the video session that did not come up in the work you did?

- Review any of the speeches from the first two chapters, looking for possible expansions and contractions.

- In working on Julia we spent some time physically marking the first syllable of reversed feet, particularly those with strong semantic content, by stomping. Look for reversed feet in the chorus from *Henry V* and Hotspur's speech in Chapter 2 and do the same.

- In working on caesuras, we marked them by turning between chairs in Julia and by rocking further and further back and forth in Shylock. Try either of those with Portia, Viola or Hamlet from Chapter 1.

- Try the physical exploration of feminine endings from *Richard III* with the Hamlet soliloquy from Chapter 1.

- As we did with Richard, Duke of Gloucester, find the reversed feet in Hotspur or Lady Macbeth from Chapter 2, then sit at a table and read the speech, pounding or slapping the table on the strong stress in each of those feet and any other word you want to emphasize.

- Use the exercise of marking line endings by either sitting or changing direction on them from our work on Richard to explore Shylock's text or Titania from Chapter 2.

- Try tapping the rhythm on a partner's breastbone, as we did with Shylock, with Hotspur from Chapter 2. Then try it with a speech that has a much rockier rhythm, for example Lady Macbeth, also from Chapter 2.

- In working on Falstaff, we 'played the drums', always hitting one on the most significant repeated words; do the same with Proteus from Chapter 1.

- With Edmund, we explored walking with the rhythm, making adjustments as it made us fall in and out of step with the meter. Try this exercise with Viola from Chapter 1 or Benvolio from Chapter 2.

- The work that we did exploring the tension that arises when a thought continues past the end of the metrical line is worth repeating with Cassius or Hamlet from Chapter 1, Edmund from this chapter, or any speech from a middle period or late play.

Further reading

Barton, John, *Playing Shakespeare*, Methuen, London, 1984. Chapter 2: 'Using the Verse'; Chapter 4: 'Using the Prose'.

Berry, Cicely, *The Actor and the Text*, Virgin Publishing, London, 1992. Chapter 3: 'Meter and Rhythm'; Chapter 4 Part 1: 'Energy Through the Text'; Chapter 7: 'Meter and Energy'; Chapter 9 Part 1: 'Prose'.

—*From Word to Play*, Oberon Books, London, 2008. Chapter 3: 'Introductory Workshop'; Chapter 4: 'Group Work on Form and Structure: Verse Rhythms', pp. 80–4, 'Prose Rhythms', pp. 84–9.

Block, Giles, *Speaking the Speech: An Actor's Guide to Shakespeare*, Nick Hern Books, London, 2013. Chapter 1: 'Why Verse?'; Chapter 2: 'Thought and Thought-Units'; Chapter 3: 'The Thought Breaks'; Chapter 6: 'Verse Irregularities'; Chapter 8: 'Why Prose?'

Carey, David and Rebecca Clark Carey, *The Verbal Arts Workbook: A Practical Course for Speaking Text*, Methuen, London, 2010. Chapter 4: 'Rhythm'.

Cohen, Robert, *Acting in Shakespeare*, Mayfield Publishing Company, Mountain View, 1991. Lesson 16: 'Scansion: A Primer'; Lesson 17: 'Using Scansion'.

Hall, Peter, *Shakespeare's Advice to the Players*, Oberon Books, London, 2003. 'Blank Verse', pp. 15–17; 'Verse', pp. 26–7; 'The Structure of the Line', pp. 28–9; 'Scansion', pp. 30–1; 'The Caesura', pp. 32–3; 'Prose', pp. 43–6.

Houseman, Barbara, *Tackling Text [And Subtext]*, Nick Hern Books, London, 2008. 'Handling Classical Text: Moving the Meter', pp. 77–84; 'Changing Directions', pp. 90–1; 'Handling the Verse', pp. 95–102.

Linklater, Kristin, *Freeing Shakespeare's Voice: The Actor's Guide to Talking the Text*, Theatre Communications Group, New York, 1992. Chapter 6: 'The Iambic Pentameter'; Chapter 8: 'Line-Endings'.

Noble, Adrian, *How To Do Shakespeare*, Routledge, London, 2010. Chapter 4: 'Meter and Pulse'; Chapter 5: 'Line Endings'; Chapter 9: 'Prose'.

Rodenburg, Patsy: *Speaking Shakespeare*, Methuen, London, 2002. Part 2: 'Structure: Rhythm', pp. 84–94; 'Pauses and Irregularities of Rhythm', pp. 95–103; 'The Line', pp. 103–7; 'The Thought and the Structuring of Thoughts', pp. 108–18.

Spain, Delbert, *Shakespeare Sounded Soundly: The Verse Structure and the Language*. Garland-Clarke Editions/Capra Press, Santa Barbara, 1988. Chapter 1: 'Attitudes on Verse'; Chapter 2: 'Analysis of the Verse'; Chapter 3: 'The Nature of Poetic Rhythm'; Chapter 4: 'Language Adjustments'; Chapter 5: 'The Variations Applied'; Chapter 6: 'Syllable Compression'; Chapter 7: 'Syllable Expansion'; Chapter 8: 'Polysyllable Accentuation'; Chapter 9: 'Lines Chiefly of Monosyllables'; Chapter 10: 'The Line As a Unit of Rhythm'; Chapter 11: 'The Short Line'.

Weate, Catherine, *Classic Voice: Working with Actors on Vocal Style*, Oberon Books, London, 2009. Chapter 4: 'Rhythm'.

4
RHETORIC AND STYLE

Framework

One of the challenges for the modern young actor facing Shakespeare's text for the first time is that the form of the language can seem so alien that it is hard to understand the content. We often hear students and actors ask, 'Why do these characters talk so much? Why can't they say what they mean? Was everybody this long-winded back then?' In answering these questions we usually say that the characters' use of such heightened language reflects the heightened state of their emotions and of the stakes at risk – they need to express themselves in this way because it's the only way they can fully communicate their thoughts and feelings. As James Bundy, Dean of the Yale School of Drama, has observed, the more language a character has the bigger the problem he or she has to solve. However, this doesn't mean that everybody spoke like this in Elizabethan times. Far from it – for one thing, nobody went around speaking in iambic pentameter! But when they went to the theatre, it was this kind of language that truly spoke to them, enthralling and entertaining them at the same time.

The English language itself was undergoing rapid and dynamic change at this time. English has an extraordinary history of absorbing many linguistic influences. It has its roots in Anglo-Saxon, which is a Germanic language, but has borrowed vocabulary from the Celtic and Scandinavian language families as well as Latin, Greek and other languages over the centuries. In particular, the Norman conquest of 1066 brought a huge French influence. In Shakespeare's day, the relatively recent invention of the printing press was giving rise to an explosion in literacy, and the English language was exploding too. It is estimated that between ten thousand and twelve thousand new words were added to the lexicon during the Renaissance (McCrum et al., 1986, p. 95). Many of these were adapted from Romance (Latin-based) languages such as French or Spanish. There was sometimes great tension between those who favoured a plainer, more Anglo-Saxon style and those who embraced a newer and more innovative use of language. Successful communication for an Elizabethan meant using the appropriate style of language for the situation – using the inappropriate style could lay you open to scorn or laughter, as we can see from the many instances of characters in Shakespeare trying to use grand words and fumbling comically with malapropisms. Even today, English evolves – there was no such thing as 'blogging' fifteen years ago. And even today, a failure to keep up with the latest slang can make one look a fool.

Elizabethan style guides identified three styles of language: **a grand or mighty style** suitable for highly charged occasions, when language was required to move or command; **a middle or small style** for more moderate occasions, when language was used to engage or amuse; and **a plain or low style** for simple, colloquial usage, when a speaker wanted to speak frankly and straightforwardly. The ability to use all three styles appropriately was considered a mark of artistry in a speaker or writer. For a dramatic writer like Shakespeare – as noted by Sylvia Adamson in her essay 'The Grand Style' (Adamson, 2001, pp. 31–50) in the Arden Shakespeare's excellent guide, *Reading Shakespeare's Dramatic Language* – the mighty style was considered appropriate for the kind of noble and commanding figures we find in the histories and tragedies; the middle style was best for romantic comedy's mix of young lovers and rich merchants; and the low style was suitable for the bawdy comedy of rustic fools and taverns. It is a sign of Shakespeare's artistry that he was able to use these styles so flexibly to create such a diverse range of individuals in his plays, characters such as Falstaff, who can navigate his way through all three styles, or Dogberry, the rural policeman who aspires to the heights of the grand style while trying to maintain command of a simple group of low-lifes.

What distinguishes the three styles linguistically is the amount of **figurative language** and **rhetoric** they use. Rhetoric can be defined as the art of using language persuasively. Ever since the ancient Greeks, people have studied how to shape and structure language so that the points the speaker is making are vivid and memorable and create a response in the listener. Figurative language is a form of rhetorical expression which uses words to convey something different than their literal meaning, e.g. 'she's as good as gold'. The low style makes use of plain English with few or no rhetorical embellishments. The middle style, as its name suggests, achieves a balanced use of plain words with an appropriate amount of rhetorical decoration. The grand style is the most extravagant, using, in the words of one Elizabethan rhetorician, 'great words … vehement figures … stirring sentences'. These terms refer to the Elizabethan fondness for rich, polysyllabic, Latinate vocabulary and elaborate figures of speech which, together, could create sentences that would excite and move an audience. Shakespeare's gift was in being able to take these stylistic elements, apply them in verse and prose, and make them serve his dramatic purposes. In his hands, rhetorical devices, such as metaphor and antithesis, become vehicles for a character's intentions and actions, and can be used to shape a speech or scene and drive towards the character's objective. The words a character chooses – whether from the newer, French-influenced, Latinate vocabulary or the older, Anglo-Saxon tradition – are not the arbitrary invention of the playwright but serve to delineate character and situation.

One choice that deserves particular attention is the use of the second person pronoun. Historically, the words 'you' and 'yours' had been used when addressing more than one person, and 'thee', 'thou', and 'thine' were used when addressing a single person. By the mid-fifteenth century, however, 'you' was also used to address a single person to whom one owed respect, so someone of lower status would use it with someone of higher status; children would use it with their elders; people of rank who were not familiar with each other would use it, etc. The use of 'thee' and 'thou' then became a mark of either talking down to someone or of intimacy with that person. Accordingly, if you wanted to distance yourself from someone, you might say 'you' to him instead of 'thee'. By Shakespeare's time, it seems that 'you' was being used more and more often when addressing a single person. We know that eventually 'thee' and 'thou' died out more or less altogether (unlike in Spanish, French and German where there are still two kinds of 'you'). Shakespeare's characters use both forms. In many instances they are used exactly as you would expect – subjects address their monarchs as 'you'; lovers address each other as 'thee'. Sometimes, however, a character will switch how he addresses another character, which is always worth noting: has something changed in their relationship? Is that character changing in order to draw closer to or create distance from someone else? Is the change an insult? A compliment? Sometimes there is no great significance – the choice merely reflects the fact that 'you' was becoming more and more common as the 'go to' pronoun. But sometimes the choice is an active choice, and you will want to play it as such.

One more point about pronouns. Sometimes when one first approaches a speech and isn't really clear about what's being said and where the argument is going, one can fall into a pattern of stressing pronouns – especially 'I' and 'you'. The impulse may be to keep focus on the interaction between scene partners, which is, in principle, not a bad thing. It can, however, make the language harder to follow as more active and important words fade in comparison. Because this happens fairly commonly in the early stages of work, sometimes one hears the 'rule': never stress pronouns in Shakespeare. This rule doesn't actually help because the fact that the pronouns are being stressed isn't the problem – it's a symptom of the problem, which is that the actor hasn't yet figured out which words are the most important to communicate the idea the character wants to convey. In most instances, once you've really thought through what your action is, you will start using the verbs and nouns much more actively and the pronouns will fade into the background. Sometimes, however, the pronoun really is an important word. This is particularly true if it's being contrasted with something, e.g. 'I don't love Hubert; I love *you*.' If you find you're giving a lot of energy to pronouns and you can't say why, try to dig deeper and find out if they really are the most important words. If, however, you find a pronoun that really feels like a key word in the point you're making, particularly if it falls in a position of metrical stress, don't shy away from it.

In this chapter, we will look at how characters pursue their intention and make points by using rhetorical devices – such as contrasts and lists. We'll also explore some of the most common Shakespearean figures of speech and how they relate to action, and consider linguistic style and word choice as important aspects of understanding a character.

Exploration

Mark Antony

Return to those first four lines of Antony's speech that we explored in the previous chapter:

Friends, Romans, countrymen, lend me your ears:
I come to bury Caesar, not to praise him.
The evil that men do lives after them:
The good is oft interrèd with their bones.   *interrèd = buried*

At first sight, this might seem to be pretty plain language. The choice of words is simple, largely monosyllabic, and mainly Anglo-Saxon in origin. And yet, Antony is using a number of rhetorical devices that lift his language out of a purely low style. We've already investigated the **metaphor** contained in the first line and why Antony might have used it. Metaphor works by imaginatively transforming the literal meaning of a word; other figures of speech work by using pairs and series of related words to create an emotional response or present a convincing argument. In this exploration we'll examine some of the most common ones.

I

- Consider that first series of three words: 'Friends, Romans, countrymen'. Speak them out loud a few times. We explored Shakespeare's use of groups of three for comic effect in the last chapter. The rhetorical term for a group of three is a **tricolon** (*tri* = three, *colon* = a phrase or clause), but it doesn't just have a comic effect, as we can see here. Why do you think Antony is using a tricolon?

- Tricolons in their very nature catch our ears; if they didn't, they wouldn't be such a common figure of speech. But this one is particularly catchy; why? Say it again, and pay attention to the number of syllables in the words.

- It's no coincidence that the words increase in number of syllables. This is a particular kind of tricolon known as a 'rising' tricolon, because the units increase in length. Not only this, but the words get larger in their meaning, growing from familiar friends to fellow citizens to all Roman nationals and so creating a form of **climax**. Why do you think Antony does this? Would the sense of climax have been the same if he had said 'Friends, people, citizens'?

- Now try reversing the order of the words: 'Countrymen, Romans, friends'. What we've created here is a 'falling' tricolon, because the units decrease in length. Does this have a different effect? Remember Antony's given circumstances and try both types of tricolon out on a resistant crowd. Did one get their attention better than the other?

II

- Look now at the next line: 'I come to bury Caesar, not to praise him.' Say it out loud a few times and notice the balance of language in the line on either side of the caesura. There is a very obvious contrast here between 'bury' and 'praise'. The two words create an **antithesis**, or a contrastive pair of opposites, in the space of one line.

- Antony uses more antitheses in the next two lines. Speak them for yourself, and feel how the two lines oppose each other quite strongly with their contrasts of 'evil/good' and 'lives/is interred'.

- Notice in all of these antitheses how the sense of opposition is increased by enclosing them in similar or parallel grammatical structures. **Parallelism** is another common rhetorical device for strengthening an argument, and it frequently involves the use of grammatical structures of the same length, when it is given the rhetorical name **isocolon** (*iso* = equal). Why do you think it's important for Antony to use such a group of antitheses at this point? Address your resistant crowd again, and feel what effect they could have.

III

- We saw how tricolons and parallelism were used to comic effect in Grumio's speech in the previous chapter. Take another look at that speech. Grumio, as a servant, might be considered a 'low' character but, while his vocabulary might be plain, he's got a great feel for rhetoric. As an actor, ask yourself why Grumio might need to express himself so vehemently at this point.

- Today, we would say the character is 'venting'. You might like to observe how twenty-first-century people vent – particularly comedians – and see if they consciously or unconsciously use any of the rhetorical devices that we've looked at so far.

Exercises

The exercises in this chapter are grouped into three sections: 'Recognizing rhetoric', 'Comedy and style', and 'Complicated characters'. In each section we will explore one verse speech and one prose. We suggest that you work through them in this order, not only because you will develop your own skill and understanding more organically, but also because we explore a different period of Shakespeare's writing in each one, as we did in the previous chapter.

Teaching Tip or Working Alone: You may wish to watch a video segment that includes exercises from this chapter before you begin practical work.

Recognizing rhetoric

The following exercises are designed to help you get familiar with many of the rhetorical devices used by Shakespeare and other classical playwrights in service of both comic and dramatic characters. We begin with a prose speech by Speed from Act 2 Scene 1 of *The Two Gentlemen of Verona*.

Speed

Speed is the quick-witted servant of one of the eponymous gentlemen, Valentine, who has fallen for Silvia, the daughter of the Duke of Milan. Speed confronts his master about the situation.

- Speak through the text quietly a couple of times without looking at the glosses.

(VALENTINE
Tell me, do you know Madam Silvia?
SPEED
She that your worship loves?
VALENTINE
Why, how know you that I am in love?)
SPEED

A
Marry, by these special marks: first, you have learned, like Sir Proteus,
to wreathe your arms, like a malcontent; to relish a love-song, like a   5
robin redbreast; to walk alone, like one that had the pestilence; to sigh,
like a school-boy that had lost his *A B C*; to weep, like a young wench
that had buried her grandam; to fast, like one that takes diet; to watch,
like one that fears robbing; to speak puling, like a beggar at Hallowmas.

B
You were wont, when you laughed, to crow like a cock; when you walked, 10
to walk like one of the lions; when you fasted, it was presently after dinner;
when you looked sadly, it was for want of money. And now you are
metamorphosed with a mistress, that when I look on you, I can hardly
think you my master.

Glosses
5, **wreathe** = fold, **malcontent** = unhappy person, **relish** = sing, warble; 6, **pestilence** = plague; 7, **wench** = girl; 8, **grandam** = grand-mother, **takes diet** = follows a diet, **watch** = stay awake; 9, **speak puling** = whine, **Hallowmas** = All Saints' Day; 10, **wont** = accustomed; 11, **presently** = immediately; 12, **metamorphosed** = transformed.

Speak

- Speak through the text quietly again, looking at the glosses as you go, even for words you think you know.

- Speak through the text again, at a more conversational volume this time, and move around the room, changing direction at every major punctuation mark (colon, semi-colon or full stop).

Question
I *Listing*

- Most rhetorical devices are of three basic types: a **pair** of units that balance meaning, such as a parallel or an antithesis; a **series** of units that extend meaning, such as a list or a climax; or the imaginative **transformation** of a unit's meaning, through a metaphor, simile or pun. This relatively simple passage has examples of all three.

- Most obviously, in the first part of the speech, Speed is making fun of his master by listing all the typical signs of a lover that he has observed in him. Speed begins his list with the word 'first', but then abandons the idea of numbers. Why might he have done this? We'd like you to re-insert those numbers and speak part A accordingly, e.g. '… second, to relish a love-song, etc.'.

- How many marks of a lover did you find? What was the effect of speaking all the numbers? Take it again, both with the numbers and without, and consciously build towards a climax.

- Now, do the same exercise with part B.

- What did you discover about this second **list**?

II *Specifying*

- The second list is half the length of the first one, but that's not the only difference. Look at the units which make up each list. In the first list, what structure unites each unit? In the second list, is there the same unity of structure?

- In the first list, all eight units consist of the same **parallel** structure: an action beginning with 'to', followed by a comic comparison beginning with 'like'.

- If you're working in a group, you can do the following exercise to help specify each of those comparisons. One person will be Speed and the other Valentine. The rest of the group should scatter through the room. Speed, take Valentine for a little walk as you speak part A. With each item on the list, approach a new person. Once you've said what Valentine has been doing and whom he's resembled, the person you are standing in front of will become that person (or animal) and do that action. Pause for a moment and let Valentine absorb how pathetic such behaviour is before you move on to the next example.

- Without pausing to talk about it, Speed should then do the speech again simply trying to persuade Valentine that he's a fool for love. Having those images in your own imagination will help you use them effectively.

Working Alone (or in pairs): Speed can act out each of the people he talks about, but it is also effective to simply 'show' Valentine imaginary examples around the room before returning to doing the speech with your focus on him.

III *Antithesis*

- The two lists are, in a way, in **antithesis** to each other – that is, there is a contrast between them. (This is one of the most common rhetorical devices Shakespeare uses and the most important to identify and actively employ.) The first list, which is introduced with the phrase 'You have learned', is a comic description of Valentine's current state; the second, introduced with the parallel but antithetical phrase 'You were wont', is a more generous description of Valentine's habitual conduct.

- Try acting out all the actions in the way they are described as you speak part B. How is it different from part A?

- While Speed uses comparisons in his first two examples of laughing and walking, he quickly becomes very concrete in describing his master's former behaviour, in contrast to the elaborate descriptions he uses in part A. The contrast in how he describes Valentine helps to establish the contrast in Valentine's behaviour.

- The general antithesis between the two lists is also pointed up by the specific antithesis between some of the units. Look at the speech and circle any words or related ideas that appear in both sections ('weep' and 'look sad', for example, could be related). Take the whole speech and, as you speak it this time, stomp with your left foot on every circled word in part A and with your right foot on every circled word in part B.

- Speed concludes his lecture with one last antithesis, in his opposition of 'mistress' and 'master'. And to emphasize his witticism, he even dresses it up with some **alliteration** in the very fancy polysyllabic word 'metamorphosed'. Take the speech one more time. And in order to explore all its potential for antithesis, imagine the former, valiant Valentine is on one side of the room and the present, love-sick Valentine on the other. As you speak the text, create each of these figures with the language, drawing out the contrast between them. End by using the word that sums up the whole problem – 'metamorphosed' – to wake Valentine up to the fact that he's turned into an idiot.

Act

- Speed is a quick-witted young man, observant and clever with language. He uses Latinate words intelligently, and often uses puns as well as the parallelism and antithesis he displays here. This style of language lifts him above the status of a slapstick clown, and shows he has some licence with his master to be a little cheeky. What do you think his intention is with this speech?

- It's possible that he's just showing off, and being funny in order to make his infatuated master smile. It's also possible that he's put out by Valentine's distracted behaviour, and so is trying to bring him to some self-awareness through humour.

- Act it both ways, either with a real or imaginary partner, and use your awareness of Speed's witty rhetoric to serve your intentions.

- What did you discover from this? Do the rhetorical devices work better as a display of wit or as a means of waking Valentine up to his situation? Did other acting intentions suggest themselves? If so, try them out as well.

- Having worked through this speech, you might like to compare it with a similar speech that Shakespeare gives to Rosalind in Act 3 Scene 2 of *As You Like It*.

Queen Margaret

Margaret is wife of King Henry VI. In *Henry VI, Part Two*, she has just arrived in England from her native France. She has only recently met her husband, since he sent William de la Pole, the Duke of Suffolk, to woo her on his behalf. She has discovered that Henry is not the man she thought he was, and the country is actually being governed by the King's uncle, the Duke of Gloucester. Here, in a speech from Act 1 Scene 3, she confronts Suffolk about the situation.

- Speak through the text quietly a couple of times without looking at the glosses.

QUEEN MARGARET
A
My Lord of Suffolk, say, is this the guise,
Is this the fashions in the court of England?
Is this the government of Britain's isle,
And this the royalty of Albion's king?
What, shall King Henry be a pupil still   5
Under the surly Gloucester's governance?
Am I a queen in title and in style
And must be made a subject to a duke?

B

I tell thee, Pole, when in the city Tours
Thou ran'st a-tilt in honour of my love   10
And stol'st away the ladies' hearts of France,
I thought King Henry had resembled thee
In courage, courtship and proportion.
But all his mind is bent to holiness,
To number Ave-Maries on his beads.   15
His champions are the prophets and apostles,
His weapons, holy saws of sacred writ;
His study is his tilt-yard, and his loves
Are brazen images of canonizèd saints.
I would the college of the cardinals   20
Would choose him Pope, and carry him to Rome
And set the triple crown upon his head:
That were a state fit for his Holiness.

Glosses

1, **guise** = custom; 4, **Albion** = England; 5, **still** = always; 6, **surly** = haughty, arrogant; **7, in title and in style** = by right and title; 10, **a-tilt** = in a joust; 13, **courtship** = courtliness, **proportion** = physique; 15, **Ave-Maries** = Hail Marys, **beads** = rosary beads; 17, **saws** = sayings; 18, **tilt-yard** = jousting ground; 19, **brazen images** = bronze statues; 22, **triple crown** = papal tiara; 23, **state** = status.

Speak

- Speak through the text quietly again, looking at the glosses as you go.

- Put one foot in front of the other and read through the speech rocking forward on each strong stress in the iambic meter.

- Speak through the text once more and move around the room, changing direction at the end of every line.

Question

I *Identifying Rhetoric*

- Margaret uses many of the same rhetorical figures as Speed, and some new ones, but she is not being humorous. As a Queen, she is talking in a largely mighty style of verse, but she is not above speaking plainly as well.

- Go through the speech, and make a note of any series (i.e. lists), parallels and antitheses that you come across.

II *Exploring Rhetoric*

- You probably found yourself making quite a few notes! The first eight lines are composed of a series of questions, some of which have a strong parallel structure, while others contain antithetical elements. The last eight lines also contain a series of more or less parallel statements, and you may also have noticed some metaphors and tricolons.

- Let's look at those first eight lines (part A) in more detail. First, ask yourself if Margaret expects Suffolk to answer any of her questions. Either with a real or imaginary partner, try these lines two ways: first, giving your partner time to answer; and then, building on each question without letting your partner answer.

- Both of these are possible, as well as a combination of the two. But what effect does each have? As you probably know, a question which the speaker doesn't expect an answer to is known as a **rhetorical question**. Let's explore these questions as potential devices to provoke a reaction rather than an answer.

- Take a look at the tricolon formed by lines 2–4 and their parallel structure:

  Is this *the fashions* IN THE COURT OF ENGLAND?
  Is this *the government* OF BRITAIN'S ISLE,
  And this *the royalty* OF ALBION'S KING?

- This is pretty artful: Margaret manages to suggest that there is something rotten in the state of England by questioning its values at several levels. And, although this isn't strictly a rising tricolon in that the units don't get any longer, the questions get stronger in two other ways: by rising up the ruling hierarchy from the fashions of court through the government of the nation to the very authority of the king, and by finding more ancient synonyms for the country (Albion being the original Roman name for the island).

- Play with a few different ways of building this list:

  – With each line, take a step closer to a real or imaginary partner.

  – Stand behind a table. Tap the table with your finger on the first 'this', 'fashion' and 'court'. Slap the table with your hand on the second 'this', 'government' and 'Britain'. Pound the table with your first on the final 'this', 'royalty' and 'king'.

  – Take the first line fairly quickly – really fire it off. Take the second line a little less rapidly, laying in the key words a bit more. And finally take the third line fairly slowly to really pound in the rhetorical question.

Teaching Tip: It can be interesting for students to take turns doing these last two in pairs and observe each other.

- Now let's look at the antitheses in lines 5–8:

  What, shall King Henry be a pupil still
  Under the surly Gloucester's governance?
  Am I a queen in title and in style
  And must be made a subject to a duke?

In the first antithesis, Margaret picks up on 'Albion's king', and makes her point more explicit by questioning the pupil/ governor relationship between 'King Henry' and 'surly Gloucester'; and in the second, she queries how a queen 'in title and in style' can be treated in reality like a subject. In this way she draws attention to what she sees as a paradoxical situation.

- Put your paper on a table in front of you or have someone hold it if you don't have these lines memorized. Read through these lines, and every time you talk about something that Margaret finds noble (or thinks should be noble, like King Henry), raise your right hand – you can wave or gesture with it too if that feels organic. Every time you talk about something Margaret finds ignoble and undesirable (like Gloucester or being a subject or a pupil), put down your right hand and raise your left hand, gesturing with it as appropriate.

- With all of this in mind, take these eight lines again, exploring how the strength of Margaret's rhetoric gives force to her intentions.

III *Landing the Point*

- The next few lines present another contrast – between Margaret's fantasy of Henry and the reality. She recalls how Suffolk's wooing of her made her imagine Henry was his equal in 'courage, courtship, and proportion' (a tricolon of nobility), but now she realizes Henry's only interest is 'holiness'. It's fairly clear that Margaret doesn't think much of 'holiness', but how does she use rhetoric and style to underline this? Does she use any particular figures of speech, or any high or low language?

- Apart from the noble tricolon, you've probably noticed that Margaret uses a couple of metaphors here: to steal someone's heart and to bend one's mind. She also speaks quite extravagantly about Suffolk and his chivalry but quite plainly about the king and his sanctity.

- That Henry's holiness annoys Margaret is made even clearer in the last eight lines of the speech. First, she emphasizes what a wimp she thinks he is by setting up a series of antitheses between some of the chivalric norms for a medieval king (champions, weapons, tilt-yard, loves) and Henry's pious equivalents. To get a feel for the dynamics of this part of the speech, go stand next to a wall, and imagine a line running down the middle of it. Every time you talk about something that has to do with chivalry and being a soldier, cross to one side of the line and slap the wall. If you use more than one martial word, slap the wall on each one of them. When you use a word or words that have to do with religion or piety, cross over to the other side of the imaginary line and slap the wall there. What patterns do you notice? How do they serve to drive home Margaret's point and her frustration?

Teaching Tip: You may want to have four groups, one working on each of the four walls of the room. The students in each group can take it in turns doing the exercise and observing.

Act

- Margaret came to England as a young queen with a fantasy of what her husband was going to be like: noble, powerful, handsome. She is sorely disappointed by the reality. In this speech, she takes the opportunity to express her dissatisfaction quite strongly to Suffolk, her confidant. It would be possible to make her a whiney teenager – Margaret was sixteen when she arrived in England – but she is going to become a powerful figure at court and Shakespeare is probably presenting us with a young woman who already has a mind of her own. Try acting it both ways, with a real or imaginary Suffolk, and see which you prefer. How does her use of rhetoric contribute to the impression Margaret makes?

Comedy and style

Comedy arises in many ways in Shakespeare, but he and his audience seem to have been very fond of verbal humour. We've already mentioned the way many of his characters reveal their pretensions by misusing or mispronouncing grand, polysyllabic words. In this section we'll examine two further examples of how linguistic style can give rise to laughter. Both are duologues between a pair of ill-matched lovers, one in prose and one in verse, and both are from *As You Like It*.

Touchstone and Audrey

Touchstone is the witty court clown who accompanies Rosalind and Celia into the Forest of Arden. There he falls for the physical charms of Audrey, a country girl who is her father's goatherd. In this comic wooing scene in prose from Act 3 Scene 3, Touchstone's sharp wit meets Audrey's blunt plainness. (We have cut from this scene a few asides delivered by a third character, Jaques.)

Teaching Tip: When working on dialogues, feel free to assign roles to students without respect to gender. We would also encourage you to have pairs of students swap roles frequently as they work on the scene. This is both because one character will often have more language than the other and also to encourage the students to approach the scene as text they are exploring together rather than get attached to performing one of the characters.

Working Alone: When working on dialogues, you should generally read both parts. It may help you to move to a different spot when you change characters.

- With a partner, speak through the text quietly a couple of times without looking at the glosses.

TOUCHSTONE

Come apace, good Audrey – I will fetch up your goats, Audrey.

And how, Audrey? Am I the man yet? Doth my simple feature content you?

AUDREY

Your features, Lord warrant us! What features?

TOUCHSTONE

I am here with thee and thy goats, as the most capricious poet, honest Ovid,

was among the Goths. When a man's verses cannot be understood, nor a   5

man's good wit seconded with the forward child, understanding, it strikes

a man more dead than a great reckoning in a little room. Truly, I would

the gods had made thee poetical.

AUDREY

I do not know what poetical is. Is it honest in deed and word? Is it a true thing?

TOUCHSTONE

No, truly; for the truest poetry is the most faining, and lovers are given   10

to poetry, and what they swear in poetry may be said, as lovers, they do feign.

AUDREY

Do you wish then that the gods had made me poetical?

TOUCHSTONE

I do truly, for thou swear'st to me thou art honest. Now If thou wert a poet

I might have some hope thou didst feign.

AUDREY

Would you not have me honest?   15

TOUCHSTONE

No, truly, unless thou wert hard-favoured; for honesty coupled to beauty is

to have honey a sauce to sugar.

AUDREY

Well, I am not fair, and therefore I pray the gods make me honest.

TOUCHSTONE

Truly; and to cast away honesty upon a foul slut were to put good meat into

an unclean dish.   20

AUDREY

I am not a slut, though I thank the gods I am foul.

TOUCHSTONE

Well, praised be the gods for thy foulness: sluttishness may come hereafter.

But be that as it may be, I will marry thee. And to that end I have been with

Sir Oliver Mar-text, the vicar of the next village, who hath promised to meet

me in this place of the forest and to couple us.   25

AUDREY
Well, the gods give us joy!
TOUCHSTONE
Amen.

Glosses

1, **apace** = quickly; 2, **feature** = looks, appearance, **content** = please; 3, **warrant** = protect; 4, **capricious** = witty, **Ovid** = Roman poet exiled to the land of the barbarian Goths; 6, **wit** = intelligence, **seconded with** = supported by, **forward** = precocious; 7, **reckoning** = tavern bill; 9, **honest** = virtuous, chaste; 10, **faining** = pleasing; 11, **feign** = invent, lie; 16, **hard-favoured** = ugly; 19, **foul** = vile, ugly; 25, **couple** = marry.

Speak

- Speak through the text quietly again, looking at the glosses as you go.

- Speak through the text again at a more conversational volume, listening for the words that connect you to your scene partner's dialogue.

Question

I *Trump Cards*

- At its heart, this scene is very simple: Touchstone wants to get Audrey to go to bed with him. If he has to, he will marry her (or pretend to), but if he can just talk her into it, so much the better. Although Touchstone considers himself to be vastly intellectually superior to Audrey, much of the scene comes down to which one of them twists the other's words around more successfully. Can he, with his suggestive puns and his claim to be a misunderstood poet, lead her to the conclusion that it would be a good idea to be morally loose (not 'true' or 'honest'), or can she, with her anti-poetic literalism, defend her virtue? Touchstone's word-play is one aspect of the court-jester's linguistic style which, while not grand, is not plain either. Other marks of this style are his allusions to Ovid and poetry and his coining of witty sayings. Audrey's plain style is characterized by simple language, repetition, and an apparent lack of understanding which leads her to question Touchstone's meaning. It is possible that Audrey misunderstands Touchstone out of ignorance, or it may be that she understands him all too well. Her use of a couple of parallel antitheses ('not fair ... gods ... honest' and 'not a slut ... gods ... foul') might suggest that there's more intelligence there than appears on the surface.

- Go through the text and circle any words that are repeated verbatim or in a variation (e.g. 'true' and 'truly') and words that sound alike (e.g. 'faining' and 'feigning').

- Get a pack of cards and cut it in half (If you don't have one handy, a small stack of notecards or post-it notes would do). Each of you take half the cards and sit at a table facing each other. Each time you introduce a new circled word, take a card from your stack and lay it on the table, as if you were making a move in a card game – a move that you probably think is pretty clever. Whenever either of you repeats that word or uses a variation or pun on it, place a new card on top of that card. The last person to use that word (or variation) gets that stack of cards. You'll have several stacks going at once as there are several words that are repeated. As the scene goes on and there are more cards on the table to keep track of, it will slow you down a bit, which is useful; it is work for these characters to track all the verbal balls that are in the air.

II *Contrasting Cards*

- You should be starting to get a feel for some of the contrasts in this scene. Go through the text and draw lines between pairs of words that are contrasted. The contrast may happen within one character's line, or it may stretch across a couple of lines – things like 'poetical' and 'honest'; 'hard-favoured' and 'beauty'; 'fair' and 'honest'; 'good' and 'unclean'.

- Get out the cards again, and this time put down one card on the first word of each contrasting pair and lay another card on top of it on the second word. If a word is contrasted to another more than once, keep laying cards on that pile.

III *Closing the Gap*

- If you have enough chairs, line up eight to ten of them; Audrey will sit in the second chair to start. If you don't have enough chairs, Audrey, sit on the floor at one end of the room.

- To start the scene, Touchstone, sit next to Audrey when you say 'Doth my simple feature content you?'

- Audrey, you will then move away from Touchstone every time your language suggests that he has said something which confuses or alarms you. You can move one chair or several depending on the strength of your reaction. If he says something that interests you, however, you can move closer to him. You can only move when it's your turn to speak.

- Touchstone, you keep trying to close the gap and move closer to Audrey, but you too can only move when you're speaking.

- If you get to the end of the row of chairs or the room, circle back to where you started and continue.

- Notice that Touchstone begins the scene by calling Audrey 'you' but then switches to the more intimate 'thee'. Audrey calls Touchstone 'you' throughout. Repeat the exercise: Touchstone try to use each 'thee' or 'thou' to get closer to Audrey, and Audrey use each 'you' to get further away.

Teaching Tip: You can probably have up to four pairs doing this at once, depending on the size of the room. More than that can get too chaotic.

IV *Wink, Wink, Nudge, Nudge*

- You will probably have noticed that there is some sexual content in this scene. While 'slut' was used to indicate a woman who was slovenly or unkempt, it could also mean one who was sexually promiscuous, and Shakespeare was definitely playing on that meaning in this scene. Shakespeare used a lot sexual puns in his comedies (and tragedies and histories as well!). Suggestive language was titillating and entertaining then and it's titillating and entertaining now – just watch any sitcom for more than five minutes. Sometimes, however, actors feel that Shakespeare's sexual puns are hard to get and that they need to explain them to the audience by adding exaggerated, crude gestures. We would argue, energetically, that this simply is not the case. In the contemporary world, people use a vast array of unlikely images to make sexual jokes which are easily recognizable because they are delivered with a clear intention. There's nothing inherently dirty about the phrase 'That's what she said.' The joke is in the situation, the timing and the intonation; and it would be dead in the water if accompanied by elaborate gestures. To tell the listener something twice – through word *and* gesture simultaneously – is ineffective storytelling. In rehearsal, it can be tempting to demonstrate to your cast mates that you get the joke, but we would strongly encourage you to try to *use the language actively* to bewitch, entertain, shock, turn on or turn off your scene partner rather than call attention to yourself with gestures. Trust that if they are delivered with a clear intention, Shakespeare's sexual references will be very easy for your audience to pick up on.

- Go through the text and highlight every word that could have a sexual connotation. If you think it could, it could.

- Play through the scene once and gently nudge your partner with your elbow on each highlighted word. Offer the word to him or her as if it were the most fun, sexy thing ever.

- Play the scene again, and this time just tap your finger on your thigh on each highlighted word and give it the lightest possible little sexy spin. Audrey, you in particular can play with how much you understand the sexual double meanings and how much you let on that you understand them.

Act

- It is important in acting comedy to play the situation and not to play for laughs. This is particularly true of Shakespeare's linguistic comedy, which can easily become tedious if the actor is trying too hard to make it funny. The comedy in this scene comes from the way the characters use different verbal tropes as tactics to get their way. Decide for yourselves whether Touchstone is genuine in wanting to marry Audrey or whether this is just a last resort to get her into bed; and ask yourselves whether Audrey is truly ingenuous and ignorant, or whether she is being disingenuous in order to get a ring on her finger. Act the scene for an audience and explore how the characters' intentions are realized or disguised through the language.

Phoebe and Silvius

Much of *As You Like It* is set in the fictional Forest of Arden, and this pastoral setting allows Shakespeare to satirize the Elizabethan fashion for rural entertainment and romanticized ideas of shepherds and shepherdesses, such as Silvius and Phoebe. Silvius is deeply in love with Phoebe, but she is a 'proud disdainful shepherdess' who scorns him. In this dialogue from Act 3 Scene 5, the two lovers both speak in a middle style, characterized by verse, a number of rhetorical figures and a mixture of plain and Latinate language.

- With a partner, speak through the text quietly a couple of times without looking at the glosses.

SILVIUS
Sweet Phoebe, do not scorn me, do not, Phoebe.
Say that you love me not, but say not so
In bitterness. The common executioner,
Whose heart th'accustomed sight of death makes hard,
Falls not the axe upon the humbled neck   5
But first begs pardon. Will you sterner be
Than he that dies and lives by bloody drops?
PHOEBE

A
I would not be thy executioner;
I fly thee for I would not injure thee.
Thou tell'st me there is murder in mine eye.   10
'Tis pretty, sure, and very probable
That eyes, that are the frail'st and softest things,
Who shut their coward gates on atomies,
Should be called tyrants, butchers, murderers.
Now I do frown on thee with all my heart,   15
And if mine eyes can wound, now let them kill thee.
Now counterfeit to swoon – why now fall down!
Or if thou canst not – O, for shame, for shame –
Lie not, to say mine eyes are murderers.

B
Now show the wound mine eye hath made in thee.   20
Scratch thee but with a pin, and there remains
Some scar of it; lean thou upon a rush,
The cicatrice and capable impressure
Thy palm some moment keeps. But now mine eyes,
Which I have darted at thee, hurt thee not,   25
Nor I am sure there is no force in eyes
That can do hurt.

Glosses
5, **Falls** = lets fall; 6, **But** = unless; 11, **pretty** = clever, **sure** = certainly;
13, **gates** = eyelids, **atomies** = specks of dust; 17, **counterfeit** =
pretend; 22, **rush** = reed; 23, **cicatrice** = scar, **capable impressure**
= receptive imprint.

Speak

- Speak through the text quietly again, looking at the glosses as
  you go.
- Speak through the text again at a more conversational volume,
  listening for the words that connect you to your scene partner's
  dialogue.

Question
I Don't Go

- At first glance, this may not strike you as a comic scene. Silvius has been hurt by Phoebe's rejection of him, but she takes no pity on him and rather mocks him all the more. However, if we consider the way each character uses language, we can discover a more humorous side to the duologue.

- To begin with, look at Silvius' first speech. Let the Silvius in your partnership speak the text while trying to prevent Phoebe from leaving the room *without touching her*. Phoebe, you want to leave, but you don't want to have to wrestle Silvius to do so. Also, if he says anything that you genuinely find interesting, you can stop and listen. Do this a couple of times – you can swap roles if you like – and notice how the language serves the intention. What type of rhetorical figures (e.g. repetition, contrasts) does Silvius use to get Phoebe's attention?

- Silvius, take your speech one more time, still with the intention of keeping Phoebe from leaving. After you get the first sentence out, start each following sentence with the phrase, 'Here's the deal'. How does this help you shape your argument? Try it again without saying 'Here's the deal', but marking the impulse to lay the problem out for Phoebe as clearly as possible.

- Does Silvius's comparison of Phoebe with an executioner feel appropriate or a little excessive? Is Silvius being sincere or making himself ridiculous? Or both?

II Get Out of My Way

- For Silvius, the likely purpose of this language is to try to increase the emotional impact of his argument: 'your rejection is killing me'. But how does Phoebe receive it?

- Phoebe, take part A of your speech once while trying to leave the room; Silvius, try to stop her without physically touching her.

- Take this section again, and this time at some point you can switch from trying to leave to trying to drive Silvius from the room. Where did that shift happen for you? Do this a couple of times – you can swap roles if you like – and notice how the language serves the intention.

- Take this section one more time, and add the word 'Seriously' at the beginning of any phrase you'd like. You can use it as a rhetorical question ('Seriously?') or as an introduction to the next phrase ('Seriously …').

III *Let's Get Literal*

- Phoebe makes use of a wide range of rhetorical devices in service of her argument. She uses a considerable amount of repetition, particularly of the words 'mine eye/eyes' but also of the word 'now' and in the phrase 'for shame, for shame'. There are antitheses, metaphors and tricolons. There is some Latinate language, and even a double negative: 'Nor I am sure there is no force in eyes'.

- Let's explore that repetition of 'eye' and the play between it and 'murder'. Get two objects and place them in front of you on a table. Every time you talk about an eye or eyes, pick up the object to your right and show it to Silvius. Hold it as long as you are talking about eyes. When you talk about murder, or anything violent, pick up the object on your left and hold it as long as you are on that subject.

- Your object is to convince Silvius that the object in your right hand is harmless, innocent; and the object in your left hand is vile. You may find, however, that the more times you say the word 'eye' in these circumstances, the more insistent and vehement (and maybe almost violent …) you become – it's a natural consequence of saying something over and over.

- Does Phoebe's response feel justified or excessive? Do you sympathize with her or Silvius?

Act

- Silvius compares Phoebe to an executioner as part of his poetical plea for kindness. She begins by denying the implied accusation, but then goes on to attack his argument by using some extended rhetoric of her own. Like a smart defence lawyer she defines the case against her on her own terms – 'Thou tell'st me there is murder in mine eye' – and proceeds to take the metaphor literally in order to utterly demolish it. Both characters indulge in some rhetorical exaggeration in order to get their point across. Play the scene together several times, exploring how far you can take the rhetorical flourishes.

- What have you discovered about the characters and how they use rhetoric and style to achieve their goals? What does it say about the characters that Silvius only addresses Phoebe as 'you' and she only addresses him as 'thou'? In watching the scene, what relationship did you find between the rhetoric and the humour?

Complicated characters

In this section we move from comedy to tragedy to examine how Shakespeare uses rhetoric and style to sharpen our understanding of characters and their complexities. We begin with a scene from *Othello*.

Desdemona and Emilia

Desdemona is the young wife of Othello, a military general. Othello has been convinced by his assistant, Iago, that Desdemona is having an affair and has accused her of adultery. In this dialogue from Act 4 Scene 3 the inexperienced Desdemona asks her maid, Emilia, who is Iago's wife, whether she could be capable of adultery.

- With a partner, speak through the text quietly a couple of times without looking at the glosses.

A

DESDEMONA

Wouldst thou do such a deed for all the world?

EMILIA

Why, would not you?

DESDEMONA

        No, by this heavenly light!

EMILIA

Nor I neither, by this heavenly light:

I might do't as well i'th' dark.

DESDEMONA

Wouldst thou do such a deed for all the world?   5

EMILIA

The world's a huge thing: it is a great price

For a small vice.

DESDEMONA

        Good troth, I think thou wouldst not.

EMILIA

By my troth, I think I should, and undo't when I had done. Marry, I would not

do such a thing for a joint-ring, nor for measures of lawn, nor for gowns,

petticoats, nor caps, nor any petty exhibition. But for all the whole world?   10

ud's pity, who would not make her husband a cuckold to make him a monarch?

I should venture purgatory for't.

DESDEMONA

Beshrew me, if I would do such a wrong

For the whole world!

EMILIA

Why the wrong is but a wrong i'th' world; and having the world for your labour, 15

'tis a wrong in your own world, and you might quickly make it right.

B

DESDEMONA

I do not think there is any such woman.

EMILIA

Yes, a dozen, and as many to th' vantage as would store the world they

played for.

But I do think it is their husbands' faults   20

If wives do fall. Say that they slack their duties

And pour our treasures into foreign laps;
Or else break out in peevish jealousies,
Throwing restraint upon us; or say they strike us,
Or scant our former having in despite,   25

C
Why, we have galls: and though we have some grace
Yet have we some revenge. Let husbands know
Their wives have sense like them: they see, and smell,
And have their palates both for sweet and sour
As husbands have. What is it that they do   30
When they change us for others? Is it sport?
I think it is. And doth affection breed it?
I think it doth. Is't frailty that thus errs?
It is so too. And have not we affections?
Desires for sport? and frailty, as men have?   35
Then let them use us well: else let them know,
The ills we do, their ills instruct us so.
DESDEMONA
Good night, good night. God me such usage send
Not to pick bad from bad, but by bad mend!

Glosses
9, **joint-ring** = a jointed ring, **measures** = amounts, **lawn** = linen;
10, **exhibition** = gift; 11, **ud's** = God's, **cuckold** = one whose wife
has cheated on him; 12, **venture** = risk; 13, **Beshrew** = curse; 18,
to th'vantage = besides, **store** = populate; 21, **slack** = neglect; 23,
peevish = foolish; 25, **scant** = diminish, **having** = pin-money, **despite**
= spite; 26, **galls** = bitter feelings; 29, **palates** = taste; 31, **sport** =
amorous amusement; 32, **affection** = desire; 37, **ills** = wrongs; 38,
usage = manners.

Speak

- Speak through the text quietly again, looking at the glosses as
  you go.

- Swap roles and speak through the text again at a more conversational volume, listening for the words that connect you to your scene partner's dialogue.

- Speak it through one more time, looking for where the language moves between verse and prose. Lean into the iambic rhythm of the verse a bit where you find it.

Question
I *Verse and Prose*

- The dialogue begins in verse but switches into prose before clearly moving back into verse at Emilia's regular iambic line 'But I do think it is their husband's fault'. However, some of Emilia's early verse lines are very irregular, while some of Desdemona's lines might just as easily be prose. To explore this further, take section A again. Desdemona, make a point of sticking with the iambic rhythm wherever you can. Emilia, make a point of speaking very freely, without regard for any metric regularity. What does this bring out in the scene? The women's relationship? Their approach to the topic?

II *Diagrams*

- When it comes to talking about sex, even today, people have different sensibilities. Some people will prefer to use euphemisms; others will call a spade a spade. Desdemona is the daughter of a Venetian nobleman, while Emilia is an army wife. Their preferences for verse and prose respectively seem to reflect this. Emilia's language is not, however, without rhetorical sophistication.

- Get a piece of paper and pen and sit down at a table with your partner. Start with Emilia's speech that begins, 'By my troth, I think I would' and read through to the end of section A. As you speak your text, Emilia, use the pen and paper to try to draw a diagram that will help Desdemona understand why it wouldn't be so bad to cheat on one's husband in exchange for the whole world. You might draw a line of dots when you make a list, or arrows when you want to show that two things are related. You could draw horns for 'cuckold' and put an equals sign between it and a crown for 'monarch'. This will slow you down, which is fine – it will also help you really connect to each detail of the argument.

III *Language Play*

- You may have found that there's actually something a bit playful about Emilia's approach to this hypothetical question of Desdemona's. Go through section A again, looking for places where Emilia repeats Desdemona's words and maybe turns them around a little. Look too for places where she plays with language, making rhymes or puns or antitheses.

- Take part A again, and explore the potential humour in Emilia's use of rhetorical tropes, by gently tickling or tapping your Desdemona on the shoulder with each playful figure. Desdemona, you will need to try to maintain your dignity.

- What discoveries do you make about the relationship between the characters? Does Emilia manage to convince Desdemona with all her rhetorical wit?

Working Alone: Play with the intention to tickle or tease an imaginary partner.

IV *Rhetorical Strategies*

- Up to the point where Emilia changes to verse, she has been responding in a playful spirit to questions or statements made by Desdemona about the sexual behaviour of women. What happens with the switch to verse? Does her rhetoric and style change?

- In the first half of the scene, where Emilia is attempting to justify female behaviour, she tends to play with the meaning of words; in this speech, however, where she is attacking male behaviour, she builds her case through creating two extended series: a list of husbands' actions and a set of rhetorical questions and answers.

- Let's start by looking at the nature of the list of husbands' actions. In section B, circle each verb Emilia describes husbands as doing – the action words like 'slack' and 'break.' Read this section and make a strong, physical gesture on each verb. It can be the action of the word, or something more abstract, like stomping. Do these words have anything in common? What would happen if you replaced 'slack' with 'neglect' or used 'diminish' for 'scant'? Try to find a longer word, one with two or more syllables, to replace each of the verbs and read the section again with the substitutions. How is it different?

- Finally, read part C aloud. As you do, walk energetically around the room and change direction sharply on each punctuation mark. Is there regularity in the rhythm of your turns? Note how one phrase seems to answer another throughout this section. Go through the text and draw lines between each question and answer and each pair of contrasts.

- Read it again while sitting facing your partner, and tap Desdemona's right knee and then her left on each set of phrases you've marked where the second phrase completes the first. Desdemona will again have to maintain her dignity.

- What discoveries did you make about Emilia's use of rhetoric? Do you think she manages to convince Desdemona this time?

Teaching Tip: If tapping knees seems inappropriate for your group, you can have them tap a table over the partner's knees.

> ***Working Alone:*** Tap a table to the right and the left as if it were an imaginary partner's knees.

Act

- Desdemona begins the scene with a very direct question, essentially asking Emilia if she would commit adultery. Emilia doesn't answer her directly at first, but replies with a question before dealing humorously with the possibility. When Desdemona denies that any woman would behave like that, Emilia turns to a more vehement argument. The relationship between the women is a complex one: Desdemona, the young noblewoman, is a relative innocent in the world; she cannot believe that women would behave immorally. Emilia, the army wife, is her social inferior but has more experience of the world, and knows what men and women are capable of. In acting this scene, you need to answer a number of questions. Why is it important for Desdemona to know if Emilia has committed adultery? Has Emilia committed adultery, or considered it? Why does she treat the subject lightly to begin with? Is she embarrassed, defensive, or trying to keep Desdemona' spirits up? Why does she feel the need to convince Desdemona that women are capable of such behaviour? Has she experienced or observed any of a husband's bad behaviour she describes?

- When you have studied the text for clues about the characters' given circumstances and intentions, act the scene together with an awareness of how the figures of speech fulfil the characters' needs.

- What have you discovered about the relationship between character and rhetoric and style?

Edmund and Gloucester

In *King Lear*, Edmund is Gloucester's bastard son. He has just tricked his father into thinking that his legitimate brother, Edgar, is plotting Gloucester's death. Gloucester is also troubled by recent events at court: the king has disinherited his daughter, Cordelia, and banished his close adviser, Kent. Here, in Act 1 Scene 2, we see the different attitudes the two characters bring to events.

- With a partner, speak through the text quietly a couple of times without looking at the glosses.

GLOUCESTER

These late eclipses in the sun and moon portend no good to us. Though the wisdom of Nature can reason it thus and thus, yet nature finds itself scourged by the sequent effects. Love cools, friendship falls off, brothers divide: in cities, mutinies; in countries, discord; in palaces, treason; and the bond cracked 'twixt son and father. This villain of mine comes under the prediction – 5 there's son against father. The King falls from bias of nature – there's father against child. We have seen the best of our time. Machinations, hollowness, treachery and all ruinous disorders follow us disquietly to our graves. Find out this villain, Edmund; it shall lose thee nothing. Do it carefully. – And the noble and true-hearted Kent banished, his offence honesty! 'Tis strange, 10 strange.

[*Exit*]

EDMUND

This is the excellent foppery of the world, that when we are sick in fortune, often the surfeits of our own behaviour, we make guilty of our disasters the sun, the moon and the stars, as if we were villains on necessity, fools by heavenly compulsion, knaves, thieves and treachers by spherical 15 predominance; drunkards, liars and adulterers by an enforced obedience of planetary influence; and all that we are evil in by a divine thrusting on. An admirable evasion of whoremaster man, to lay his goatish disposition on the charge of a star. My father compounded with my mother under the dragon's tail and my nativity was under Ursa Major, so that it follows I am 20 rough and lecherous. Fut! I should have been that I am had the maidenliest star in the firmament twinkled on my bastardizing.

Glosses

1, **late** = recent; 2, **wisdom of Nature** = natural philosophy, **reason** = argue rationally, **scourged** = lashed; 3, **sequent** = ensuing; 4, **mutinies** = riots; 6, **bias** = tendency; 7, **Machinations** = plots, **hollowness** = hypocrisy; 8, **disquietly** = uneasily; 9, **lose** = harm; 12, **excellent foppery** = utter foolishness; 13, **surfeits** = sickening results of; 15, **knaves** = rogues, **treachers** = traitors, **spherical predominance** = astrological influence; 17, **thrusting on** = compulsion; 18, **admirable** = marvellous, **whoremaster** = lecherous, **goatish disposition** = lust; 19, **charge** = responsibility, **compounded** = joined; 20, **dragon's tail** = a particular phase of the moon, **nativity** = birth; **Ursa Major** = the Great Bear constellation, **maidenliest** = most virginal.

Speak

- Speak through the text quietly again, looking at the glosses as you go.

- Speak through the text again at a more conversational volume.

- Speak it through a few more times, so you get a clear sense of the meaning. Take it in turns to be Gloucester and Edmund.

Question

I *Identifying Rhetoric*

- Let's focus on Gloucester first. While paying some lip-service to science (the wisdom of nature), he tends to believe the portents of astrology. How does he use rhetorical tropes to support this belief? Take the text again with one of you as Gloucester, trying to convince a sceptical Edmund. Find how the various pairings, tricolons, antitheses, metaphors and parallels help you persuade him.

- Gloucester has a fondness for tricolons, except he has a tendency to amplify them with an extra unit. What does this suggest about Gloucester's mental or emotional state? Take the text again, and explore with your sceptical Edmund the climactic effect of the added items.

II *Anticlimax*

- Edmund clearly doesn't believe in astrology, but takes a lot of pleasure in telling us how foolish are the people who do so. Take his speech again with one of you as Edmund, using your Gloucester as the living model of what he's describing. Explore how Edmund uses many of the same rhetorical devices to make fun of his father's beliefs and mannerisms.

- Edmund takes Gloucester's fondness for tricolons and amplifies it to the point of exaggeration. But now take the following version of the middle section of the speech, where we have edited out all of the tricolons, and focus on all the 'by' phrases. Find a different physical representation for each of them as you speak the text:

  > We make guilty of our disasters the sun and moon,
  > as if we were villains on necessity, fools by heavenly
  > compulsion, knaves by spherical predominance,
  > drunkards by an enforced obedience of planetary
  > influence, and all that we are evil in by a divine thrusting on.

- A build-up of parallel phrases like this would normally lead to a climax at the end but, given that Edmund is so dismissive of astrology, what sort of climax might this be? Take the original text again, and find how you can link the tricolons with the parallel 'by' phrases to create an exaggerated climax. How is this climax undercut by what follows?

- From all this grand talk of the heavens, Edmund takes the sexual innuendo of 'divine thrusting on' and turns it into the explicit sexual epithet of 'whoremaster man' and the bestial metaphor of 'goatish disposition'. This kind of anticlimax is known rhetorically as **bathos**. Take the whole speech again, and explore how the excessive rhetorical energy of the first half's tricolons and parallels is deflated by what follows.

- How does this shift in rhetorical energy reflect Edmund's argument? What is his purpose with all this satire?

- From a humorous attack on all believers in astrology, Edmund shifts to a personal attack on the man responsible for his 'bastardizing'. In doing so, he reveals just how much respect he has for his father.

Act

- Both Gloucester and Edmund speak in prose, but this is not plain language. They both use elaborate figures of speech and some grand Latinate words, but without the support of verse. Edmund is clearly making fun of his father, but how seriously are we to take Gloucester? Explore the scene in at least two ways: one where Gloucester is a reasonable man with reasonable fears and outrage; and the other where he is rather gullible and his fears and outrage are slightly ridiculous.

- How far did the rhetoric support either of these choices? What effect did each choice have on Edmund's behaviour? What other choices now suggest themselves for each character?

Follow-up

- Watch a video segment that includes work from this chapter. How did your exploration connect to what you see in the video? Are there any points from the video session that did not come up in the work you did?

- Look for the lists in Grumio's and Falstaff's speeches in Chapter 3, Titania's in Chapter 2, or Lady Percy's in Chapter 1 and try numbering each item out loud, as we did with Speed.

- In Helena from Chapter 2 and Proteus from Chapter 1, try stomping with your left and right foot alternately on items that you are contrasting, as we also did with Speed.

- In Margaret's speech, we explored raising one hand on words associated with being noble and the other on words associated with being ignoble. See what happens if you do this with Richard III's speech from Chapter 3. How is his relationship to these concepts different from Margaret's?

- In Audrey and Touchstone, we worked on tracking the points and counter-points made in an exchange between two characters using a pack of cards. You can also experiment with laying down and stacking up cards to make points in many speeches, such as Margaret, Lady Macbeth and Titania from Chapter 2 and Joan Puzel from Chapter 1.

- You can try using the phrase 'Here's the deal' to help find the shape of the argument and the fresh impulses within it with many speeches and scenes, as you did with Silvius. Cassius and Viola from Chapter 1 are good ones to start with.

- Drawing a diagram using lines and arrows as you work your way through an argument is also a great technique that would work with Phoebe, Shylock from Chapter 3 and Joan Puzel from Chapter 1 as well as Emilia.

- Just as we tried tickling and tapping a partner on puns and antitheses with Emilia and Desdemona, you could try the same with Phoebe and Silvius.

Further reading

Berry, Cicely, *The Actor and the Text*, Virgin Publishing, London, 1992. Chapter 4 Part 2: 'Antithesis'; Chapter 4 Part 7: 'Word Games and Patterns'.
—*From Word to Play*, Oberon Books, London, 2008. Chapter 4: 'Group Work on Form and Structure, The Word Itself', pp. 99–104.
Carey, David and Rebecca Clark Carey, *The Verbal Arts Workbook: A Practical Course for Speaking Text*, Methuen, London, 2010. Chapter 3: 'Sense'; Chapter 4: 'Argument'.
Cohen, Robert, *Acting in Shakespeare*, Mayfield Publishing Company, Mountain View, 1991. Lesson 4: 'Oppositions and Builds'; Lesson 5: 'Antithesis'; Lesson 7: 'The Straight Build'; Lesson 8: 'The Nature and Structure of Builds'; Lesson 9: 'Platforms, Cutbacks, and Interpretation'; Lesson 10: 'Shared Builds'; Lesson 14: 'Shakespearean Language'; Lesson 15: 'Word Choice'; Lesson 18: 'Shakespearean Rhetoric'.
Hall, Peter, *Shakespeare's Advice to the Players*, Oberon Books, London, 2003. 'Rhetorical Devices', pp 42–9, 50–1.
Houseman, Barbara, *Tackling Text [And Subtext]*, Nick Hern Books, London, 2008. 'Language Patterns', pp. 127–38.

Linklater, Kristin, *Freeing Shakespeare's Voice: The Actor's Guide to Talking the Text*, Theatre Communications Group, New York, 1992. Chapter 5: 'Figures of Speech: Antithesis', pp. 82–92; 'Puns', pp. 92–5; 'The Ladder', pp. 95–8; 'Interlude: Thee's and Thou's and You's', pp. 112–17; Chapter 9: 'Verse and Prose Alternation'.

Noble, Adrian, *How To Do Shakespeare*, Routledge, London, 2010. Chapter 2: 'Apposition'; Chapter 6: 'Word Play'; Chapter 12: 'Comedy'.

Rodenburg, Patsy, *Speaking Shakespeare*, Methuen, London, 2002. Part 2: 'Structure: Antithesis', pp. 121–6; 'Puns', pp. 169–72; 'Language Games', pp. 173–6.

Spain, Delbert, *Shakespeare Sounded Soundly: The Verse Structure and the Language*, Garland-Clarke Editions/Capra Press, Santa Barbara, 1988. Chapter 13: 'The Language'.

Weate, Catherine, *Classic Voice: Working with Actors on Vocal Style*, Oberon Books, London, 2009. Chapter 3: 'Word'.

5
PREPARATION FOR PERFORMANCE

Framework

The work we've laid out so far in this book will do a lot to help you prepare to perform Shakespeare's text. Investigating the language closely so that you can make informed, active choices to get the most out of its extraordinary poetic and rhetorical richness is a vital first step. It is a long way, however, from being the whole story. Performances of plays happen in contexts, and those contexts are also very important. Performing in a park without microphones places very different demands on an actor than performing in a ninety-nine-seat theatre does. Performing for school children is different from performing for a West End audience. Embodying a character who lives in nineteenth-century Vienna is different from embodying a character who lives in twenty-first-century Brooklyn. Part of the greatness of Shakespeare is that his writing is so compelling, so beautiful and persuasive, so immediate in its portrayal of human experience that it can speak to audiences in all of these contexts and more. We can think of no other theatre artist who enjoys a popularity that has spread so far and lasted so long, and the scope of his appeal invites us to enlarge the scope of our imaginations and our skill to meet it.

When you come to rehearse a Shakespeare play, there will be a number of circumstances particular to that production that will influence how you craft your performance: the space you'll be working in; the director's and designers' vision of the world the story takes place in; the audience you'll be performing for; the nature of your rapport with your fellow actors, etc. In this chapter, we're going to look particularly at how you can prepare yourself to perform in a variety of different spaces and within a variety of imaginative circumstances. Developing the flexibility necessary to speak the language with energy and conviction under a range of conditions is a very important step in moving out of the classroom and onto the stage.

At the time Shakespeare was writing, the playhouse, or theatre building, was a relatively new invention. For much of his career, he wrote for a circular (or twenty-sided) playhouse with an open roof. The stage jutted quite far forward, and the audience surrounded it on three sides. Most of the audience stood on the main floor; others, who could afford it, sat in one of three sheltered galleries, each stacked on top of the other. The diameter of the playhouse is estimated to have been about a hundred feet, so the audience was in close proximity to the players. The frequent use of asides and soliloquies suggests that the actors interacted openly with the audience; the idea of an imaginary, invisible 'fourth wall' sealing the stage off from the auditorium would have been completely alien. Despite the physical closeness to and overt relationship with the audience, however, the actors could not take their attention for granted. Performances happened during the day, and because of the way the space was arranged, large swaths of the audience were visible to and able to distract each other at all times. Refreshments were sold and consumed during performances, and prostitutes soliciting business as well as pickpockets were reported to circulate freely.

Costumes in Shakespeare's time were impressive. Often they were donated by wealthy patrons and were beautifully crafted. Because there were rigid codes dictating who could wear what, the costumes would have helped the audience recognize instantly a character's social class and rank. The costumes were not, however, designed for specific plays, but were used over and over. While it's possible that a sartorial gesture might be made to Roman dress in a play like *Julius Caesar*, most of the actors would have worn contemporary clothing. Set pieces were minimal – a chair here, a bed there. Visually, there was little to distinguish the ancient Britain of *King Lear* from the Renaissance Italy of *The Merchant of Venice*. There would have been musicians present and songs were used in many plays, but otherwise the actors really only had the words to grab the audience's attention and pull them into the story. In the later stages of his career, Shakespeare's company moved indoors where performances were lighted with candles and there would have been fewer distractions. There are some stylistic changes to his plays around this period, but the conventions of performance were still very different from what we know today.

In the intervening centuries, Shakespeare's plays have been presented in a wide range of circumstances and styles, and a hefty load of opinions about the 'right' way to do them has accumulated. Many of the practices that are widely considered to be 'traditional' only go back a century or two, and sometimes approaches that are hyped as fresh and new have little in them that is truly innovative. For the actor the fundamental task is the same: *to engage the audience's attention and draw them into the story moment by moment.* Changes in theatrical fashions and audience expectations as well as the nature of the space you perform in will all influence how you approach that task, but we believe that the *event* is the same as it was over four hundred years ago when Shakespeare's plays were first performed: human beings using all their skill and passion to bring to life some of the most thrilling, moving, shocking and entertaining language ever written in the service of storytelling.

Note: Since this chapter is less about working on text and more about working on context, we are not including either an 'Exploration' or a 'Follow-up' section here.

Exercises

Space

Because language is the main event in a Shakespeare play, it is absolutely vital that you be heard and understood at all times. Some theatrical spaces make this easier than others. In general, the larger a space is, the larger your sense of truth needs to become. An intimate, domestic space allows you to find the truth in and to portray intimate, domestic human behaviour. A larger space asks you to seek for truth in more energetic expressions of human wants and needs – in larger communicative impulses. The good news is that Shakespeare's language itself is muscular and energetic and invites the speaker to be vigorous in speaking it. As we've discussed,

Shakespeare was interested not in recreating ordinary conversation but in using heightened language to command his audience's attention, rouse their emotions and awaken their imaginations. In whatever space you are performing, the following exercises will help you to fill both the size of the room and the size of the language.

Sound the Space

- Getting a feel for the acoustic properties of the space you'll be performing in is important whether it's a thousand-seat outdoor amphitheatre or a forty-seat black box. Rarely does one get the chance to rehearse in the theatre more than once or twice before technical rehearsals, which is not necessarily a bad thing; sometimes rehearsing on the stage can lead one to stint on the exploration part of the process and jump into performance mode too soon. It is always a good idea, though, to get into the performance space as early as you can and do some exploration to get a feel for it.

- Start by warming up your voice in the space. There is a good general warm-up in Appendix 1. We recommend that your warm-up include some work on stretching and opening the body, connecting to the breath, releasing the tongue and jaw, working through the pitch range and, particularly when you are working in larger spaces, waking up your forward or mask resonance – the part of your voice that has the most easy carrying power. There are exercises for all these in our *Vocal Arts Workbook and DVD* and other books in the Bibliography.

- If you are working in a group, stand in a circle and number off (one person says 'one'; the person to his right says 'two' and so on around the circle). Take a moment to memorize who was before you and who was after. Take a moment as well to agree on a nursery rhyme or a similar text that everyone knows the words to.

- Scatter through the space – some people on the stage and some people in every part of the house (including the balcony if there is one). Find the person who was before you and the person after and stand facing the person who was before you.

- Number one, call out the first word of the nursery rhyme to two. Number two, turn quickly to three and call out the next word of the rhyme to him. Three, turn quickly to four and call out the next word, and so forth. If you finish the nursery rhyme before every one has had a chance to speak, simply start it again.

- It is also good to use some Shakespearean text with this exercise – perhaps one of the chorus speeches from *Henry V* – with each individual taking not just words but also phrases and lines.

- Working individually now, stand in the middle of the stage and look straight out into the house, where the audience will sit. Plant your feet firmly on the ground and let your breath settle, so that it is full and present, neither held nor forced. Imagine that you want to call out to a person in the furthest seat away from you. Breathe in with the intention of doing so – you don't actually have to call yet, just feel the energy of the in-breath. Repeat the exercise, turning to face the audience to your right and then your left.

- Come back to facing centre. Engaging again with an energized, purposeful in-breath, call out to the back, 'Hey you, listen to this.' Repeat this four or five times, looking for the exact amount of energy you need to feel that you are engaging with an imaginary person at the back without shouting at him. Repeat to the right and the left.

- Move to a new part of the stage and pick any seat in the house as your target. Take the first line of your text and, remembering to start with an in-breath, speak the line with the intention of communicating with someone in that seat. Do likewise from different parts of the stage to different parts of the house.

- If you have a scene partner, stand on the stage together (use an imaginary partner if you don't). Try playing the first few lines of the scene or speech with the same amount of vocal energy that you were using when speaking to the back of the house. This may feel odd at first. Stop and shake out. Close your eyes, and think about what your character is trying to accomplish. Think about his desire to meet this objective. Think about any obstacles he might face and the effort he will need to overcome them. Open your eyes and play the beginning again trying to match the acting energy with the vocal energy. Experiment with this until using your voice in a way that fills the space feels appropriate as you play the scene.

- When you are back in the rehearsal room, warm up your voice before every session, focusing on using breath, resonance and articulation actively. As you work, continually look for ways to fill your performance with an energy that will fill the space.

Follow-through

- In our experience, one of the primary things that make actors hard to hear and understand in any space is dropping vocal energy at the ends of phrases and sentences. It is an insidious habit and one that you should be vigilant about overcoming from the first stages of rehearsal. Not only is it technically ineffective, but the impulse to 'throw away' the ends of lines will ultimately thwart your efforts to pursue your character's intentions effectively. Unlike many modern characters who will begin a speech or sentence with what's important to them, Shakespearean characters frequently build towards the point they wish to make or will finish a sentence with a significant piece of information. You will also find that words at the end of verse lines often carry significance, and so need your energy. The actor must, therefore, maintain her commitment through to the very end of the thought or the character's intention is not being served fully. Disengagement and commitment cannot co-exist, and commitment is what makes your acting compelling.

- Any of the following speeches will work well for this exercise, or you can use another speech you are working on:

    Portia from Chapter 1
    Cassius from Chapter 1

Shylock from Chapter 3
Phoebe from Chapter 4.

- Get a partner. Deliver the speech to your partner. On the last word of every sentence, either reach out and give your partner's arm/shoulder a little squeeze or a (gentle!) little shove. Which action you do will depend on whether you are trying to get the sympathy of or challenge your listener. Don't worry too much about which to do – just follow your impulse. Some speeches will be all or nearly all one action or the other, while others may mix them up more. The important thing is that you are physically transmitting energy to your partner on the last word of the sentence.

- Switch roles so that the listener now becomes the speaker. The new speaker will now squeeze or shove the other's arm not only on words that appear before full stops (periods), but on every word that is followed by a punctuation mark and at the end of every verse line.

- Finally, each partner should play the speech focusing on actively using the words at the ends of phrases, lines and sentences to have an impact on their listener.

Working Alone: Hold a pillow and either squeeze or shake it a bit on the last word of sentences and then before all punctuation.

Teaching Tip: If the word 'shove' seems like an invitation to chaos, you might use 'poke' or 'nudge'.

Launch

- The beginnings of sentences can also be hard to catch sometimes, regardless of the size of the theatre. Actors often snatch at or rush through the first few words in a mistaken attempt to convey urgency or immediacy. This is particularly frustrating for an audience, who must then try to catch up with them as they continue speaking. That tendency to glide into a thought rather than launching into it with energy and clarity also weakens your ability to have an impact on your partner. Shakespeare's characters are intent on getting what they want and can't afford to waste time garbling any of their words.

- Any of the following speeches would be good for this exercise, or use something else you're working on:

    Lady Percy from Chapter 1
    Viola from Chapter 1
    Titania from Chapter 2
    Richard from Chapter 3.

- Get a number of full bags – handbags, backpacks, gym bags – and scatter them around the room. When you start the speech, reach down and scoop up a bag with energy and purpose and lift it above your head. You can't say the first word of the speech until you have hoisted the bag to at least shoulder level.

- Walk around the room holding the bag over your head until you get to a full stop. You will then put the bag down, but you cannot let it drop below your shoulder until you have at least started the last word of the sentence.

- Go find a new bag to lift up as you begin the next sentence.

- You can repeat this exercise and change the direction you're walking in on every punctuation mark within the sentence as well as lifting and lowering the bag at the beginning and end.

- When you finish, you might want to try a little negative practice: begin the speech by rushing through the first two or three words, and then go back and start with a more deliberate attack.

Teaching Tip: Depending on the size of your group, you may want to have a portion of the class do this at a time with the others watching. If your students work particularly well together, you can assign each one who is doing the exercise a buddy who will watch her and let her know if she's starting the sentence before getting the bag up in the air or letting it droop before the sentence is over. You'll need one more bag on the floor than the number of students who are doing the exercise. It's generally better for students in a group to do it in their own time than in unison.

Muscularity and Definition

- Often what seems to be a problem with volume is actually a problem with clarity. If words lack definition, it will be hard for the audience to grasp what is being said even in smaller spaces. If, however, words are formed with muscularity and commitment, they will carry in a large space without the need for pushing or shouting. Working on not rushing the first few words in a phrase or dropping off the last is very important, but clarity of articulation throughout goes hand in hand with clarity of intention and thought, which is what makes a persuasive performance.

- Start by warming up a bit; do some exercises to help you connect to your breath and stretch your lips and tongue. We include some of this work in Appendix 1; you can find more in our *Vocal Arts Workbook and DVD* and other books in the Bibliography.

- Any of the following speeches would work well for this exercise, or you can use one of your own:

  Proteus from Chapter 1
  Hamlet from Chapter 1
  Titania from Chapter 2
  Hotspur from Chapter 2.

- Go through the first eight or nine lines and circle two or three words in each line that you feel are particularly important to the point you are making or are particularly interesting in their own right. Read those lines aloud, and when you come to the circled words, give extra strong energy to the sounds in those words – so you might draw out an M or Z sound or give extra punch to a B or K or let your pitch glide on an EE or EYE. Go much further than you ever would in real life. Try to use the sounds to get inside the brain of your listener and burn the words into his memory. Stand as you do this exercise – you'll probably find that you'll want to move a bit as you say those sounds.

- Read the same lines again. This time, use the sounds of the circled words as more of a stealth attack on your listener: lean into them, punch them, point them just enough to make the words as vivid as possible without drawing attention to the sounds at the expense of the meaning.

- Standing comfortably about a metre away from your partner (or a wall if you're on your own), whisper your text to him. Use a true whisper, which is a well-supported flow of air without any constriction in the throat, not an unhealthy and raspy forced whisper. Because you don't have any vocal dynamics to convey your meaning, you'll find that you need to work your lips and tongue more energetically (and probably your breath as well).

- Once both partners have done this, stand with your backs to each other. Now speak your text at a conversational volume thinking about using a similar engagement of your articulators to reach your partner behind you.

- Finally, stand a few metres away from your partner and explore how the work you've just done can support your intention to communicate as you rehearse the speech or scene.

- As a rehearsal exercise, have everyone in a scene (or even act or whole play if you have the time and inclination) lie on the floor with their eyes closed. Play the scene this way. You will most likely find yourselves speaking more clearly and listening more carefully to each other when you have nothing visual to aid your communication.

- Include some articulation work in your warm-up before every rehearsal, and consciously pay attention to how giving definition to the words helps give definition to your intentions and actions as you rehearse.

Orientation

- In many modern theatre spaces, the audience wraps around the stage to a greater or lesser extent. In Shakespeare's time, too, there would have been audience around three sides. This means that, unless you are very far upstage facing straight ahead, your back is going to be to part of the audience whenever you speak. It's important, therefore, to think about the space all around you as you prepare your performance.

- As an exploration, start to notice how you position yourself physically when you have conversations. How often do you directly face someone for a long period of time? When you are sitting, do you always keep your face pointed directly at the person you are talking to? You may be surprised to find that statically facing a conversation partner dead on for a sustained period of time doesn't happen all that often in real life. When you are rehearsing scenes and speeches, look for opportunities to move and to open your body up so that it faces more of the audience. Try to avoid standing in profile, facing only your scene partner, as this closes you off from the audience. It's not only more theatrically effective, it's also truthful human behaviour.

- The following is a particularly important exercise to do if you are working in the round (with the audience sitting all around the performance space), as it helps bring your awareness into your back and the space behind you. You can do it with any text.

- Hang over in a roll down, and have a partner give your back a little rub-down. Then have your partner place her hands in the middle of your back, cupping your ribs, and feel your back expanding as you breathe in and out deeply a few times.

- Slowly roll up to standing, and have your partner place her hands on the middle of your back. Begin to hum, imagining that you are filling your partner's hands with vibrations. Have your partner move her hands to a different place on your back and hum again on a new pitch (stay near the middle of your range). Repeat a few more times. You can open the hum into a 'maaaah', still imagining filling your partner's hands with your vibrations.

- Your partner will now go back to rubbing your back. This should be an open-handed rub down the whole back rather than a massage of specific muscles. As your partner rubs, chant the first line of your text (like singing it on one note), and then speak it. Chant, then sing, the first eight or nine lines this way. Finally, speak your complete text with your partner simply holding her hands against your back to help you maintain your awareness of how your voice fills the space behind you as well as the space in front of you.

Working Alone: Stand with your back to a wall to help you become more aware of vibrations there.

- As in the Muscularity and Definition section, rehearse a speech or scene standing or sitting back to back with your partner. Feel how you need both strong articulation and strong vibrations to reach each other.

- As in Sound the Space, go into the theatre as a group and scatter throughout the space. Take turns speaking words, phrases or lines. Practise communicating with those behind you as well as those in front of you, using just the energy necessary to fill the space with your ideas.

Circumstances

One of the wonderful things about live theatre is that, though they start with the same script, no two productions of a play are ever the same.

Each one will reflect the unique sensibilities of the particular group of artists who have collaborated to tell the story at that particular moment in time and that particular place for that particular audience. One reason that Shakespeare's plays are still produced as often as they are four hundred years after his death is that the stories and the characters are not tied to his time and place. He did, of course, write in response to the world around him, but he set many of his plays in far-off lands and distant times (without much regard for geographic or historical accuracy, it should be noted), and he probed relentlessly not only the question of what it meant to be an Elizabethan person, but what it means to be a person, full stop. Generation after generation since has looked into his plays and seen its own image reflected back.

In contemporary theatre, many producers and directors seek to explore the universality of Shakespeare's stories by placing them in specific settings. We have seen wonderful productions set in twentieth-century America, twenty-first-century Britain, nineteenth-century Italy, as well as Elizabethan London. At their best, each one has helped us to hear the text with fresh ears and understand the humour and heartbreak of the stories more profoundly. In each of these productions that we have found so effective, the creative team was able to create a world that was specific, consistent and convincing – that created a framework in which the particular events of the story made sense and which did not distract from that story. The actors, then, were able to find behaviours that were appropriate to both the world of the production and the given circumstances of the play; they found what is universal and immortal about the need to use language actively to work one's way through the problems of human existence.

When you come to do Shakespeare's plays as an actor, you will most often have little or no say in decisions about setting and design – all that will have been determined long before you are cast. What you need to do is develop the flexibility of imagination to be able to marry the given circumstances created by your director and designers to your character's story. When you are lucky, the setting and design will feed and fire your imagination; they will help you connect to the character's dilemmas and desires and make sense of why you say the things you say and do the things you do. Sometimes you will be luckier than others. Sometimes you will need to dig deeper. Theatre in its essence, though, is one big 'what if', so we would encourage you to keep an open mind and keep questioning the text until you find the specific human impulse behind the words.

In this section, we're going to introduce you to a few exercises to help you expand your sense of what Shakespearean characters can be and embrace and use their language effectively under a variety of circumstances. One thing to keep in mind is that, while we encourage you to explore the interpretive possibilities that different given circumstances open up for you, we would caution against over-embellishment. If Shakespeare has created a character who is sexually aggressive, and your designer has given you a costume that is sexually aggressive, by all means do your best to really inhabit that characteristic, but don't feel that you need to exaggerate it. Just because it's Shakespeare and the language is big and sometimes unfamiliar doesn't mean the audience needs you to over-illustrate the point. Trust the language and the design, and commit to pursuing your intentions in the given circumstances.

Shoes

- Assemble several pairs of shoes. Try to find at least one pair that is formal; one that is soft soled, like trainers or sneakers; and one that is heavy, like boots. If you don't have a wide enough range, see if you can borrow some from a friend who wears the same size or get some from your drama department's costume shop, if you have one.

- Find a speech or scene you have worked on and would like to explore further. Given what you know about the character's age and social status and the given circumstances of the scene, which shoes does it seem most likely he or she would wear?

- Put on that pair of shoes and have a walk around the room. Vary your pace and stride to explore the range of walking possibilities these shoes afford you. Just as an exploration, lean into any particular quality the shoes seem to suggest – so if boots make you feel like stomping, really stomp, or if slippers make you feel like shuffling, really shuffle. After a minute of that, ease off that quality; notice how the energy of a stomp can still be present in your walk even if you're not pounding your feet down on each step.

- Stop and stand for a moment. Turn your attention to your breath. Try to take a nice, full, engaged breath. Does it feel tight or stopped anywhere? Though given circumstances may make it difficult for characters to breathe sometimes, anyone who wants to express himself verbally needs breath, so your character will always *want* to breathe as fully as he is able. See if there are any adjustments you can make in your stance to facilitate your breath.

- Begin your text and start to pace. Notice where you speed up and where you slow down. Notice where you have an impulse to turn or stop. Notice if the shoes are influencing how you use your pitch range – is your voice higher or lower than usual? Are you moving through your range more or less?

- Now think about what other shoes your character might wear in the scene or speech. This might take some creativity. Say you picked formal heels for Lady Macbeth because you know she has wealth and status and she seems like someone who would want to present herself as being well put together. Is it possible that she might wear slippers in the scene you're doing if it happens at night? Or could the messenger who brings her the letter she's reading have caught her on her way into the house after a tennis match? Maybe you put Hotspur in boots because he's a soldier. What if he had to wear a dress uniform with dress shoes to meet the king? Or what if his boots were so wrecked after the battle that he changed into the first thing he could find, which happened to be trainers? How would he maintain his military authority without military footwear?

- Take a walk around the room *as your character* in the new shoes. Stop and breathe in your new shoes.

- Play the speech or scene in the new shoes, moving and walking whenever you feel the impulse to do so. Did the shoes change anything in your approach to the text? Repeat it, exaggerating any changes and then do it again, making them as subtle as possible.

- Many actors like to begin rehearsing as soon as possible with the actual shoes they will be wearing. The shoes you wear have a big influence on how you hold your body, which is a large component of your characterization. If you can't get the actual costume shoes before tech, we would encourage you to find out what kind of shoes you'll be wearing and use a pair from your own closet that are of the same general type to wear in rehearsal.

Furniture

- Any of the following would work well with this exercise, or you can pick another piece you've been working on:

  Cassius from Chapter 1
  Proteus from Chapter 1
  Helena from Chapter 2
  Speed from Chapter 4.

- Run through your piece once without any furniture.

- If you have one, grab a straight-backed chair. If you don't, imagine that the chair you have has a straight back. Run through your piece again. You can start standing up or sitting on the chair, but if you start standing up, you must sit down at least once. Otherwise you can sit or stand whenever you have the impulse. Try to maintain a very formal relationship to the chair, so always sit up straight in it and never cross your legs. This may feel very natural for your character in these circumstances; if it doesn't, think of reasons why your character might particularly want to be 'at attention' in this speech or scene.

- Do the piece again. This time you can have a slightly more relaxed relationship with the chair. You can lean forward or back or cross your legs at any point. Try to notice where and how these impulses are related to what you're doing with your language. What changed between the first time you used the chair and the second?

- Try the speech or scene one more time, and look for places where you can use a casual attitude towards the chair to reinforce a point you're making. Maybe lean back and stretch your legs in front of you to show your listener how comfortable and confident you are, or hunch forward to establish more intimacy with the person you're talking to. This may feel very natural for your character, or it may not. If it doesn't, think about what in the given circumstances might drive him to break out of his usual physicality. Try to find something in the language that would prompt the move.

Accent and Character

- In Britain, there is a long-established theatrical tradition of certain types of characters speaking with certain types of accents. Aristocratic characters have usually spoken in what is known as Received Pronunciation. Rural characters often have a West Country accent. Cheeky servants like Speed from *The Two Gentlemen of Verona* might use an East London accent. This is beginning to change, however. A wider variety of regional accents is being heard on the stage, and they're not always done 'to type'. In addition, directors are more frequently setting plays outside of England. Recent productions have set *Much Ado About Nothing* in India and *Julius Caesar* in Africa and used accents from those locales.

  In America, there has not generally been as much use of accents in Shakespeare productions. There was a period when Shakespearean actors were widely expected to use a kind of 'classical' accent that borrowed some of its sounds from Britain. This has fallen out of favour in many circles, but Shakespeare plays are still largely performed in a non-regionally-specific, 'general' American accent. This too, however, is beginning to change. We know of several productions in the last few years that have been set in areas where Spanish is the predominant language and different accents of Spanish have been used to a greater or lesser extent. Some directors are also becoming interested in using accents to distinguish between nationalities and social classes.

  It's important that you as a young actor don't get locked into thinking that Shakespeare in general or any character in particular should sound any one way. In the following exercises, we're going to ask you to experiment with some different sounds. The point is not to do a given accent perfectly, but to start to feel how the language can adapt to different circumstances.

- Let's start with a speech of Edmund's from *King Lear* which we already worked on in Chapter 3:

EDMUND
Thou, Nature, art my goddess; to thy law
My services are bound. Wherefore should I
Stand in the plague of custom, and permit
The curiosity of nations to deprive me?
For that I am some twelve or fourteen moonshines
Lag of a brother? Why bastard? Wherefore base?
When my dimensions are as well compact,
My mind as generous and my shape as true
As honest madam's issue? Why brand they us
With base? With baseness, bastardy? Base, base?
Who in the lusty stealth of nature take
More composition and fierce quality
Than doth within a dull stale tirèd bed
Go to the creating of a whole tribe of fops
Got 'tween a sleep and wake. Well, then,
Legitimate Edgar, I must have your land.
Our father's love is to the bastard Edmund
As to the legitimate. Fine word, 'legitimate'!
Well, my legitimate, if this letter speed
And my invention thrive, Edmund the base
Shall top the legitimate. I grow, I prosper:
Now gods, stand up for bastards!

- We know that Edmund has been away from the court for nine years and that his father is planning to send him away again. We also know that Edmund seems to have some military training as he steps very naturally into a leadership role when war breaks out between France and Britain.

- Imagine that Edmund has been in an elite military academy training to be an officer. Stand at attention, salute, and call out 'Sir, yes sir.' What kind of vocal energy are you using? What kind of rhythm? How would you characterize your articulation? Play the speech through once with a very military attack as if you were a soldier of high rank with an excellent education. Where did this vocal characterization seem to work best with the language? Were there places where you felt it was in conflict with the text?

- Play the speech again. Continue to work with this vocal characterization, but let it move to the background a bit more. If there are places where you feel Edmund would want to distance himself from the very correct officer his father has tried to make him into, let that come through in how you speak.

- Let's imagine now that Edmund has been living with his working-class mother in an inner city (choose a city that has an accent you feel you can have a good go at). He hasn't had much success at school there and has joined the army as a way out.

- To shake off the military bearing and get more into a street-smart physicality, play a minute or two of pantomime basketball (or real basketball if you happen to have one to hand).

- Try the speech once through and lean into the urban accent of your choice (don't worry if it feels a bit silly!). Use it to call attention to the fact that you are rough and proud of it. Where did this vocal characterization seem to work best with the language? Were there places where you felt it was in conflict with the text?

- In many accents words are abbreviated ('running' becomes 'runnin'' or 'bottle' becomes 'bo'ul'). This doesn't, however, have to make them hard to understand. If you found yourself slurring a bit or letting ends of thoughts slide away, take the speech again and invest in Edmund's drive and determination – use it to keep the language sharp and energized. Look too for places where Edmund might minimize or maximize his accent to make a point.

- Let's turn now to Joan Puzel, whom we looked at in Chapter 1. We have removed Burgundy's lines in this instance:

  JOAN PUZEL
  Brave Burgundy, undoubted hope of France,
  Stay, let thy humble handmaid speak to thee.
  Look on thy country, look on fertile France,
  And see the cities and the towns defaced
  By wasting ruin of the cruel foe,
  As looks the mother on her lowly babe
  When death doth close his tender-dying eyes.
  See, see the pining malady of France,
  Behold the wounds, the most unnatural wounds,
  Which thou thyself hast given her woeful breast.
  O, turn thy edgèd sword another way,
  Strike those that hurt, and hurt not those that help:
  One drop of blood drawn from thy country's bosom
  Should grieve thee more than streams of foreign gore.
  Return thee therefore with a flood of tears
  And wash away thy country's stainèd spots.
  Besides, all French and France exclaims on thee,
  Doubting thy birth and lawful progeny.
  Who join'st thou with but with a lordly nation,
  That will not trust thee but for profit's sake?
  When Talbot hath set footing once in France
  And fashioned thee that instrument of ill,
  Who then but English Henry will be lord,
  And thou be thrust out, like a fugitive?
  Call we to mind – and mark but this for proof –
  Was not the Duke of Orleans thy foe?
  And was he not in England prisoner?
  But when they heard he was thine enemy
  They set him free without his ransom paid,
  In spite of Burgundy and all his friends.
  See, then, thou fight'st against thy countrymen
  And join'st with them will be thy slaughter-men.
  Come, come, return; return, thou wandering lord.
  Charles and the rest will take thee in their arms.

- Joan is French. In this speech, she is speaking to a Frenchman, but one who has left France and joined with the English. For the purposes of this exercise, let's imagine that Burgundy's English is actually better than his French and Joan is speaking English to him as a courtesy. She is doing so, however, with a French accent. Try the speech once with this accent. Don't worry about getting it 'right' – if it gets a little Italian at times, for example, that's not a problem. Do focus on using the accent tactically. When might Joan want to lean into the soft and luxurious aspect of French sounds? When might she want to minimize her accent to show Burgundy that they're not really foreign to each other?

- Another important aspect of Joan's character is that she is from the country. She is an 'ordinary' woman, not a sophisticate or a politician. To bring this out, let go of the French accent for now and think about how you might speak if you wanted to convince someone that you are down to earth. Try the speech this way. What subtle shifts did you make in your own way of speaking? How well did they fit with Joan's intentions and her use of language? Is there another accent you can think of that is associated with simple, rural life? Try the speech once in that accent. Did this change your approach to the language or your relationship with Burgundy? Were there places where it felt right to lean into it or to back away from it?

Further reading

Berry, Cicely, *Text in Action*, Virgin Publishing, London, 2001. 'Style and Space', pp. 73–5.
—*From Word to Play*, Oberon Books, London, 2008. Chapter 6: 'Working the Space'.
Cohen, Robert, *Acting in Shakespeare*, Mayfield Publishing Company, Mountain View, 1991. Lesson 6: 'The Demands of Shakespeare'; Lesson 12: 'Costume and Character'; Lesson 19: 'Speeches Into Scenes'.
Rodenburg, Patsy, *Speaking Shakespeare*, Methuen, London, 2002. Part 2: 'Structure: Location', pp. 184–5; 'Stage Directions, Props, Entrances and Exits', pp. 186–7.
Weate, Catherine, *Classic Voice: Working with Actors on Vocal Style*, Oberon Books, London, 2009. Chapter 10: 'Performing Outside'.

APPENDIX 1
VOCAL WARM-UP

Shakespeare's language is highly energetic, articulate and nuanced, and you will give your best performance of it when your voice and body are energized, free of tension (unnecessary effort), and responsive to thought and impulse. We would recommend that you do at least a five- to ten-minute warm-up before every classroom session or rehearsal. If you have built a role while physically or vocally tight and disengaged, a warm-up before performances will do little to dislodge the constricted, under-energized muscular patterns you established in rehearsal.

Below is a warm-up you should be able to perform in about ten minutes in a relatively small space. Most of the exercises in it come from our *Vocal Arts Workbook and DVD*. There are also warm-ups in the appendices of that book and *The Verbal Arts Workbook*, and in many other voice and text books. As well as physically preparing your body and voice to work, a warm-up can also be a useful opportunity to focus mentally and develop a habit of awareness. As you work, then, you will be better able to notice when you are pushing or straining and have the tools to release physically and vocally.

1. Start by stretching and yawning, making stretching and yawning sounds as you do so.

When you've finished stretching and yawning, stand with your feet hip-width apart. With your feet planted, bounce up and down from your knees for 10 to 15 seconds; imagine your shoulders and jaw loosening as you do so.

Keeping the feet planted, begin swinging your arms and shoulders from side to side, but keep your hips and waist still.

After ten to fifteen seconds let your waist join in the swing, but keep your hips still. You'll feel a nice stretch in your ribs and back as you do this.

Next let your hips join in the swing, which will become bigger and more energetic.

Let the energy of the swing begin to pull your heels up off the ground on either side.

After ten to fifteen seconds, widen your stance and bend your knees a bit in a little lunge as you swing to each side.

Deepen the lunge until finally you can touch the floor with your fingertips on either side.

After five or six deep lunges, return to swinging and pulling the heels up off the floor on either side.

Plant the heels on the floor and swing from the hips.

Let the hips be still and swing from the waist.

Let the waist be still and swing from the shoulders.

Come to stillness and feel how the breath has been energized.

2. Standing with your feet about hip-width apart, lift your arms in the air and imagine your shoulder blades sliding down your back, so your shoulders are not hunched up by your ears.

Imagine that there is a large barrel to your left and stretch your waist up and over it so that you are stretching the ribcage on your right side.

Drop your left arm down and reach it across your body to hold your ribs to the right. Imagine those ribs expanding to fill your hand as you take a full, energized breath in.

Continue breathing in this position for 20 to 30 seconds; then release the stretch by relaxing your arms and torso forward into a roll-down position.

Roll up and repeat the sequence to the right.

3. Still standing with feet hip-width apart, bend your knees a bit, as if you were starting to sit down, but rather than sticking your bottom out, think of curling your tailbone under your spine.

Let your head, shoulders and upper back hang forward.

Cross your arms in front of your body as if you were hugging yourself. Try to grab the edges of your shoulder blades with your fingertips.

Take a nice, full breath and feel your back and ribs expanding as you do. Let the breath out on a voiced sigh.

Repeat five or six times, and then release your arms and gently roll back up.

4. Place your hands on your lower belly, at least three inches below the navel, then move your hands forward about a foot. Imagine that you are holding a beach ball against your lower belly.

Breathe in, and then blow out a short, energized 'fff', moving your hands in an inch or two as if you were pressing sharply on the beach ball.

Repeat, and this time follow the initial short burst of 'fff' with a more sustained flow of 'fff', moving the hands in towards the belly as if continuing to press on the beach ball. As soon as you begin to run out of breath (just when your chest begins to feel tight), let your hands spring forward, as if releasing pressure on the beach ball, and let your breath drop in.

Repeat and notice if you are using more effort in the jaw, the underside of the chin or the neck than you need. Imagine those areas releasing and the effort/energy focusing in your lower abdomen.

Repeat using a 'vvv' sound.

Shake out for a moment. Then, let your jaw hang slightly open, noticing the space between your back teeth. Let your tongue rest in your mouth with the tip resting gently behind your bottom teeth and the body releasing away from the palate. Try yawning without moving your jaw or pulling the tip of your tongue away from your bottom teeth. Keeping a sense of space at the back of your mouth (yawn again if you're not feeling it), close your lips.

Repeat the beach ball exercise on a hum instead of a 'vvv'. Do this a few times on different pitches in the middle of your range.

Repeat, and after a couple of seconds of sustained humming, let your lips fall open and imagine the inside of your mouth also stretching open on a 'mah'.

Repeat, and when you open your mouth, instead of simply sustaining a 'mah' for the length of your breath, chant (sing on one note) a line of text – it can be poetry or dramatic verse. Do as many lines of text as you'd like this way, changing pitch from time to time and maintaining an awareness of engaging the lower abdomen on the out-breath and releasing it on the in-breath.

5. Rub your face all over with your hands.

Wrinkle your nose and lift your top lip in an exaggerated sneer. Holding the sneer, massage the sides of your nose. As you do, say 'meeee', holding the 'ee'. The sound will be quite nasal and not necessarily pleasant; that's just fine for now.

Repeat, and this time, after you've held the 'meeee' for several seconds, move your fingers over so you are massaging your cheekbones under your eyes, and say 'may'. Repeat, and after you've said 'may' once, flick your fingers away from your face several times and say 'may' each time. Think of the sound shooting out of your cheeks like lasers.

Repeat the above, and at the end bring your fingers back to your face and sweep them across your face and out to the side until your arms are wide open. Say 'maaaaah' as you do this, and imagine your throat getting wider as your arms open out.

Stay on the 'mah' and shake your whole body.

Send some 'mees', 'mays' and 'maaahs' across the room, making a throwing motion with your arms and imagining your voice easily arching through the space as you do so. You can have a 'mee', 'may', 'mah' conversation with a friend if you like.

6. Stick your little fingers inside your mouth (make sure your hands are clean!), and use them to stretch your lips out in every direction.

Exaggerating the movement of your lips, energetically repeat 'ee-you-ee-you-ee-you' for fifteen to twenty seconds.

Move your top lip up and down; thinking of sneering can help.

Move your bottom lip up and down; thinking of a little kid who's about to cry can help.

Blow through your lips. Add some voice, making a shivering sound, then glide from the bottom of your pitch range to the top and back down again while blowing through your lips.

Cradle your jawbone in your hands and let their weight gently pull it down until there is about a centimetre (half an inch) of space between your back teeth. Leave your hands there as you work your tongue.

Stick your tongue out as far as it will go.

Reach your tongue up to your nose and then move it up and down a centimetre or so six or seven times, making a little 'huh' sound on each pulse.

Point your tongue over towards your right ear and push it in that direction six or seven times. Repeat, pushing the tongue down towards the chin, and finally over towards the left ear.

Make a big circle with your tongue in one direction and then the other.

Let your tongue come back into your mouth and trill an R sound. Move up and down your pitch range as you trill.

7. Speak the following lines from *Hamlet* slowly, being very mindful that the motions of the lips and the tongue are full and energetic. If you feel your jaw tightening, you can rest your hands on the side of the face to encourage it to stay as released as possible. You may find yourself exaggerating the speech sounds a bit, which is fine; just don't overdo it to the point where your delivery becomes tense and forced:

'Speak the speech, I pray you, as I pronounced it to you – trippingly on the tongue. But if you mouth it as many of our players do, I had as lief the town-crier spoke my lines.'

Repeat five or six times, trying to get a little faster each time without losing any of the definition of the sounds.

APPENDIX 2
CURRICULUM CHOICES

We provide here two outline programmes: a fifteen-week model and a ten-week one. In both cases we assume that the class will take place either in Year 2 of a three-year course or as a module in a postgraduate degree. These are provided to indicate two ways in which the work of this book might be incorporated into a formal curriculum. They are not meant to be definitive models, as we expect teachers to adapt them to suit the learning needs of their particular students; for example, by applying the exercises to further scenes and monologues from Shakespeare's plays.

Fifteen-week model (one semester)

Each session in this model is conceived as a two- to three-hour workshop.

Session 1

Introduction to the Shakespeare workshop: how the work of these classes connects with previous acting training, and where it differs. The nature of heightened language and its relationship to dramatic actions. Recommended reading in advance of the class:

Introduction and Chapter 1: 'Language and Action: Framework'.
'Exploration' exercises from 'Language and Action'.
Explore the Speak and Question work for either Joan Puzel or
    Lady Percy in 'Having an effect'.
Discussion.

Session 2

Explore the Speak and Question work for either Cassius or Portia in 'Negotiating complications' from Chapter 1.
Discussion.
Explore the Speak and Question work for either Proteus or Viola in 'Solving problems' from Chapter 1.
Discussion.
Ask students to choose one of the speeches explored for Act work in the following session.

Session 3

Explore the Speak and Question work for Hamlet in 'Solving problems' from Chapter 1.
Discussion.
Explore the Act work for students' chosen speeches.
Discussion.
Set the Framework and Exploration sections from Chapter 2: 'Language in Action: Imagery, Sound and Story' as preparatory homework for the following session.

Session 4

Discussion of the nature of imagery, sound and storytelling in relation to acting Shakespeare.
Explore the Speak and Question work for both Chorus and Titania from 'Picture painting' in Chapter 2.
Discussion.

Session 5

Explore the Speak and Question work for either Lady Macbeth or Helena in 'Ear catching' from Chapter 2.
Discussion.
Explore the Speak and Question work for either Benvolio or Hotspur in 'Storytelling' from Chapter 2.

Discussion.
Ask students to choose one of the speeches from Chapter 2 for
Act work in the following session.

Session 6

Explore the Act work for students' chosen speeches.
Discussion and constructive feedback.
Set the Framework section from Chapter 3: 'Rhythm and Meter' as
preparatory homework for following session.

Session 7

Discussion of verse and iambic pentameter.
Exploration exercises from Chapter 3.
Explore the Speak and Question work for both Julia and Richard in
'Finding the rhythm' from Chapter 3.
Discussion.
Set the Speak and Question work for Grumio in 'Finding the
rhythm' from Chapter 3 as homework.

Session 8

Explore the Speak and Question work for Shylock, Portia/Lucius
and Falstaff in 'Mastering the rhythm' from Chapter 3.
Discussion.

Session 9

Explore the Speak and Question work for Edmund and Hermione
in 'Breaking the rhythm' from Chapter 3.
Discussion.
Ask students to choose one of the speeches from Chapter 3 for
Act work in the following session.

Session 10

Explore the Speak and Question work for Antony/Cleopatra in
'Breaking the rhythm' from Chapter 3.
Explore the Act work for students' chosen speeches.
Discussion and constructive feedback.
Set the Framework and Exploration sections from Chapter 4:
'Rhetoric and style' as preparatory homework.

Session 11

Discussion of rhetoric and style.
Review the Exploration section from Chapter 4.
Explore the Speak and Question work for both Speed and Queen
Margaret in 'Recognizing rhetoric' from Chapter 4.
Discussion.

Session 12

Explore the Speak and Question work for both Touchstone/Audrey
and Phoebe/Silvius in 'Comedy and style' from Chapter 4.
Discussion.

Session 13

Explore the Speak and Question work for both Desdemona/Emilia
and Edmund/Gloucester in 'Complicated characters' from
Chapter 4.
Discussion.
Ask students to choose one of the speeches/scenes from Chapter
4 for work in sessions 14 and 15.

Session 14

Explore the exercises in the Circumstances section of Chapter 5: 'Preparation for performance', using the speeches and scenes chosen by the students.
Discussion.

Session 15

This session should take place in a large theatre. Prepare the students for their Act work on their chosen speeches/scenes by using the exercises from the Space section of Chapter 5 as part of an extended warm-up in the theatre and auditorium.
Discussion following the Act work.

Ten-week model (one term)

Each session in this model is conceived as an eighty- to ninety-minute class.

Session 1

Required reading in advance of the class: Introduction and Chapter 1: 'Language and Action: Framework'.
Exploration exercises from 'Language and Action'.
Explore some of the Speak and Question work for either Joan Puzel or Lady Percy in 'Having an effect'.
Home study task: reflective journal report on personal discoveries.

Session 2

Explore some of the Speak and Question work for Portia in 'Negotiating complications' from Chapter 1.
Explore some of the Speak and Question work for either Proteus or Hamlet in 'Solving problems' from Chapter 1.

Discussion.
Home study task: students choose one of the speeches from
   Chapter 1 to explore for Act work in the following session.

Session 3

Explore the Act work for students' chosen speeches.
Discussion.
Home study task: reflective journal report on personal discoveries.
   Also, set the Framework and Exploration sections from
   Chapter 2: 'Language in Action: Imagery, Sound and Story' as
   preparatory reading for following session.

Session 4

Explore some of the Speak and Question work for either Chorus or
   Titania from 'Picture painting' in Chapter 2.
Explore some of the Speak and Question work for either Lady
   Macbeth in 'Ear catching' or Hotspur in 'Storytelling' from
   Chapter 2.
Discussion.
Home study task: reflective journal report on personal discoveries.
   Also, ask students to choose one of the speeches from Chapter
   2 for Act work in the following session.

Session 5

Explore the Act work for students' chosen speeches.
Discussion.
Home study task: reflective journal report on personal discoveries.
   Also, set the Framework section from Chapter 3: 'Rhythm and
   Meter' as preparatory reading for the following session.

Session 6

Exploration exercises from Chapter 3.

Explore some of the Speak and Question work for either Julia or Richard in 'Finding the rhythm' from Chapter 3.

Discussion.

Home study task: reflective journal report on personal discoveries. Also, set the Speak and Question work for Grumio in 'Finding the rhythm' from Chapter 3 as homework.

Session 7

Explore some of the Speak and Question work for either Shylock or Falstaff in 'Mastering the rhythm' from Chapter 3.

Explore some of the Speak and Question work for either Edmund or Hermione in 'Breaking the rhythm' from Chapter 3.

Discussion.

Home study task: reflective journal report on personal discoveries. Also, ask students to choose one of the speeches from Chapter 3 for Act work in the following session.

Session 8

Explore the Act work for students' chosen speeches.

Discussion.

Home study task: reflective journal report on personal discoveries. Also, set the Framework and Exploration sections from Chapter 4: 'Rhetoric and style' as preparatory homework.

Session 9

Explore some of the Speak and Question work for either Speed or Queen Margaret in 'Recognizing rhetoric' from Chapter 4.

Explore some of the Speak and Question work for either Touchstone/Audrey or Phoebe/Silvius in 'Comedy and style' from Chapter 4.

Discussion.

Home study task: reflective journal report on personal discoveries. Also, ask students to choose one of the speeches/scenes from Chapter 4 for Act work in the final session.

Session 10

Explore the Act work for students' chosen speeches.

Discussion.

Home study task: set Chapter 5: 'Preparation for performance' as follow-up reading. Students to write reflective journal report on how they would prepare one of the roles they chose during the term for performance in a specified theatre.

APPENDIX 3
PROFESSIONAL
HISTORIES

David Carey

David Carey trained during the 1970s as a speech and drama teacher at the Royal Scottish Academy of Music and Drama in Glasgow, where his voice teachers were John Colson, Jacqui Crago and Jim House. John was the husband of Greta Colson, Co-Director of the New College of Speech and Drama, London. Greta Colson was a graduate of the Central School of Speech and Drama and author or co-author of a number of books on voice, speech and phonetics. The New College of Speech and Drama, which was later absorbed by Middlesex Polytechnic (later Middlesex University), was one of a number of drama schools in the 1960s which were training voice teachers in the UK. Jacqui Crago and Jim House were both graduates of New College. Jacqui's classes in phonetics and poetry were a particular influence on David's decision to become a voice teacher.

However, David's initial introduction to voice and speech work was literally at his mother's knee. Elna Carey (née Graham) trained during the 1930s as a Speech Teacher at the Central School of Speech and Drama under Elsie Fogerty. Gwynneth Thurburn and J. Clifford Turner were also on the Central faculty at this time. She married actor Brian Carey, who came from a theatrical family in Dublin, and so David was brought up with a deep awareness of the importance of voice, speech and articulate communication.

Following his training in Glasgow, David completed a BA degree in English Language and Linguistics at Edinburgh University before taking up a position as Lecturer in Voice and Speech at Queen Margaret College,

Edinburgh, where he taught on the College's undergraduate drama programme for five years. His work at this time was strongly influenced by both Cicely Berry and Kristin Linklater through their seminal books, *Voice and the Actor* (first published in 1973) and *Freeing the Natural Voice* (first published in 1976). Berry had trained under and worked with Gwynneth Thurburn at the Central School of Speech and Drama (CSSD), while Linklater had trained under and worked with Iris Warren at the London Academy of Music and Dramatic Art (LAMDA). David found that the rigorous and muscular work of Berry was complemented by the more kinaesthetic and image-based approach of Linklater, and that a combination of the two was well suited to the needs of developing students.

David left Edinburgh in 1982 to join the Royal Shakespeare Company as Assistant Voice Director, working under Cicely Berry and alongside Patsy Rodenburg. The four years that David spent at the RSC were a rich period in the company's history. Judi Dench, Fiona Shaw, Juliet Stevenson and Harriet Walter, Kenneth Branagh, Brian Cox, Derek Jacobi, Alan Rickman and Antony Sher were all members of the acting company. In addition to Joint Artistic Directors, Terry Hands and Trevor Nunn, other directors included Bill Alexander, John Barton, Ron Daniels, Howard Davies, Barry Kyle and Adrian Noble. Notable plays and productions of this period with which David was associated were *Richard III* with Antony Sher, *Henry V* with Kenneth Branagh, and the world premieres of Christopher Hampton's *Les Liaisons Dangereuses* and Howard Barker's *The Castle*. David's understanding of voice, text and acting was deeply informed by the opportunity to observe these actors and directors, but most especially by the experience of watching Cicely Berry's unique collaboration with these theatre artists. Her passion for language and its ability to express human experience, particularly through the work of Shakespeare, left an indelible impression on David and continues to influence his work to this day.

David left the RSC to take up the post of Senior Lecturer (later, Principal Lecturer) in Voice Studies at the Central School of Speech and Drama, where he was responsible for developing and sustaining the School's postgraduate programme in Voice Studies, a course of professional development for graduates who wished to follow a career in voice teaching. David was responsible for all aspects of teaching and learning, from course design and admissions to assessment, timetabling and pastoral care. He taught modules in vocal anatomy, vocal pedagogy, voice and text, and phonetics, as well as supervising dissertations and independent practical projects.

Under his leadership, the course became recognized as a national and international benchmark in the field. British graduates were regularly employed by all of the leading HE drama training institutions in England and Wales. As UK universities diversified their provision with respect to practice-based drama courses, graduates also found employment in this part of the sector. The course also served a worldwide demand for well-qualified teachers of voice and speech, attracting a regular number of international applicants from North America, Europe, Asia and Australia. In the USA, graduates went on to work at (among others) Yale University, Southern Methodist University and the University of Utah. Other graduates were successfully employed in HE drama training institutions in Australia, Canada, Japan, Singapore, South Africa, Holland and Denmark. In his seventeen-year tenure, David was responsible for training over two hundred voice teachers, many of whom are now at the top of their profession, including the Heads of Voice at the Royal National Theatre in London, the Stratford Ontario Festival Theatre, and the Oregon Shakespeare Festival.

Through the course at CSSD, David introduced a generation of voice teachers to the work of a wide range of practitioners, including Frankie Armstrong, Kevin Crawford, Meribeth Bunch Dayme, Catherine Fitzmaurice, Nadine George, Barbara Houseman, Gillyanne Kayes, Christina Shewell, Andrew Wade and Joanna Weir-Ouston.

In 2000, recognizing the need for a major resource facility that was designed to serve the professional development of teachers of voice and speech and to contribute to the wider international community in HE actor training, David established the International Centre for Voice at CSSD. During his term as Director of the International Centre for Voice he organized a number of events intended to support and influence colleagues.

David left Central in 2003, returning to the vocal training of actors as a Senior Voice Tutor at the Royal Academy of Dramatic Art. In 2004 he revisited the RSC to coach their touring productions of *Julius Caesar* and *The Two Gentlemen of Verona*. In 2005 he spent two months with the Oregon Shakespeare Festival as Voice and Text Director for productions of *The Philanderer* by George Bernard Shaw and *By the Waters of Babylon* by Robert Schenkkan. He returned to Oregon in 2008 as Voice and Text Director for productions of *Coriolanus* by William Shakespeare and *The Further Adventures of Hedda Gabler* by Jeff Whitty; and again in 2010 for a production of *Hamlet* by William Shakespeare. He also established a relationship with the Stratford Ontario Festival in Canada, where he was vocal coach for the 2007 production of Oscar Wilde's *An Ideal Husband*. He was an Associate Editor for the *Voice and Speech Review*, the journal of the Voice and Speech Trainers Association, from 2002 to 2009.

David left his position at RADA at the end of 2010 to become a Resident Voice and Text Director with the Oregon Shakespeare Festival, where he is currently responsible for voice, text and dialect work for four to five productions each season. At the same time, he has maintained his connection with the Royal Shakespeare Company through work on the following productions: *Written on the Heart* by David Edgar (2011), *The Orphan of Zhao* by Ji Junxiang and adapted by James Fenton (2012), *King Lear* by William Shakespeare and adapted by Tim Crouch (2012), and *Antony and Cleopatra* by William Shakespeare and adapted by Tarell Alvin McCraney (2013).

David's pedagogy is an eclectic one which draws on the work of the leading voice teachers of today, such as Cicely Berry, Kristin Linklater and Patsy Rodenburg. His academic interest in Linguistics – he has a Masters in Contemporary English Language and Linguistics from Reading University – also informs his practice through a deep understanding of language, vocal anatomy, phonetics and dialects. He also draws actively on his experience of Alexander Technique and T'ai Chi. He places emphasis on exploring and developing the natural potential of the voice, with equal attention paid to physiological function and imaginative intention, so that fundamental work on breathing, alignment, resonance and articulation is integrated with expressive work on text and communication.

David was awarded a prestigious National Teaching Fellowship in 2007 by the UK's Higher Education Academy in recognition of his contribution to vocal pedagogy.

Rebecca Clark Carey

Rebecca Clark Carey received her BA in History and Literature from Harvard University. She focused particularly on the history of drama in Germany and wrote her undergraduate thesis on Weimar theatre. She went on to train as an actress in the University of California at Irvine's Master of Fine Arts programme. Her principal voice and speech teacher there was Dudley Knight, and she continues to draw heavily on Dudley's teaching in her own work. Dudley himself studied voice with Kristin Linklater and Catherine Fitzmaurice, both of whom did their initial training in London; Kristin at the London Academy of Music and Dramatic Art with Iris Warren and Catherine at the Central School of Speech and Drama with Cicely Berry and Gwynneth Thurburn.

Rebecca's principal acting teacher at Irvine was Robert Cohen, author of *Acting in Shakespeare*, among other titles. Robert's approach to Stanislavski-based actor training continues to influence Rebecca's approach to text work. While at Irvine, working with Joan Melton, Rebecca first read Kristin Linklater's *Freeing Shakespeare Voice*. Kristin's thoughts on the power of the individual word to open up a world of associations to both the speaker and the listener profoundly influenced Rebecca's understanding of not only language but also of what it is to act truthfully. Her Master's thesis at Irvine focused on the encounter between speaker, word and listener. When teaching, she often tells her students that the essence of their job is to mean what they say, which creed grew out of her thinking on this subject.

After leaving UC Irvine, Rebecca worked as a professional actress, primarily on the west coast of the United States. She gained skills in classical text particularly through her work with the California Shakespeare Festival, Shakespeare Santa Cruz, and the Oregon Shakespeare Festival. While in Los Angeles, she also had the good fortune to study Shakespeare at the Antaeus Company with Dakin Matthews, from whom she learned an enormous amount about prosody and acting. While still working as an actor, Rebecca was invited to teach voice and text at Palomar College in San Diego County. She coached every Shakespeare play produced at the college for a number of years.

When Rebecca decided to make the transition to teaching and coaching full time, she went to London to study at the Central School of Speech and Drama. While working on her MA in Voice Studies there, she had the opportunity to receive instruction from many prominent voice practitioners, including Cicely Berry, Andrew Wade, Joanna Weir-Ouston, Gillyanne Kayes and Meribeth Bunch Dayme. Her dissertation was on speaking Shakespeare's late plays (an edited version was published in *Film, Broadcast and e-Media Coaching: And*

Other Contemporary Issues in Professional Voice and Speech Training, Applause Books, New York, 2003). In preparing it, she drew heavily on the works of Cicely Berry and Patsy Rodenburg and their thoughts about the embodied exploration of text.

Shortly after completing the Central course with distinction, Rebecca joined the Oregon Shakespeare Festival (OSF)'s education department, headed by Joan Langley. Among her responsibilities was developing workshops with another actor/teacher, Kirsten Giroux, to be delivered by members of the company to the hundreds of students who visit the festival every year. The experience she gained in finding ways to actively engage young people with Shakespeare has been invaluable to her later teaching. The work on laying out a programme of exercises so other teachers could follow it was also excellent preparation for writing this book.

In her first year at OSF, Rebecca was invited to assist voice and text directors Scott Kaiser and Ursula Meyer on productions of *Handler*, by Pulitzer Prize winner Robert Schenkkan, and *A Winter's Tale*. Their expertise and generosity continues to inform and inspire her coaching work. The following year she served as voice and text director on *Hedda Gabler* and *Wild Oats*. She has since returned regularly to coach plays including *King Lear*, *Much Ado About Nothing*, *The Taming of the Shrew*, *The Tempest*, *Measure for Measure*, *Love's Labour's Lost*, *Troilus and Cressida* and *A Midsummer Night's Dream*, as well as many modern plays.

Rebecca is currently the head of voice and text at OSF. She has also worked in England as a voice teacher at the Central School of Speech and Drama, The Italia Conti Academy of Theatre Arts, The Oxford School of Drama, and for five years as a senior voice tutor at the Royal Academy of Dramatic Art. She frequently coaches British actors on American accents and was the accent coach for the Royal and Derngate's productions of Tennessee Williams' *Spring Storm* and Eugene O'Neill's *Beyond the Horizon* and their revivals at the Royal National Theatre in 2010. She was also the accent coach for Robert Schenkkan's Tony Award-winning *All the Way* at the American Repertory Theatre and on Broadway.

APPENDIX 4
BIBLIOGRAPHY AND RESOURCES

Shakespeare editions

There are many good editions of Shakespeare's plays: the Arden Shakespeare, the New Cambridge Shakespeare, and the Oxford Shakespeare offer helpful and scholarly editions of each play. The following are good editions of the complete works: *The Arden Shakespeare*, *The Oxford Shakespeare*, *The Riverside Shakespeare* and *The RSC/Modern Library Shakespeare*.

For this book we have used the following editions of the complete works:

The First Folio of *The Complete Works of William Shakespeare*, editor: Herbert Farjeon, The Nonesuch Press, London, 1953.
William Shakespeare: The Complete Works, general editors: Stanley Wells and Gary Taylor, The Clarendon Press, Oxford, 1986.
PlayShakespeare.com, 2013. *Shakespeare Pro*. [computer program] Readdle Inc. Available at: http://www.playshakespeare.com

We have also used the following individual plays in their current Arden edition:

Antony and Cleopatra, editor: John Wilders, *The Arden Shakespeare* (Third Series), Bloomsbury Publishing plc, London, 1995.
As You Like It, editor: Juliet Dusinberre, *The Arden Shakespeare* (Third Series), Bloomsbury Publishing plc, London, 2006.
Hamlet, editors: Ann Thompson and Neil Taylor, *The Arden Shakespeare* (Third Series), Bloomsbury Publishing plc, London, 2006.

Julius Caesar, editor: David Daniels, *The Arden Shakespeare* (Third Series), Bloomsbury Publishing, London, 1998.

King Henry IV, Part 1, editor: David Scott Kastan, *The Arden Shakespeare* (Third Series), Bloomsbury Publishing, London, 2002.

King Henry IV, Part 2, editor: A. R. Humphreys, *The Arden Shakespeare* (Second Series), Bloomsbury Publishing, London, 1967.

King Henry V, editor: T. W. Craik, *The Arden Shakespeare* (Third Series), Bloomsbury Publishing, London, 1995.

King Henry VI, Part 1, editor: Edward Burns, *The Arden Shakespeare* (Third Series), Bloomsbury Publishing, London, 2000.

King Henry VI, Part 2, editor: Ronald Knowles, *The Arden Shakespeare* (Third Series), Bloomsbury Publishing, London, 2000.

King Henry VI, Part 3, editors: John D. Cox and Eric Rasmussen, *The Arden Shakespeare* (Third Series), Bloomsbury Publishing, London, 2001.

King Lear, editor: R. A. Foakes, *The Arden Shakespeare* (Third Series), Bloomsbury Publishing, London, 1997.

King Richard III, editor: James R. Siemon, *The Arden Shakespeare* (Third Series), Bloomsbury Publishing, London, 2009.

Macbeth, editor: Kenneth Muir, *The Arden Shakespeare* (Second Series), Bloomsbury Publishing, London, 1997.

The Merchant of Venice, editor: John Drakakis, *The Arden Shakespeare* (Third Series), Bloomsbury Publishing, London, 2010.

A Midsummer Night's Dream, editor: Harold F. Brooks, *The Arden Shakespeare* (Second Series), Bloomsbury Publishing, London, 1979.

Othello, editor: E. A. J. Honigmann, *The Arden Shakespeare* (Third Series), Bloomsbury Publishing, London, 1997.

Romeo and Juliet, editor: René Weis, *The Arden Shakespeare* (Third Series), Bloomsbury Publishing, London, 2012.

The Taming of the Shrew, editor: Barbara Hodgdon, *The Arden Shakespeare* (Third Series), Bloomsbury Publishing, London, 2010.

Twelfth Night, editor: Keir Elam, *The Arden Shakespeare* (Third Series), Bloomsbury Publishing, London, 2008.

The Two Gentlemen of Verona, editor: William C. Carroll, *The Arden Shakespeare* (Third Series), Bloomsbury Publishing, London, 2004.

The Winter's Tale, editor: John Pitcher, *The Arden Shakespeare* (Third Series), Bloomsbury Publishing, London, 2010.

Reference texts

Crystal, David and Ben, *Shakespeare's Words: A Glossary and Language Companion*, Penguin Books, London, 2004.

McArthur, Tom (ed.), *The Oxford Companion to the English Language*, Oxford University Press, Oxford, 1992.

Onion, C. T., *A Shakespeare Glossary* (enlarged and revised by Robert D. Eagleson), Oxford University Press, Oxford, 1986.

Schmidt, Alexander, *Shakespeare Lexicon and Quotation Dictionary* (3rd edition, revised and enlarged by Gregor Sarrazin), Dover Publications Inc, New York, 1971.

Shorter Oxford English Dictionary (5th Edition), Oxford University Press, Oxford, 2002.

Wells, J. C., *Longman Pronunciation Dictionary*, Longman, Harlow, Essex, 1990.

Recommended and referenced texts

Adamson, Sylvia, 'The Grand Style' in Lynette Hunter, Lynne Magnusson and Sylvia Adamson (eds), *Reading Shakespeare's Dramatic Language: A Guide*, The Arden Shakespeare, Bloomsbury Publishing, London, 2001, pp. 31–50.

Barton, John, *Playing Shakespeare*, Methuen, London, 1984.

Berry, Cicely, *The Actor and the Text*, Virgin Publishing, London, 1992.

—*Text in Action*, Virgin Publishing, London, 2001.

—*From Word to Play*, Oberon Books, London, 2008.

Block, Giles, *Speaking the Speech: An Actor's Guide to Shakespeare*, Nick Hern Books, London, 2013.

Carey, David and Rebecca Clark Carey, *Vocal Arts Workbook and DVD*, Methuen, London, 2008.

—*The Verbal Arts Workbook: A Practical Course for Speaking Text*, Methuen, London, 2010.

Cohen, Robert, *Acting in Shakespeare*, Mayfield Publishing Company, Mountain View, 1991.

Crystal, Ben, *Shakespeare on Toast*, Icon Books Ltd, London, 2009.

Dal Vera, Rocco (ed.), *Film, Broadcast and e-Media Coaching: And Other Contemporary Issues in Professional Voice and Speech Training*, Applause Books, New York, 2003.

Donnellan, Declan, *The Actor and the Target*, Nick Hern Books, London, 2002.

Edelstein, Barry, *Thinking Shakespeare: A How-to Guide for Student-actors, Directors, and Anyone Else Who Wants to Feel More Comfortable with the Bard*, Spark Pub Group, New York, 2007.

Ford Davies, Oliver, *Performing Shakespeare: Preparation, Rehearsal, Performance*, Nick Hern Books, London, 2007.

Gaskill, William, *Words into Action*, Nick Hern Books, London, 2010.

Gielgud, John, *Acting Shakespeare*, Applause Theatre Book Publishers, New York, 1999.

Hall, Peter, *Shakespeare's Advice to the Players*, Oberon Books, London, 2003.

Harrison, G. B., *Introducing Shakespeare* (3rd edition), Penguin Books, Harmondsworth, 1966.

Houseman, Barbara, *Tackling Text [And Subtext]*, Nick Hern Books, London, 2008.

Kaiser, Scott, *Mastering Shakespeare: An Acting Class in Seven Scenes*, Allworth Press, New York, 2003.

Kermode, Frank, *Shakespeare's Language*, Penguin Books, Harmondsworth, 2001.

Leech, Geoffrey, *A Linguistic Guide to English Poetry*, Longman, London, 1969.

Leith, Sam, *You Talkin' to Me: Rhetoric from Aristotle to Obama*, Profile Books, London, 2011.

Linklater, Kristin, *Freeing Shakespeare's Voice: The Actor's Guide to Talking the Text*, Theatre Communications Group, New York, 1992.

Marlowe, Christopher, *Tamburlaine the Great, Part Two*. [Online]. Available at http://www.gutenberg.org/ebooks/1589 [accessed May 2014].

McCrum, Robert, William Cran and Robert MacNeil, *The Story of English*, Faber and Faber Ltd, London, 1986.

Noble, Adrian, *How to Do Shakespeare*, Routledge, London, 2010.

Norwich, John Julius, *Shakespeare's Kings*, Penguin Books, London, 1999.

Pennington, Michael, *Sweet William: Twenty Thousand Hours with Shakespeare*, Nick Hern Books, London, 2012.

Rodenburg, Patsy, *Speaking Shakespeare*, Methuen, London, 2002.

Sher, Antony, *Year of the King*, Chatto & Windus: Hogarth Press, London, 1985.

Spain, Delbert, *Shakespeare Sounded Soundly: The Verse Structure and the Language*, Garland-Clarke Editions/Capra Press, Santa Barbara, 1988.

Weate, Catherine, *Classic Voice: Working with Actors on Vocal Style*, Oberon Books, London, 2009.

Wikipedia. *Blank verse*. [Online]. Available at http://www.en.wikipedia.org [accessed August 2013].

—*Enjambment*. [Online]. Available at http://www.en.wikipedia.org [accessed August 2013].

—*End-stopping*. [Online]. Available at http://www.en.wikipedia.org [accessed August 2013].

—*Iamb (foot)*. [Online]. Available at http://www.en.wikipedia.org [accessed August 2013].

—*Papal tiara*. [Online]. Available at http://www.en.wikipedia.org [accessed August 2013].

—*Syncopation*. [Online]. Available at http://www.en.wikipedia.org [accessed August 2013].

—*Systems of Scansion*. [Online]. Available at http://www.en.wikipedia.org [accessed August 2013].

LINKS TO WORKBOOK VIDEO

To view a particular video, please visit its URL below, or go to http://vimeo.com/channels/shakespeareworkbook

INDEX

This index covers the study of Shakespeare's plays: featuring performance, language, speaking, questioning and acting, in all chapters; these topics are categorized by further headings. Play titles follow the style of names used in Appendix 4.